Sex and the State

Abortion, Divorce, and the Family Under Latin American Dictatorships and Democracies

Abortion, divorce, and the family: How did the state make policy decisions in these areas in Argentina, Brazil, and Chile during the last third of the twentieth century? As the three countries made the transition from democratic to authoritarian forms of government (and back), they confronted challenges posed by the rise of the feminist movement, social changes, and the power of the Catholic Church. The results were often surprising: Women's rights were expanded under military dictatorships, divorce was legalized in authoritarian Brazil but not in democratic Chile, and no Latin American country changed its laws on abortion. *Sex and the State* explores these patterns of gender-related policy reform and shows how they mattered for the peoples of Latin America and for a broader understanding of the logic behind the state's role in shaping private lives and gender relations everywhere.

Mala Htun is a member of the faculty of the political science department at New School University and a Fellow at the Radcliffe Institute for Advanced Study of Harvard University.

Sex and the State

*Abortion, Divorce, and the Family Under
Latin American Dictatorships
and Democracies*

MALA HTUN

CAMBRIDGE
UNIVERSITY PRESS

PUBLISHED BY THE PRESS SYNDICATE OF THE UNIVERSITY OF CAMBRIDGE
The Pitt Building, Trumpington Street, Cambridge, United Kingdom

CAMBRIDGE UNIVERSITY PRESS
The Edinburgh Building, Cambridge CB2 2RU, UK
40 West 20th Street, New York, NY 10011-4211, USA
477 Williamstown Road, Port Melbourne, VIC 3207, Australia
Ruiz de Alarcón 13, 28014 Madrid, Spain
Dock House, The Waterfront, Cape Town 8001, South Africa

http://www.cambridge.org

First published 2003

Printed in the United States of America

Typeface Sabon 10/12 pt.   *System* LaTeX 2$_\varepsilon$ [TB]

A catalog record for this book is available from the British Library.

Library of Congress Cataloging in Publication Data

Htun, Mala, 1969–
Sex and the State : abortion, divorce, and the family under Latin American
dictatorships and democracies / Mala Htun.
    p.   cm.
Includes bibliographical references and index.
ISBN 0-521-81049-3 – ISBN 0-521-00879-4 (pb.)
1. Family policy – Argentina.   2. Family policy – Brazil.   3. Family policy – Chile.
4. Sex role – Argentina.   5. Sex role – Brazil.   6. Sex role – Chile.   I. Title.

HQ590 .H78   2003
306.85′098–dc21   2002031349

ISBN 0 521 81049 3 hardback
ISBN 0 521 00879 4 paperback

To my parents

Contents

Acknowledgments

Friends, colleagues, and mentors in the United States and Latin America helped me complete this book. The project began as a Ph.D. dissertation in the Department of Government at Harvard University. My greatest thanks are owed to my dissertation chair Jorge Domínguez, who was indispensable to the project. He helped me to articulate my ideas and craft an analytical framework, and he rescued me from despair on countless occasions. Theda Skocpol's theoretical instincts and outlook on comparative historical analysis were a major inspiration. Jenny Mansbridge pushed me toward the disaggregated approach that is the centerpiece of this book and greatly improved its readability. I am grateful to the friends and colleagues who read parts of the manuscript: Andrew Arato, Lisa Baldez, Lawrence Broz, Gelson Fonseca, Jr., Elisabeth Friedman, Ira Katznelson, Olivia Newman, David Plotke, Jack Snyder, Juan Vaggione, Bernard Wasow, Andrew Weiss, and Aristide Zolberg. Bill Burck, Courtney Jung, Sankar Muthu, and Smita Singh helped in a crunch.

Experts and participants in Brazil, Chile, and Argentina kindly shared their thoughts and experiences. Lena Lavinas and Hildete Pereira offered me an affiliation with the IPEA in Rio de Janeiro, Brazil. Thanks go to the staff of CFEMEA, the Archivo Nacional, the library of the National Senate, and the archives of the Planalto, as well as to my friends and colleagues Albertina Costa, Sonia Corrêa, David Fleischer, Maria Goreti, Olaya Hanashiro, Comba Marques, Rosinethe Monteiro Soares, Jacqueline Pitanguy, and Marcos Tenório. In Chile, Gloria Claro sharpened my thinking and offered an introduction to the world of politics and society, Katherine Gilfeather educated me on the Roman Catholic Church, and Bonnie Shepard and David Holmstrom housed and fed me. I am grateful for access to the archives of the National Congress, ISIS, the Fundación Jaime Guzmán, the Corporación 2000, and the Instituto Libertad y Desarollo. Silvina Ramos invited me to work at CEDES in Buenos Aires, and Mariano Grondona and Enrique Zuleta provided invaluable contacts. The personal archives of Ethel

Diaz and Cecilia Grosman greatly expedited my search for information, and Marcela Durrieu briefed me on the intricacies of the real gender politics of Argentina.

The National Science Foundation, the National Security Education Program, the Social Science Research Council, and Harvard University financed my field research in Latin America. Joan Caivano and Peter Hakim of the Inter-American Dialogue deserve particular thanks for involving me in the Women's Leadership Conference of the Americas, which provided extensive contacts throughout the region. I am grateful for the help of Phil Satterfield of the International Legal Studies Library at the Harvard Law School, and my research assistants at the New School, Renata Segura and Myra Waterbury. Participants in panels at meetings of the American Political Science Association and the Latin American Studies Association, and in seminars and workshops at Harvard, the New School, Northeastern University, New York University, and Columbia University offered useful comments and perspectives.

Finally, I acknowledge the solidarity of my colleagues from the Harvard Government Department's entering class of 1993 – Gary Bass, Ben Berger, Rory MacFarquhar, Kim Reimann, and Smita Singh; my Weatherhead Center friends Marc Busch, Kathleen O'Neill, and Mike Tomz; and my Latin American studies colleagues Juan Enriquez, Alejandro Poiré, and Deborah Yashar. My father, Ko Moe Htun, and my family in Burma would have been satisfied with nothing less than another academic in the family. As in everything else, the love and support of my mother, Helen Muller, pulled me through.

Note on Translations

All translations from Spanish and Portuguese, including text and interviews, are the author's.

Sex and the State in Latin America

One of the more contentious developments of modern politics is the claim of the state to regulate family life and gender relations. How and on what grounds should states organize the rights of parents over children, allocate property within marriage, offer the possibility of and grounds for divorce, and allow women the choice to terminate a pregnancy? In most countries around the world, laws on these issues historically conformed to religious and patriarchal models. State policy granted men almost complete power in the family and limited citizen discretion over decisions about marriage and reproduction. Between the 1960s and the 1990s, the rise of the feminist movement brought new ideas about women's roles, while changes in social practices and the consolidation of democratic politics put pressure on old laws. Lawyers, feminist activists, and liberal and socialist politicians organized to demand reform of laws on family equality and divorce; many also favored decriminalizing abortion. Some states introduced major liberalizing changes in what Glendon has called "the most fundamental shift since family law had begun to be secularized at the time of the Protestant Reformation" (1987: 63). Other countries continued to uphold restrictive laws, often stressing the importance of traditional gender norms to cultural integrity and national identity.

This book studies the experiences of Argentina, Brazil, and Chile during the last third of the twentieth century to understand how and why states make decisions about policy on gender issues. Through comparative analysis, it assesses how the transition from dictatorship to democracy, relations between Church and state, the mobilization of liberal and feminist reformers, and international norms shaped state policy on abortion, divorce, and gender equality in the family. The book reaches some surprising conclusions, and proposes a new, disaggregated approach to studying gender policy and the state. All three countries in this study modified laws to grant women greater rights in marriage. By contrast, only two out of three legalized divorce and none liberalized abortion. This suggests that differences among gender issues are politically consequential. Rather than treating "women's rights" or "feminist policies" as a single issue area, we should disaggregate gender issues. The book also stresses how political institutions, including the expert policy-making commissions of military dictatorships and the party systems of democratic polities, shaped the ability of elite reformers to enact policy changes. We also see that, in spite of their vociferous opposition to divorce and abortion, under certain circumstances Roman Catholic bishops can be defeated. Armed with the disaggregated approach, this book explores the conditions in which the partisans of reform "hooked into" state institutions, including the institutions of the military authoritarian state, to bring about change in abortion, divorce, and gender equality in the family.

The last third of the twentieth century witnessed significant economic and political transformations in Latin America. Argentina, Brazil, and Chile experienced military coups in the mid-1960s to early 1970s, prolonged periods of military rule, and transitions to democracy in the 1980s. They passed through state-led economic growth in the 1960s and 1970s, economic crises in the early 1980s, and market-oriented reforms in response to their respective crises. In the 1990s, the three countries together shed their authoritarian and statist pasts and embraced democracy and freer markets. These changes affected the power of the Roman Catholic Church and the status of Catholic values, and altered the role of women in society and the place of the family in citizens' lives. Argentina, Brazil, and Chile thus provide interesting territory to explore how countries in transition and countries with hegemonic religious institutions negotiate complicated questions about abortion, divorce, and gender equality in the family. The conclusions reached here may have a broader meaning as well, for Latin American experiences mirror the dilemmas faced by many societies in the last decades of the twentieth century. The greater embrace of principles of individual rights and citizen equality produced a tension with models of family life and gender relations upheld by religious doctrine, patriarchal traditions, and conservative and nationalist movements. These conflicts over gender and the state are prominent in national politics, and their outcomes have profound implications for people's lives.

In the civil law countries of Latin America, laws on abortion, divorce, and family relations are embedded in civil and criminal codes. They are not short-term policies introduced and withdrawn by each incoming government but weighty tomes passed from one generation to the next. The historical institutions of the civil and criminal codes are decades, and often centuries, old. Most predate the imposition of military rule in the region and some date from the nineteenth century. Historically, these codes have provided a continuous framework for the administration of justice amidst coups, constitutional changes, and chaotic economic conditions. Like other institutions, the civil and criminal codes structure social action over time and serve as transmitters of common values, providing "moral or cognitive templates for interpretation and action" (Hall and Taylor 1996: 939). The law "tells stories about the culture that helped to shape it and which it in turn helps to shape: stories about who we are, where we came from, and where we are going" (Glendon 1987: 8). The civil and criminal laws of Latin America thus have a strong ethical component, making ideas an important part of debates about legal change.

This book shows that liberalizing reforms on gender and the family may come about in surprising ways. Between 1960 and 1990, conservative military governments in Latin America introduced liberalizing reforms to laws on gender and the family. In Argentina in the late 1960s, the military government of General Juan Carlos Onganía promulgated major changes to the civil and criminal codes to grant married women more property rights, permit couples to obtain judicial separations by mutual consent, and make it clear that abortion was permitted for women who had been raped.[1] In Brazil in the 1970s, the military government legalized divorce, altered the marital property regime to grant women more rights, and liberalized laws on family planning. Brazil's military rulers introduced a national women's health program, designed, in part, by feminists, in 1983. In Chile, on the eve of its departure from power in 1989, the Pinochet government introduced changes to the civil code, granting married women full civil capacity and erasing the requirement that wives owe their husbands unconditional obedience.

By contrast, though we might expect democratic governments committed to citizen equality and human rights to respect women's equal rights, the freedom to divorce, and the choice to terminate a pregnancy, this did not occur. Latin American democracies uniformly failed to change old laws on abortion. Argentina and Brazil introduced changes to family law, including, in Argentina, the legalization of divorce. But in Chile, even twelve years after the democratic transition, laws remain restrictive. Chile presents a puzzling combination of economic modernization and social conservatism. It has enjoyed the region's most rapid rates of economic growth and is considered a model of successful economic reform, rational state institutions, and pioneering social programs. But Chile is the only country in the world (besides Malta) where divorce is not legal and is among the small group of countries where abortion is banned under all circumstances, even to save the mother's life.

Until now, virtually no scholarly work on Latin American politics has explored these puzzles. Various studies have documented the rise of

---

[1] As Chapter 6 explains, the Argentine Criminal Code of 1922 was ambiguous on the point of whether abortion was permitted in the event of the rape of *all* women or only the rape of mentally handicapped or mentally ill women. Differing interpretations of the code gave way to a vigorous debate among criminologists. Reformists working under the Onganía regime attempted to give closure to this debate by redrafting the law.

second-wave feminist activism in the region, the multiplication of feminist and feminine groups, and the relationship between these groups, political parties, and the state (Alvarez 1990; Baldez 2002; Charlton, Everett, and Staudt 1989; Craske 1999; Friedman 2000; Gonzales and Kampwirth 2001; Jaquette 1994; Jaquette and Wolchik 1998; Luciak 2002; Matear 1996; Navarro and Bourque 1998; Pitanguy 1996; Rodriguez 1998; Waylen 1994, 2000). More historical analyses have studied the achievement of suffrage and documented early legal reforms expanding women's rights (Dore and Molyneux 2000; Lavrín 1995; McGee Deutsch 1991; Miller 1991). These studies have proposed useful conceptual frameworks for analyzing the genesis of women's activism, and the effects of the democratic transition on women's political participation and women's groups in civil society. There are fewer works that engage in comparative historical analysis of the state and its approach to gender issues.[2] To be sure, there are several studies of gender-related public policies in Latin America, though most focus on a single country (Alatorre 1999; Baldez 2001; Friedman 2000; Haas 1999; Schlueter 2000; Stevenson 1999) or have a descriptive character (Htun 2001a). A few works explore the influence of international norms and treaties on local policy on domestic and sexual violence, women's political participation, and the formation of state agencies on women in different countries (Htun 1998; Htun and Jones 2002; Keck and Sikkink 1998). Yet no one has adopted a comparative, macrohistorical approach to explain variation in gender policy[3] changes across Latin American countries making transitions from dictatorship to democracy.

In this book, I introduce an approach that stresses the distinctiveness of different gender issues. Issues differ in how they are processed politically, the groups that weigh in on policy debates, and the ideas at stake in change. Some policy issues provoke rhetorically charged public debate informed by clashing world views, principled beliefs, and religious and ethical traditions. Other policy issues occupy small groups that spend days arguing over details of syntax and sequence. The prospect of change on some issues threatens the status of Catholic values, prompting bishops to defend the Church's position

[2] One study with an approach similar to this book is Mounira Charrad's *States and Women's Rights: The Making of Postcolonial Tunisia, Algeria, and Morocco* (Berkeley: University of California Press, 2001). Charrad proposes that the relationship between states and tribes was the decisive variable influencing different approaches to family law in the three Maghribi countries.

[3] From this point on, this book uses the terms "gender policies" and "gender rights" to refer to laws and policies on divorce, abortion, and gender equality in the family. In general, however, "gender policies" and "gender rights" may refer to a broader range of policy issues than those considered in this book. "Gender rights" are not the same as "women's rights," for they also involve men. Though gender is frequently used as a synonym for women (Scott 1988), it is better understood to refer to the social organization and cultural interpretation of sexual differences. Gender policies and rights are thus the legal regulations, obligations, and privileges that refer to or reinforce sex relations and sex differences.

in the public sphere. The Church is disinterested in other issues and neglects to flex its muscles in policy debates. These differences among issues stem in large part from how policies are framed (Yishai 1993: 208). "Absolutist" policies tend to be seen in symbolic terms, provoke gut responses and value clashes, and "more likely deal with policy ends than means" (Carmines and Stimson 1980: 80). Religious institutions are likely to weigh in on changes to an absolutist agenda. "Technical" policies, by contrast, demand expert knowledge and provoke little public controversy. Change on technical issues is less likely to put religion on the defensive. In short, "gender rights" is not one issue but many. Opportunities for reform on one issue may not lead to reform on others. To explain policy change, we must disaggregate gender issues.

The book emphasizes the role of "issue networks" – elite coalitions of lawyers, feminist activists, doctors, legislators, and state officials – in bringing about policy change. These issue networks, inspired by ideas of modernity, equality, and liberty; changes in other countries; and international treaties constituted the impetus behind reform. The growth of the second-wave feminist movement, in particular, helped put gender equality and reproductive rights on the policy agenda in many countries. Feminist movements in all three countries raised public awareness about questions of gender, lobbied state officials, and worked with or within the state to help formulate state policy. Yet many members of issue networks were not feminist activists but middle-class male lawyers. These lawyers, who played decisive roles in early abortion reform, the legalization of divorce, and changes promoting equality in the family, have been the unsung heroes of much of gender law liberalization in Latin America. Their activism on gender rights serves as important evidence that gender, far from being a "woman question," involves and affects all of society.

The possibilities for policy change depended on whether and how these elite issue networks were able to hook into state institutions. Institutional features of military and democratic regimes and the relationship between Church and state shaped this "fit" between issue networks and the state (the notion of "fit" comes from Skocpol 1992: 54–7). Military governments created technical commissions charged with modernizing the civil law, opening a privileged window of influence for lawyers to bring cosmopolitan legal theories to bear on domestic policy. The closed nature of these governments insulated technical decisions from societal input, thus expediting change. As a result, military rulers in Argentina, Brazil, and Chile presided over important reforms advancing gender equality in the family. Under democratic rule, the success of issue networks was more varied, for it depended on the weight of the authoritarian legacy, the political party system, and the strength of executive and partisan commitment to women's rights. Not all democratic governments were able to complete an agenda of gender equality, reneging on promises made during the transition and contributing to the trend toward illiberal democracy in the region (Diamond 1999; O'Donnell 1994; Zakaria 1997).

The other major factor shaping issue network success was the relationship between Church and state. For partisans of legal divorce to succeed, the bishops had to be overpowered and defeated. The eruption of Church-state conflict over human rights, economic policy, and authoritarian rule performed this function, opening a window of opportunity for liberal issue networks to promulgate divorce.

Abortion is a special case in this book, because it provoked considerably more moral conflict than other issues. Even when citizens in Latin America came to accept divorce, they remained deeply ambivalent about abortion. Though the practice is widespread, abortion laws are rarely enforced. Since middle-class women generally have access to safe abortions in private clinics, many see little reason to press for the liberalization of abortion laws. It is primarily poor women who suffer the consequences of clandestine abortions. At the same time, the political clout of abortion opponents grew, particularly after John Paul II became Pope of the Roman Catholic Church and antiabortion movements organized at the global level. Whereas abortion was once considered a technical issue of interest to criminologists and health practitioners, by the 1970s the abortion debate became polarized around a clash of absolutist values, frustrating political compromise over abortion legislation.

By studying three issue areas in three countries across two time periods (pre- and postdemocratization),[4] the book has a total of eighteen observations with which to test hypotheses and draw conclusions about the causes of policy change (see Table 1.1).[5] Table 1.1 shows that, in spite of their superficial similarities, the timing and content of gender policy in Argentina, Brazil, and Chile differed significantly. This variation is striking across countries and across issues. Brazil started to change its laws first, and these changes continued throughout the period of military rule. Argentina introduced major civil law reforms during military rule, though most of its changes came after the 1983 democratic transition. Chile, by contrast, which waited until 1989 to grant married women full civil status (also under military rule), has still not legalized divorce, and abortion remains illegal under all circumstances. In fact, no Latin American country has liberalized its laws on abortion since the 1940s.[6]

---

[4] For the most part, the book studies the period between the early 1960s and the end of 1999.

[5] Including several issue areas and distinct time periods in the analysis is one way to multiply observations and minimize the small-number problem in qualitative research (King, Keohane, and Verba 1994).

[6] One exception must be mentioned here. In 2000, the legislature of Mexico City approved changes to the city's criminal code to expand the conditions of legal abortion. Based on a bill introduced by then mayor Rosario Robles, the reforms granted women permission to abort if the pregnancy threatened their health (not just their life), or in the event of fetal abnormalities.

TABLE I.I. *Dates of Major Gender-Related Legal Reforms in Three Countries*

Country	Issue	Time period	
		Predemocratization	Postdemocratization
Argentina	Family equality	1968 law granted married women full civil capacity and equal property rights	1985 law granted mothers equal parental rights
	Divorce	No change	1987 law legalized divorce
	Abortion	No change	No change
Brazil	Family equality	1962 married women's statute granted married women full civil capacity[a] 1977 law granted married women equal property rights	1988 Constitution upheld principle of sex equality in the family, including parental rights
	Divorce	1977 constitutional amendment permitted legal divorce	
	Abortion	No change	No change
Chile	Family equality	1989 law granted married women full civil capacity	1998 law granted mothers equal parental rights
	Divorce	No change	No change
	Abortion	1989 law withdrew permission for therapeutic abortion	No change

[a] Brazil's 1962 reform came at the end of a democratic period (1946–64), but still preceded the major wave of democratic transitions of the 1980s.

How can we make sense of this variation? This book discerns four patterns in the timing and content of gender policy. Using a common set of variables, each pattern is described in one of the four empirical chapters of the book. Chapter 3 addresses the question of why military governments alleged to be patriarchal and conservative initiated civil law reforms to expand women's rights in Argentina, Brazil, and Chile. It shows that military governments seeking to modernize state and society turned to experts to advise them on legal reform. By creating small, official commissions where experts could deliberate about the law, modernizing military leaders opened a window of opportunity for liberalizing policy changes. Influenced by international trends and the ideas circulating in cosmopolitan legal circles, these experts proposed reforms that in some cases brought about major modifications to women's civil status and property rights.

Chapter 4 focuses on divorce. Opposition from Roman Catholic bishops can pose an enormous obstacle to divorce, particularly when no other civil society institutions can act as countervailing influences to Church power. As a result, restrictive laws may endure in spite of social changes, international pressures, and widespread acceptance of new ideas about gender and the family. Argentina, Brazil, and Chile were among the last Latin American countries to legalize divorce.[7] Yet the patterns of change differ significantly in the three countries. In Brazil, a military government approved a divorce law in 1977. Argentina legalized divorce following the return to democracy in 1983. In Chile, divorce remained illegal in 2002, twelve years after the transition. The chapter shows that conflict between Church and state creates an opportunity for change, while Church-state cooperation precludes it. In Argentina and Brazil, governments clashed with the bishops over education, human rights, and economic policy. Triggered by the political repression and human rights abuses of military dictatorships, these moments of Church-state conflict enabled liberal and feminist partisans of divorce to defeat the Church. In Chile, Church-state collaboration posed an obstacle to divorce. Chile's progressive Church helped usher in the transition to democracy and was seen to play a crucial role in the consolidation of democratic rule and the protection of human rights. Having built ties to democratic parties and politicians during the struggle against military rule, the Church took advantage of its clout by vetoing the legalization of divorce under democratic governance. In this way, the same Church that helped bring about the fact of democratization later curtailed the extension of democratic rights and liberties.

Chapter 5 analyzes the varied success of democratic governments in completing the family equality reforms begun under military rule. After the political transition, feminist activists joined with male lawyers and officials in state women's agencies to see that married women and mothers had equal rights with men. They were inspired by changes to family law in European countries and a growing body of international agreements such as the Convention on the Elimination of All Forms of Discrimination against Women (CEDAW). Though an emerging national and international consensus favored reform, the configuration of national political institutions shaped patterns of policy. In Argentina, strong parties in Congress and a commitment from actors in the Executive helped the cause of reform. In Brazil, the formulation of a new constitution in 1988 provided an opportunity to advance gender equality, but it took thirteen more years to change the civil code because of the weakness of the party system and the state women's agency. In Chile, policy making was more affected by an authoritarian legacy than in the other two countries, as agreements made at the time of transition preserved the power and prerogatives of the military and its allies. There, "authoritarian enclaves" in the political system and coalitional dynamics among governing parties delayed and thwarted family equality reform.

---

[7] Other countries where the legalization of divorce was delayed include Colombia, where divorce was legalized for non-Catholics in 1976 and for Catholics in 1991, and Paraguay, where divorce was legalized in 1991.

Chapter 6 considers the question of abortion. In spite of the growing influence of feminist reproductive rights movements, Latin American countries have failed to loosen abortion restrictions. Much of the resistance to change comes from the Roman Catholic Church and antiabortion movements, who have redoubled their efforts to fight abortion at home and at United Nations conferences. Yet most politicians show little enthusiasm to confront conservative forces; consequently, big coalitions backing reform, so important in the case of divorce, have not yet materialized. Though illegal abortion is prevalent and disastrous for women's health, punitive abortion laws are almost never enforced and there is little public support for major changes. Beyond the general failure to decriminalize, however, there are differences in abortion politics in the three countries. Argentina and Brazil permit abortions in the event of rape or when the pregnant woman's life is at risk; Chile forbids abortion under all circumstances. Brazilian feminists have organized a legal abortion movement to see that rape victims have access to free abortions (though abortion is *legal* in the case of rape, it may not be *available*), and the Ministry of Health responded by requiring all public hospitals to perform those abortions permitted by law. By contrast, due to the antiabortion posture of most of the political elite, Argentine and Chilean feminists have been unable to provoke serious debates about legal abortion and have focused instead on reproductive health and family planning legislation.

These chapters make propositions about the causes of change on individual issues; these propositions are summarized in the conclusion. Chapter 2 continues the theoretical background begun in this chapter by sketching the evolution of ideas about gender and the family in Roman Catholicism, liberalism, feminism, and socialism. After offering some brief background on Latin American legal systems, the remainder of this introductory chapter introduces the main causal variables used in the rest of the book: issue differences, the role of elite issue networks, and the factors determining the "fit" between these networks and the state, such as military technical commissions, democratic political institutions, and Church-state relations. Reform on each gender issue was a shared process, but national specificities sometimes generated dissimilar outcomes.

Latin American Legal Systems

Two aspects of Latin American civil law systems will be unfamiliar to readers who know the common law tradition of the Anglo-American world. The first is the mechanism of legal change. The power of the judicial branch to issue binding interpretations of existing laws is more circumscribed in Latin American civil law systems than in common law countries (although Latin American high court judges have historically been invested with the power of judicial review). In civil law systems, most judges have the authority to decide only individual cases; their decisions are not binding on later cases or on the lower courts.[8] Reformers seeking legal change must direct their energies to the national legislature and not the courts.[9] In the common law system, by contrast, judges are far more empowered to make law by issuing interpretations that are binding on subsequent judicial decisions. These precedents are as much a source of law as the original laws crafted by the legislature (Glendon, Gordon, and Osakwe 1982). As a result, reformers in the Anglo-American system exert pressure not only on the legislature responsible for enacting statutory changes but also on the various federal and state courts.

The second distinguishing feature of Latin American laws is their hortatory nature. Gender rights conflict everywhere may assume dimensions of a cultural struggle among competing world views. The thick normative content of Latin American civil and criminal codes increases the symbolic stakes in legal reform. That the law should have a role in enforcing the moral order is an idea more deeply rooted in continental European and civil law than in the Anglo-American common law. Civil law has preserved an older Platonic tradition that invests laws with a rhetorical and pedagogical function. As Plato wrote in the *Laws*, the objective of the law is not merely to control social behavior but, through powers of persuasion, to "lead the citizens toward virtue, to make them noble and wise" (Glendon 1987: 6). As Glendon puts it, "the civil law systems retain vestiges of the classical view of law as educational. The great codifications, especially those modeled on the French, kept alive a certain rhetorical tradition of statutory drafting and a certain story-telling aspect of law that is notably absent from the Anglo-American legislative tradition." Lawmakers in Europe "took from Montesquieu and his followers an awareness of how culture shapes law, and from Rousseau and his followers a belief that law can help to shape society and the individuals who compose it" (1987: 130–1). In the Anglo-American common law system, by contrast, legal positivist notions of the law as a set of rules that impose duties and confer powers are dominant (Hart 1994). Common law consists of a slow accretion of judicial decisions, while civil laws reflect the strenuous efforts of legal scholars to apply reason to the meticulous ordering of human affairs. The content of the law establishes not merely the hedges constraining individual freedom but the moral rules by which people live and the symbols that shape their social identities.

---

[8] According to Glendon, Gordon, and Osakwe (1982), however, several civil law systems have mitigated this rule in practice, and judges have at times exercised vast discretion in developing the law.

[9] Although Argentina and Brazil are federal systems, civil and criminal law is established at the national level. Mexico is the only Latin American federal system where each state has its own civil and criminal code.

Due to the hortatory nature of civil and criminal laws in Latin America, gender-related legal reform involves more than a mere policy shift. It can represent a transformation in the social and moral norms governing an important sphere of human behavior. When gender rights change, so do definitions and understandings of gender roles and relationships. Liberals who favor the legalization of divorce seek to replace the traditional image of marriage as an indissoluble and sacred relationship with a modern notion of a civil contract rooted in the will of individuals. Conservatives who resist divorce insist that marriage is not a contract but a bedrock institution of the social order. Prochoice groups favoring the decriminalization of abortion aim to make motherhood elective, not compulsory. Antiabortion groups maintain that an ethic of life in the post-Holocaust era requires the unconditional defense of the weak and innocent, including the unborn. As so much is at stake, government officials, elected representatives, and other policy experts take change in gender rights very seriously. They do want not to impose one vision of gender on the rest of society but to convince other citizens that it is the appropriate vision for the times. Gender-related legal reform is not usually imposed through executive decree or party discipline, but evolves through prolonged deliberation. Legislative decision making on divorce and abortion, for example, usually follows the principle of *voto de consciencia*, according to which parties free each legislator to vote her or his conscience on the issue.

The importance of deliberation has been highlighted in recent literature in normative political theory by scholars such as Jürgen Habermas, Seyla Benhabib, Amy Gutmann, and Dennis Thompson. Although these scholars begin from different philosophical premises, they converge in the conviction that the legitimacy of collective decisions lies in the extent to which they result from "processes of collective deliberation conducted rationally and fairly among free and equal individuals" (Benhabib 1996: 69). Deliberation is particularly appropriate to modern democracies characterized by a "pluralism of ultimate value orientations." Habermas's discourse theory of morality and democracy identifies deliberative argumentation as the way to reach consensual agreements among peoples with different views of justice and of the good life (Habermas 1990, 1996b). As Benhabib puts it: "Agreements in societies living with value pluralism are to be sought for not at the level of substantive beliefs but at that of procedures, processes, and practices for attaining and revising beliefs" (1996: 73). Gutmann and Thompson argue that deliberation is the best means to deal with persisting moral conflict in politics. Even when citizens' views prove incompatible, "deliberation promotes an economy of moral disagreement in which citizens manifest mutual respect as they continue to disagree about morally important issues in politics" (1996: 43).

These claims about norms suggest that deliberation about policy changes allows reformers and their opponents to persuade, not just impose. Latin

Americans involved in major changes in gender rights often believed that
the legitimacy of legal reforms would be enhanced through ethical deliberation. Some recent literature in the field of international relations similarly
highlights the role of moral argumentation and persuasion in human rights
policy changes. While not denying that many states initially conform to
international human rights norms for instrumental reasons, this literature
maintains that states eventually get caught in moral discourses and rational
argumentation about human rights, and are then socialized into the norms
governing the society of "civilized nations" (Risse and Sikkink 1999).

To be sure, domestic political deliberation over the reform of the civil code,
the legalization of divorce, and the decriminalization of abortion merely ap-
proximated the ideal deliberative conditions posited by democratic theorists
such as Jürgen Habermas and Seyla Benhabib. For the most part, participants were not mass democratic publics but educated elites with access to
policy makers. In the 1990s, as Argentina, Brazil, and Chile have grown
more democratic, the deliberative circle on gender rights has widened beyond elites to include a broader set of organizations, or, as Benhabib aptly
puts it, "a public sphere of mutually interlocking and overlapping networks
and associations of deliberation, contestation, and argumentation" (1996:
74). As we see below, however, the democratization of deliberation did not
always prove conducive to liberalizing reforms.

Issue Differences

In his classic 1964 *World Politics* article, Ted Lowi argues that different types
of public policies involve distinct structures of power, systems of group relations, and policy processes. As a result, different models of politics char-
acterize decision making on different types of policies. Decision making on
distributive issues, or pork barrel programs such as public works, defense
procurement, and research and development, occurs through the formation
of "log-rolling" coalitions whose members have nothing in common and
operate under a principle of "mutual non-interference" (1964: 693). Power
elite models apply to *redistributive* issues where conflicts tend to occur along
class lines, while pluralist models more accurately describe *regulatory* issues
where groups united by shared, though temporary, interests bargain for relative advantage. One of the key insights of the article is that by disaggregating
policies in this way, we can expand the explanatory power of political theories. Lowi argues that the "relevance" of a theoretical approach "becomes
stronger as the scope of its application is reduced and as the standards for
identifying the scope are clarified" (ibid.: 715). Power elite and pluralist
models fail as *general* theories of politics, but succeed when applied to *specific* types of issues.

This book applies Lowi's insights to the realm of gender policy. Like Lowi's
distributive, redistributive, and regulatory policies, different gender policy
issues may engender distinct types of politics. Specifically, policies differ in

terms of the involvement of the Roman Catholic Church and whether they are treated as "technical" or "absolutist." Roman Catholic bishops opposed policy change on divorce and abortion,[10] but did not contest, and sometimes even supported, advancing gender equality in the family. As Chapter 2 describes, Church doctrine began to change in the 1960s. From its earlier support of a patriarchal household, the Church came to endorse men and women's equal rights in family matters. The presence or absence of Church opposition was highly consequential for the politics surrounding policy change. Gender equality, moreover, was often treated as a technical issue of civil law. One had to have legal training (and considerable patience) to understand the nuances of marital property arrangements. Divorce and abortion, by contrast, were policies that invoked gut responses from novice and expert alike. Divorce and abortion called on people to assume absolutist moral positions; with rare exceptions, these two issues were never treated as technical matters.

Lowi's analysis points out that the locus of decision making may differ across policy types. Decisions on *distributive* issues tend to be taken in congressional committees and sometimes in specialized government agencies. Executive and peak associations make the relevant decisions about *redistributive* issues, while the policy process on *regulatory* issues tend to be centered in Congress (1964: 713). On gender issues as well, decision making venues vary. Decision making on technical policies could often be delegated to small commissions of experts. These commissions applied specialized knowledge to issues such as marital property and parental rights and the conditions under which abortion should be legally permitted. Working out the details of these reforms often took years, for it involved organizing studies, consulting data, and revising numerous drafts. Significantly, even when they closed Congress, military governments did not shut down expert commissions; in fact, military rulers frequently created such commissions to formulate state policy. Absolutist policies, by contrast, were decided in Congress. Decision making on these policies was preceded by principled deliberation among elected representatives, policy experts, activists, members of the media, and so on. While some ended up convinced by the views of their opponents, many continued to disagree. Resolving conflicts over an absolutist agenda thus required a congressional vote. After the 1970s, no president – not even a military president – was willing to impose radical changes to divorce and abortion law by executive decree on the recommendations of a small group of experts.[11] Table 1.2 summarizes some of the differences among gender issues.

---

[10] Before *Roe v. Wade*, however, the Church declined to contest some reforms that exempted from criminal punishment abortions performed on women who had been raped.

[11] A partial exception must be mentioned here. In 1989, the outgoing Chilean military government modified the country's Health Code to make therapeutic abortions (performed in case of grave risks to the mother's life or health) illegal. This reform was supported by military elites but not preceded by deliberation among regime officials or society at large. I

TABLE I.2. *Differences among Gender Issues*

Issue	Bishops contest change	Nature of issue	Decision venue
Civil code (civil capacity, property rights, parental rights) Conditions of legal abortion (early twentieth century)	No	Technical issue: expert knowledge required	Small expert commissions
Divorce Liberalization of abortion	Yes	Absolutist issue: symbolic, invoking "gut" response	Congress

Issue differences need to be taken into account by theories of change. To be sure, the gender policy issues considered in this book share some common features. Laws on gender are normative as opposed to merely distributive, redistributive, or regulatory. As argued earlier, the normative power of the law enhances the role of deliberation, emotion, and the weight of principled ideas in policy change. But it would be a mistake to assume that all normative policies follow the same logic. Just because ideas are at stake doesn't mean they are the same ideas. Emotional investment, too, can vary in degree. For example, though divorce and abortion both engendered ethical conflict, the degree of moral polarization surrounding abortion made the issue far more politically intractable than divorce. By disaggregating gender issues, we may, as Lowi suggests, reduce the scope of the application of causal theories and thereby enhance their explanatory power. Though we may never have a *general* theory of gender and the state, we may be able to arrive at *specific* theories of the politics surrounding different gender issues.

Issue Networks

New paradigms of gender rights became politically salient in Latin America when they were debated within elite "issue networks" of lawyers, feminists, and reformist politicians. The concept of "issue network" was coined by Hugh Heclo (1978) to describe "specialized subcultures of highly knowledge-able policy watchers." Issue networks involve people at many levels, such as interest groups who directly lobby policy makers, knowledgeable individuals

---

call this a "partial" exception because the criminal code, which criminalized abortion under all circumstances, was not modified.

who publish and offer expert advice, professional associations, grassroots movements circulating information about social conditions, and state officials with particular policy interests or competencies (Berry 1989; Heclo 1978; for the related concept of "policy communities," see Baumgartner and Jones 1993). This concept usefully captures the range of actors and interests who have contributed to gender-related reform in Latin America in the last third of the twentieth century. Feminist activists interested in women's emancipation participated in gender-related issue networks, and so did jurists influenced by legal changes in other countries and rational principles of law, liberal and socialist politicians interested in social reform, doctors, and representatives of the media. Issue networks were the key advocates for gender rights reform. These networks, which mobilized around specific issues such as divorce, abortion, or family law reform, brought issues to the public agenda, circulated information and recommendations, and mobilized public opinion.

"Issue networks" may be influenced by, or even grow out of, social movements. Yet "social movements" is a much broader term, which can be understood to refer to sequences of collective action among social actors seeking a variety of goals. These goals may be instrumental (such as the desire to influence state policy), normative (the assertion of collective identity or common values), or defensive (resistance to encroachment or "colonization" by the market economy or the state) (Cohen and Arato 1992: 526; Tarrow 1998: 2). Issue networks, by contrast, mobilize around specific policy issues, and may involve actors from both state and society. What links members of issue networks is interest in a particular policy area, not collective identity, occupational category, place of residence, shared values, or ideological orientation (though members of issue networks may share these things). For example, the mobilization of the second-wave feminist movement in the mid- to late 1970s contributed to the growth of issue networks favoring liberal policy changes. Many activists from the feminist movement joined with others to mobilize support for change on gender equality, divorce, and abortion. Yet the goals of feminist movements may include consciousness raising, empowerment, and cultural transformation, not merely policy change. A lot of the force behind change on gender equality and the family and divorce came from middle-class male lawyers. These lawyers, motivated by the social problems they encountered in their legal practices, changes in other countries, and international norms, played a central role in issue networks. Yet until now, these unsung heroes have not received much attention in the scholarly literature on gender and the state.

Issue networks were the mechanism through which international developments influenced domestic political changes. International conferences, interstate agreements, and demonstration effects generated ideas and proposals within domestic issue networks. In the first few decades of the twentieth century, for example, participants in criminology conferences in Europe and

Latin America debated the legalization of "compassionate" abortions performed on women who had been raped. By approving proposals based on these new legal theories, promoted most notably by Spanish criminologist Luis Jimenez de Asúa, Argentina and Brazil became among the first countries in the world to permit "compassionate" abortion. Beginning in the 1940s, lawyers attending the annual meetings of the Inter-American Bar Association (IABA) deliberated civil law reforms to grant married women more rights in family matters. For IABA delegates, who passed several resolutions pertaining to married women's civil capacity and property rights, modern law meant law based on principles of equality. Lawyers who attended these conferences came home armed with proposals for domestic policy reform. In this way, many members of domestic issue networks were simultaneously participants in transnational advocacy networks (Keck and Sikkink 1998).

Later, international agreements such as the Inter-American Convention on Women's Civil and Political Rights (1949) and the United Nations' Convention on the Elimination of All Forms of Discrimination Against Women (CEDAW, endorsed by the General Assembly in 1979 and ratified by the vast majority of Latin American countries in the 1980s and 1990s) helped consolidate global norms of gender equality that helped issue networks to pressure local governments for change. In theory, the CEDAW has the force of law in ratifying countries. This boosts the standing of gender equality advocates, who may make the argument not that their government change its policies, but that it comply with already existing law. Liberal issue networks were also inspired reforms in other countries. After the vast majority of North American and European states reformed laws on divorce, family relations, and abortion in the 1970s and 1980s, many members of Latin American issue networks argued that their countries had to adopt similar reforms in order not to lag behind the rest of the "civilized world."

International influences were also channeled through conservative issue networks. United Nations conferences in Cairo in 1994, Beijing in 1995, and New York in 2000 provided a focal point for antiabortion groups and created an opportunity for Latin American antiabortion activists to build connections and acquire skills and resources. These groups mobilized to prevent the consensus documents produced by U.N. meetings from endorsing broad definitions of reproductive rights, which they argued legitimized the legalization of abortion (Franco 1998; Shepard 1999a). Antiabortion transnational advocacy networks also fed domestic political mobilization. Abortion reforms in Western Europe and the United States left behind disgruntled opponents who took an interest in preventing similar reforms in other countries. Human Life International, a U.S. antiabortion group that mobilized in the wake of the *Roe v. Wade* decision, has affiliates around the world that played active roles in opposing the liberalization of abortion in

Latin America. Meanwhile, studies about the pernicious consequences of divorce law liberalization in the United States motivated Latin American conservatives to contest divorce reform at home (Díaz Vergara 1997). High rates of teenage pregnancy in the United States, interpreted as the result of liberal state policies on reproductive issues, shored up the arguments of Latin Americans opposed to sex education, family planning, and abortion (e.g., Santa Cruz 1996: 20).

Though they were the central actors in gender rights reform, policy change required more than the mobilization of issue networks. Gender rights reform was not a reflex of societal and elite demands. The possibilities for change depended on whether and how elite issue networks were able to hook into state institutions. As Skocpol puts it, "degrees of success in achieving political goals – including the enactment of social legislation – depend on the relative opportunities that existing political institutions offer to the group of movement in question (and simultaneously deny to its opponents and competitors)" (1992: 54). To explain reform, we need to direct our attention to the "fit" between elite issue networks and the state (ibid.). This project employs a middle-level, polity-centered approach, proposing that institutional features of military and democratic regimes as well as the relationship between Church and state shaped this "fit" between actors demanding reform and state agencies with the power to make changes.

State Institutions

A key insight of an institutionalist perspective on politics is that the configuration of governing institutions and political party systems shapes the relationships among political actors and the possibility for policy change (Hall and Taylor 1996; Pierson 1994; Skocpol 1992; Thelen and Steinmo 1992). For many years, major works of Latin American studies had used regime type and transition as proxies for the institutional configurations that mattered for political outcomes. Yet as we have seen, liberalizing reforms on gender and the family occurred under both military and democratic regimes, before and after democratic transitions. This lack of correspondence between forms of political regime and liberalizing gender policies caused scholars to call for a more complex analysis of the relationship between institutions and gender-related reform (Alvarez 1990; Jaquette 1994; Molyneux 2000; Waylen 1998). The field of economic policy making has arrived at a similar conclusion. In an earlier era, scholars relied on regime type and transition to explain the adoption of market-oriented economic policies. The conventional wisdom was that authoritarian regimes were better able to implement liberal economic policies than democracies because of "executives that could operate with limited institutional restraints and . . . extensive bureaucratic or coercive control of popular sector protest" (Kaufman

TABLE 1.3. *Regime Types in Argentina, Brazil, and Chile since 1960*

Country	Democratic	Military	Democratic
Argentina	1962–6	1966–73	1983 to present
	1973–6	1976–83	
Brazil	1946–64	1964–85	1985 to present
Chile	1925–73	1973–90	1990 to present

and Stallings 1989: 207).[12] In the 1990s, a wave of studies cast doubt on this conventional wisdom, finding that authoritarian governments did not implement deeper market-oriented reforms than democracies (Remmer 1990), that social groups expected to oppose reform did not behave as anticipated (Geddes 1995), and that democratic governments with neoliberal policies were rewarded at the ballot box (Domínguez 1998). As a result, economic policy-making scholars turned their focus away from regime type and transition to intraregime characteristics such as the interests of state officials and the relationship between politicians and bureaucrats (Geddes 1995). In this spirit, the present study analyzes how middle-level features of military and democratic governments and the relationship between Church and state shaped the prospects for reform.

Military Governments
Military coups and military governments have been a recurrent feature of Latin American politics in the twentieth century. In Argentina, the armed forces overthrew elected civilian governments in 1930, 1943, 1955, 1962, 1966, and 1976. The Brazilian armed forces staged coups d'etat in 1930, 1937, 1945, 1954, and 1964. In Chile, armed force intervention has been more infrequent: Following the 1924 coup, the armed forces did not seize power until 1973. Not until the 1960s, however, did military rule become a long drawn-out affair. After seizing power in the 1964 coup, the Brazilian military remained in control of the national government until 1985. In Argentina, the military ruled from 1966 to 1973, and then again from 1976 to 1983. The Chilean coup of 1973 initiated a period of military governance that lasted until 1990 (see Table 1.3).

The military coups of the 1960s and 1970s differed from their predecessors in one central way. Whereas earlier coups lacked any defined programmatic goals beyond restoring order or saving the fatherland, later coups were backed by a specific political ideology elaborated by senior military leaders.

[12] Kaufman and Stallings argued that not only authoritarian regimes, but also established democracies, were better able to implement adjustment policies than transitional democracies. Still, of the countries considered in their sample, the authoritarian regimes of Chile and Mexico handled the debt crisis of the early 1980s better than the established democracies of Costa Rica, Colombia, and Venezuela (1989).

Coups of the 1960s and 1970s were organized and executed by the military acting as an institution and aiming to reorder state and society (Cardoso 1979). Military rulers developed a national security ideology that justified their seizure of power to avert threats posed by politically mobilized popular classes and leftist movements; they also felt that military governance would create the political stability necessary to encourage investment for the "deepening" of import substituting industrialization (O'Donnell 1979; Stepan 1978, 1988).

Military discourse had a significant gendered component. "Gender is a primary way of signifying relationships of power," notes Joan Scott (1988: 42). Many of the world's political regimes have expressed authority relations in polity and society through gendered imagery. Conservative, fascist, and fundamentalist governments, for example, upheld the patriarchal family as the basis of public order. Regimes from Nazi Germany and Vichy France to Afghanistan under the Taliban have emphasized male power in the household, traditional motherhood, and a rigid sexual division of labor (McGee Deutsch 1991; Pollard 1998; Scott 1988). Latin American military governments similarly expressed their right and reason to rule in gendered terms, and appealed to traditional virtues of feminine care and devotion (Chuchryk 1989, 1994; Filc 1997; Kirkwood 1990; Munizaga and Letelier 1988; Tabak 1983; Valenzuela 1987). Military ideologies thus reinforced traditional gender roles and identities, presenting a seeming obstacle to liberalizing change on gender rights. Indeed, some Latin American feminists have seen military authoritarianism as the "highest expression of patriarchal oppression" and argued that stability of military authoritarianism depends on authoritarian patriarchy in the household (quoted in Alvarez 1990). Political democratization is therefore a precondition for advances in family law and women's rights. As Chilean feminist theorist Julieta Kirkwood argued: "There is no democracy without feminism, and no feminism without democracy" (1990). To be sure, the patriarchal military project was not seamless. Latin American militarism produced contradictory effects on gender relations and women's positions. In spite of their conservative discourse, military economic policies pushed unprecedented numbers of women into the work force, breaking down public-private distinctions and creating social dynamics that challenged traditional gender roles (Alvarez 1990; Jaquette 1994; Waylen 1996).

Given these conservative ideologies, how could military governments preside over important reforms on married women's civil rights and, in the Brazilian case, legalize divorce? To understand why, we need to look at the policy-making institutions created by military governments as well as how Church-state relations developed under military rule (this latter point is dealt with in the next section). Military governments overhauled national laws, constitutions, state bureaucracies, economic policy, and state-owned enterprises in line with principles of technical efficiency and cosmopolitan standards of modernity. The infamous "technocrats," exemplified by the "Chicago Boys" working in the Chilean Ministry of Finance during the Pinochet dictatorship, executed many of these policies. Though we commonly think of technocrats working on economic reforms, the legal field also had its fair share. Legal technocrats included lawyers, legal scholars, and judges who published in professional journals and participated in national and international legal conferences. When they decided to modernize the law, military rulers created small commissions of legal technocrats to draft proposals for change based on the newest ideas and approaches. For example, the Argentine government of General Juan Carlos Onganía organized dozens of legal commissions to overhaul the country's civil, commercial, and criminal legislation. The existence of these commissions provided a window of opportunity for elite issue networks to influence state policy, even under authoritarian conditions.

One important difference between military governments that affected their policy-making capacity was the existence of Congress. Brazil, which Juan Linz aptly calls an "authoritarian situation" as opposed to an "authoritarian regime," did not follow the usually military pattern and close its Congress (Linz 1973). To be sure, the military government circumscribed the activities of the legislature and continually rigged electoral rules to privilege the party aligned with the government (ARENA, later PDS) (Lamounier 1999; Skidmore 1988). But Congress continued to debate and approve legislation throughout most of the period of military rule. The existence of this policy-making arena enabled prodivorce coalitions to gain force during authoritarian conditions in Brazil, something that did not occur in the other two countries.

Democratic Governments

Latin American countries commonly made the transition to democracy in the 1980s and 1990s. Yet the political institutions of democratic governance – electoral rules, federalism, presidentialism, legislative procedures, party systems, and so on – contain important variations that have proven consequential for democratic stability, political practice, and policy outcomes (Ames 1995a, b, 2001; Baldez and Carey 2001; Carey 1997, 2002; Figueiredo and Limongi 1999, 2000; Jones 1997a, 2002; Jones, Saiegh, Spiller, and Tommasi 2002; Mainwaring 1999; Mainwaring and Scully 1995; Mainwaring and Shugart 1997; Morgenstern 2002; Samuels 2003; Siavelis 2002). Mainwaring and Scully show that the region's party systems vary from the highly institutionalized to the inchoate (1995). Parties in institutionalized systems, such as Chile, Costa Rica, and Uruguay, have clear internal structures and relatively stable political support, and are seen as legitimate and important political actors. Parties in inchoate systems, including Bolivia, Brazil, Ecuador, and Peru, rank low on these criteria. Parties and party systems, in turn, are significantly affected by electoral rules. Ames (1995a, b), Carey

(1997, 2002), Jones (2002) and Mainwaring (1999), among others, identify the ways that different electoral systems shape party unity by influencing the degree of nomination control exercised by party leaders and the incentives for personalistic or party-oriented activity by politicians. Meanwhile, the contributors to Mainwaring and Shugart find that variation *among* Latin America's presidential systems of government is often greater than variation *between* presidentialism and parliamentarianism (1997), while contributors to Morgenstern and Nacif (2002) explore intercountry variation in executive-legislative relations, internal legislative organization, and the legislature's role in policy making.

These institutional differences help to account for distinct patterns of policy making across countries. In Brazil, a combination of a fragmented party system, weak party discipline, and "robust federalism" thwarted the executive's attempts to fight inflation and reform the state during three administrations in the mid- to late 1980s and early 1990s (Mainwaring 1999). Problems with the party system can be largely attributed to Brazil's electoral rules, which combine an extreme form of proportional representation (a low threshold and high district magnitude) with a preference-voting system that encourages personalistic behavior. Historically, moreover, Brazilian legislators have enjoyed the automatic right to stand for reelection, further reducing the leverage of party leaders. Lamounier, one of the most prominent critics of Brazil's combination of presidentialism and fragmented multipartyism, argues that the country suffers from a "hyperactive paralysis syndrome" which thwarts significant attempts at reform on gender as well as other issues (1999). Nonetheless, there is evidence that this traditional pattern may have changed as parties became more disciplined throughout the 1990s. Whereas some attribute this evidence of increased party unity in roll-call voting to the legislative powers of the president and the strength of party leaders (Figueiredo and Limongi 2000), others argue that pork-barrel expenditures, constituency structure, popularity, ideology, and other factors are better predictors of how deputies vote and that party unity in Brazil is considerably lower than in other countries (Ames 2001).[13]

In Argentina, by contrast, a two-party-dominant system and moderate to high degree of party discipline in the legislature contributed to the country's *relative* policy success, particularly its ability to weather a severe economic crisis at the end of the 1980s. Electoral rules, including a closed-list proportional representation system, relatively low district magnitude (an average of five deputies per district), and plurality elections for senators and governors, helped maintain the two-party system and party discipline, as did the ability of party leaders in Congress to affect, by determining committee memberships and allocating budgetary resources, legislators' ability to deliver goods to their constituencies (Jones 2002). Compared with their counterparts

---

[13] For a good review of this debate, see Amorim Neto (2001).

in Brazil, moreover, Argentine legislators are more likely to focus on national policy issues than on pork-barrel projects for their constituents. Only 14 percent of the bills introduced in 1994, for example, could be classified as pork (Jones 1997a: 277–8). To be sure, Argentine democracy has its problems, including lack of judicial independence, limited provincial autonomy, and the excessive use of presidential decree powers, though many of these issues were addressed in the 1994 constitutional reforms (ibid.). The relative inclination of Argentina's parties and institutions toward policies of national importance is reflected in the Radical Party's championing of liberal changes to family law, and of a multipartisan advocacy of divorce, in the mid-1980s. Argentine liberal lawyers and feminist activists found common ground with liberal parties in Congress and actors in the executive branch committed to reform.

Chile's democratic political institutions have been far more affected by an authoritarian legacy than counterparts in Brazil or Argentina. Democrats agreed to respect the constitution promulgated by military rulers in 1980, which established, among other problematic features, the presence of eight "institutional" senators appointed by Pinochet (the so-called *designados*). The presence of the *designados* increased the power of the socially conservative voting bloc in the Senate, frustrating reform on even mildly controversial gender issues (Londregan 2000). Military rulers also changed the electoral norms to create incentives for a de facto two-party system by creating sixty two-member districts to elect the lower house and requiring that a party or coalition receive twice as many votes as the runner-up in order to capture both seats (Rabkin 1996; Siavelis 1997). These rules required Chile's historic multiparty system essentially to squeeze itself into a two-coalition framework. The two coalitions have proven durable and unified throughout the 1990s (Carey 2002). Nonetheless, to maintain unity and their hold on power against opposition from the right-wing coalition, members of the governing coalition, comprised of Christian Democratic, Socialist, and Democratic (PPD) parties, have sought to avoid potentially divisive issues such as divorce and abortion. Coalition politics in Chile has generally impeded policy changes favored by feminists (Baldez 2001). In short, though Latin American democratic governments rhetorically committed themselves to an agenda of liberal rights on family law and gender equality, not all were able to deliver. The authoritarian legacy in the political system, coalitional dynamics, party systems, and electoral rules affected the prospects for reform on gender issues.

Church-State Relations

The final variable affecting the "fit" between issue networks and the state is Church-state relations. Seen most broadly, the process of gender law liberalization described in this study involved the replacement of laws inspired by traditional Roman Catholic ethics on male authority, indissoluble marriage, and the crime of abortion with new laws inspired by feminism and liberalism. Though this makes the Church an integral part of the story, it is important to bear in mind that Roman Catholic bishops did not contest all gender-related policy changes. By the 1960s, Roman Catholic doctrine had replaced a traditional model of male authority with acceptance of sex equality within marriage. As a result, the bishops did not act to oppose reforms advancing family equality. Church doctrine on divorce and abortion did not change. The Church always opposed the legalization of divorce and the decriminalization of abortion. Yet historically the Church acted to oppose divorce more vehemently than abortion because of the threat to its values posed by pro-divorce movements. Issue networks of lawyers, socialists, and liberals had mobilized to demand divorce since the nineteenth century. A large movement proposing alternative ideas about abortion, however, emerged only in the late twentieth century. The general social consensus that abortion was morally wrong assured the Church that its position was safe, and it chose not to contest some early, liberalizing reforms to abortion laws. After the middle of the twentieth century, the diffusion of feminist liberal ideas about elective abortion compelled the Church firmly to defend the sanctity of embryonic life under all circumstances.

The evolution of Church doctrine and the perceived threat to core Church principles shaped the Church's decision on whether or not to contest reforms. Yet even when the Church contested reform, it could still be defeated (see Fig. 1.1). Cracks in the Church-state relationship opened a window of opportunity for liberal issue networks to defeat the Church. How did this come about? Though the Latin American Church had historically allied itself with the conservative oligarchy and the military, many bishops transferred their allegiances in the 1970s and 1980s. Latin American bishops influenced by liberation theology condemned the human rights abuses of military governments, introduced new participatory structures, and worked

FIGURE 1.1. The Church and gender policy reforms.

with social movements and labor unions to demand social justice (Gilfeather 1979; Levine and Mainwaring 1989; Mainwaring and Wilde 1989; Moreira Alves 1984; Smith 1982). In many countries, the Church hierarchy formally opposed the military government and supported social movement networks struggling to bring about an end to authoritarian rule (Mainwaring 1986; Smith 1982).

These shifting relationships between Church and state produced by military rule and democratic transition were consequential for Church influence over policy issues it cared about. During periods of Church-state cooperation, state leaders realized benefits from the Church's political support and were unwilling to make moves that would incur episcopal wrath. When the Church turned against the state, opportunities emerged for opposing coalitions to step in and produce shifts in gender rights legislation. When national governments clashed with the Church over policy issues such as human rights, economic development, and education, liberal issues networks could overpower the Church. At other times, the Church elected to contest reform and succeeded.

In summary, differences among issues, political institutions, and Church-state relations shaped the ability of issue networks to produce policy change. Figure 1.2 illustrates how these variables affect the "fit" between issue networks and the state (cf. Skocpol 1992: 54). Large coalitions of feminists, middle-class male lawyers, and liberal and socialist politicians endorsed change on gender equality in the family and divorce. Under military rule, the creation of expert policy-making commissions opened a window of opportunity for these coalitions to produce policy change on gender equality in the family. Under democratic conditions, the possibility for change turned

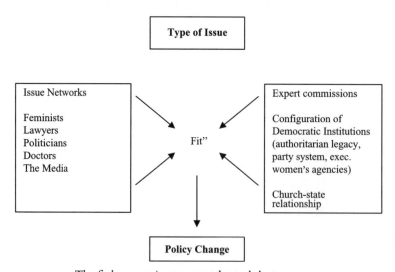

FIGURE 1.2. The fit between issue networks and the state.

on the military legacy, the party system, and executive commitment. For divorce to be legalized, however, the Church needed to be defeated. Cracks in the Church-state relationship allowed the liberal partisans of divorce to overpower the Church. On abortion, fewer people supported change, and fierce opposition grew over time. Partisans of liberal abortion have been unable to defeat the Church and antiabortion movements. At the same time, they also have been unable to persuade average citizens – who offer moral support to restrictive abortion laws, while undermining them in practice – to come to terms with the inherent contradictions of such a position.

Other Hypotheses: Modernization and Culture

At this point, the skeptical reader may be wondering, Why focus on issue differences, issue networks, and political institutions? Couldn't the legal changes in question merely be a function of socioeconomic development or a transformation in cultural values? After all, economic development involves the incorporation of women into the work force, a rise in women's education, and a drop in fertility, trends that transformed family structures and gender roles in many countries. As women's social and economic status has increased, they have become less dependent on men, altering marriage dynamics as well as traditional sexual mores. The law must respond to these social changes. Moreover, theories maintaining that developmental trajectories are best explained by a country's culture, attitudes, and values are enjoying a renaissance in political science (Fukuyama 1995; Grondona 1999; Harrison and Huntington 2000; Inglehart 1997). Even if one doesn't buy the proposition that culture accounts for political and economic performance (Jackman and Miller 1996), it seems plausible that culture would exert a major influence on state decisions to regulate family life and intimate relationships. A central theme of most cultures is "the sphere of personal, sexual, and reproductive life," and the enforcement of rules governing intimate behavior is a crucial indicator of the cohesiveness and survival of cultural groups (Okin 1999: 13). To make the analysis of this book more convincing, we should pause and evaluate the merit of modernization and cultural explanations for policy change.

If modernization arguments are correct, we would expect indicators of national wealth, women's labor force participation, and fertility to correspond to policy outcomes on gender and the family in Latin America (see Tables 1.4–1.6). Argentina had the highest overall level of economic development and the least inequality, and Chile the fastest economic growth. Brazil lagged both. If *levels* of modernity explain policy, then laws on gender in Argentina and Chile should be the most "progressive." Argentina granted women equal property rights in 1968, but waited until 1987 to legalize divorce. Chile, meanwhile, waited until 1989 to change a law stating that women owe obedience to their husbands, and has failed to legalize divorce or

TABLE I.4. *Economic Indicators*

Country	GDP per capita, 1998 ($)	Average growth of GDP per capita, 1989–98 (%)	Gini coefficient, latest available data (measure of income inequality)
Argentina	6,720.40	2.4	0.46
Brazil	3,195.60	0.4	0.63
Chile	4,047.00	5.9	0.57

Source: Inter-American Development Bank.

TABLE I.5. *Women as Percentage of the Labor Force*

Country	1950	1960	1970	1980	1990	2000
Argentina	20	21.2	24.8	28	29	33
Brazil	15.4	17.8	20.4	28	35	36
Chile	25.2	22	22.2	26	30	34

Source: FLACSO (1995); World Bank (2002).

TABLE I.6. *Changes in Fertility (number of children born per woman)*

Country	1950–5	1970–5	1980–5	1990	2000
Argentina	3.2	3.2	2.8	2.9	2.5
Brazil	6.2	4.7	2.8	2.7	2.2
Chile	5.1	3.6	2.7	2.6	2.2

Source: FLACSO (1995); World Bank (2002).

make the marital property regime fully equal. Brazil – the poorest and most unequal country of the three – was the first to legalize divorce and the first to grant married women full legal agency. These differences in the timing and approach of policy persisted even though levels of women's labor force participation and fertility were similar in the three countries (in 2000, women accounted for 33 to 36 percent of the labor force in all three countries and fertility rates were 2.2 to 2.5 children per woman).

A hypothesis linking the *rate* of modernization to legal outcomes might be more promising. Karl Deutsch, for example, argued that people experiencing dislocations in their daily lives would increase the demands on governments, prompting major changes in political practice and institutions (1971: 390–1). By implication, we might expect to see legal reform in countries such as Brazil that underwent extensive modernization within a short time period. Until 1970, Brazil lagged behind Argentina and Chile in women's labor force participation and fertility. By the 1990s, Brazil had pulled ahead. A "rate of modernization" hypothesis thus might explain why some of Brazil's laws changed before those of the other two countries. However, a "rate of modernization" hypothesis cannot account for the differences between Argentina and Chile, where the rates of change are more similar, but legal outcomes different.

Does state policy on gender and the family reflect more liberal or more conservative cultures? If cultural arguments are correct, we should see a correlation between national cultural variables (such as religious values, beliefs about gender roles, and public opinion) and policy changes.[14] Yet in Latin America, cultural arguments have limited predictive power. The intensity of religious beliefs does not correspond to the course of gender rights reform. The World Values Survey data indicate that religious devotion is strongest among Brazilians and weakest among Argentines, with Chile occupying a middle ground.[15] However, it is in Brazil where the debate about the decriminalization of abortion has advanced the farthest and divorce was first legalized. Nor do patterns of reform correspond to public attitudes toward gender roles and relationships. Based on data about gender role beliefs in the World Values Survey, we would expect married women to have more, or at least as many, rights in Chile as in the other two countries. In reality, Chile's laws were the last to change and as of 2002 remained more inegalitarian than laws in Argentina and Brazil.[16] Finally, the pace of reform does not

[14] To study culture systematically and cross-nationally, political scientists long ago decided to take political culture to mean "attitudes toward the political system and its various parts, and attitudes toward the role of the self in the system" (Almond and Verba 1963). Other social scientists find such an approach too limited, agreeing with Clifford Geertz that culture is not subjective but "public." In Geertz's view, culture lies not in the beliefs we hold inside our heads but in the intersubjective "webs of significance" collectively spun by societies (1973). Geertz's approach (which is, in my view, the best way to think about culture) makes it methodologically impossible to study culture as a causal variable. Conceived as "webs of significance," culture is both an independent and a dependent variable – there is no way to step outside of it. At any rate, the purpose of this section is not to adjudicate competing definitions or approaches to culture, but merely to evaluate the analytical plausibility of hypotheses based on the operational political science definition of culture as subjective attitudes and values.

[15] The World Values Survey provides data on church attendance, one indicator of religious devotion. On a scale of one to eight (one the lowest attendance and eight the highest), the country means are 3.71 in Argentina, 4.68 in Brazil, and 4.36 in Chile (Blofeld 1998: 10). The values on the survey range from 1 (never attend church), 2 (less than once a year), 3 (once a year), 4 (holidays), 5 (Christmas/Easter), 6 (once a month), 7 (once a week), and 8 (attend church more than once a week).

[16] The World Values Survey shows that attitudes toward women's work are most "liberal" in Brazil and Chile and least "liberal" in Argentina, while attitudes toward motherhood are most "liberal" in Argentina and Chile and least "liberal" in Brazil. Seventy-three percent of Brazilians and 70 percent of Chileans agreed that having a job is the best way for a woman to be an independent person, compared with 58 percent of Argentines. Ninety-three percent of Brazilians and 86 percent of Chileans agree that both a husband and wife should contribute to household income, compared with 75 percent of Argentines. When asked whether a working mother can establish just as warm and secure a relationship with her children as a mother who does not work, 71 percent of Chileans and 72 percent of Argentines agreed or

always correspond to the extent of public support for new laws and policies. In Chile, for example, national public opinion polls demonstrate overwhelming public support for the legalization of divorce, yet divorce remains illegal. On the other hand, the failure of public opinion to endorse elective abortion more enthusiastically makes the issue unattractive to politicians, helping to account for the lack of change in abortion politics, as Chapter 6 discusses. In short, though socioeconomic modernization and cultural transformation are important shapers of the context of gender policy, explaining change requires that we turn to politics.

strongly agreed, compared with 62 percent of Brazilians. World Values Survey (available at the Harvard-MIT Data Center: http://data.fas.harvard.edu/).

2

Four Normative Traditions

Struggles over state policy on divorce, abortion, and family equality revolve around competing ideas of how state institutions should regulate citizen's intimate lives and relationships. Should the law uphold the husband's authority in marriage, or recognize equality between the sexes? Ought the family be protected through prohibitions on divorce, or does this violate the separation of Church and state? Must the law protect life at the moment of conception by forbidding abortion, or grant women the freedom to choose? These conflicting positions are not of recent vintage, but rooted in decades- and even centuries-old normative traditions offering distinct models of men and women's roles, reproduction and the family, and the appropriate use of state power. The normative traditions of gender and the state found in Roman Catholicism, liberalism, feminism, and socialism contextualize the political struggles depicted in this book. The agreements and disagreements among Catholicism, liberalism, feminism, and socialism helped frame gender policy debates and opposition to proposals for change.

This chapter sketches the evolution of ideas about gender policy issues in four normative traditions of gender and the state and describes the historical development of Latin American civil and criminal codes. In many ways, these normative traditions resemble the "policy paradigms" described by Peter Hall in his analysis of competing approaches to economic management (1992, 1993). A policy paradigm consists of an overarching set of ideas about how problems are to be perceived, policy goals, and techniques to achieve these goals. Hall notes that competing economic policy paradigms are based on different models of the economy, which, as "a set of human relationships and material flows that cannot be perceived by the naked eye ... must be interpreted or modeled to be understood, and from divergent models flow different prescriptions for policy" (1992: 92). Gender, like the economy, needs to be interpreted to be understood. Policy paradigms of gender and the state resemble economic paradigms in that they provide interpretation, analysis, and prescription.

Yet the ideas studied here differ in two ways from the kinds of ideas analyzed in literature on economic policy making, such as the work by Peter Hall (1992, 1993) and Kathryn Sikkink (1991) on Keynesianism and developmentalism, respectively. Whereas ideas about economic policy focus on *means* (how best to achieve economic growth, for example), ideas about gender are usually about the *ends*, or the ultimate justifications, for law and policy. They are principled, rather than instrumental, ideas. And whereas Keynesianism and developmentalism are twentieth-century concepts, certain ideas about gender are very old. Christian teachings on family relations and abortion originate in the New Testament, and Church rules against abortion date from the fourth century. Liberal ideas about the separation of Church and state are at least as old as Locke's *Letter Concerning Toleration* of 1788. The longevity and the principled nature of ideas about gender raise the stakes in debates on policy reforms. Conflicts between Roman Catholic bishops, state officials, politicians, lawyers, and feminist activists are about competing visions of the normative order, not merely the distribution of political power and resources.

As Chapter 1 argued, gender policy issues need to be disaggregated. One way to do this is to differentiate the ideas behind various policy options. Though Roman Catholic doctrine initially endorsed the patriarchal family, Church views changed. After the 1960s and 1970s, Catholicism, liberalism, feminism, and socialism generally supported sex equality in marriage and the family. Social changes and the influence of feminism helped propel a convergence of traditions on this issue. Divorce, on the other hand, divides Catholics from liberals, feminists, and socialists. Catholic doctrine maintains that marriage is an indissoluble institution; the secular traditions see marriage as a civil contract terminable at the will of the parties involved. Conflicts over divorce revolved around whether the law should guarantee individual liberties or reflect ideas of the good rooted in Catholic ethics. Abortion is another issue that generates deep conflict between world views. Whereas feminists view abortion as a woman's right and a question of individual liberty and privacy, bishops of the Roman Catholic Church, among others, contend that abortion is murder. In other countries of the world, liberalism and socialism have come to endorse a woman's right to terminate her pregnancy. In Latin America, however, many defenders of these traditions have persisted in condemning abortion.

The Roman Catholic Tradition

Roman Catholicism, from the teachings of the New Testament to the natural law philosophy of Saint Thomas Aquinas (1225–74) and the pronouncements of Roman Catholic popes and bishops' councils, is the oldest and most influential ethical tradition in the Latin American region. The importance of Catholic thought for state organization and public policy has been well documented. The "organic-statist" model of governance proposed by Aristotle, Aquinas, and the modern papal encyclicals *Rerum novarum* (1891) and *Quadragesimo anno* (1931) have served as the intellectual guide and philosophical rationale for twentieth-century Latin American corporatist[1] arrangements (Stepan 1978; Wiarda 1973). The governments of Juan Perón in Argentina in the 1940s, Getulio Vargas in Brazil in the 1930s, Lazaro Cárdenas in Mexico in the 1930s, the Peruvian experiment of General Velasco in the 1960s and 1970s, and General Onganía in Argentina of the late 1960s all exhibited strong corporatist features. Thomist natural law philosophy and Catholic social thought spawned the emergence of Latin America's Christian Democratic parties and inspired their political programs (Lynch 1993; Sigmund 1988; Williams 1967). In line with general principles of Catholic social thought, these parties have emphasized the "moral and spiritual nature of human beings," a relatively high level of state social spending, and the idea that people be "induced to act morally with the fruits of their labor and investment" (Lynch 1993: xiv).[2]

Thomist philosophy and Catholic doctrine on morality and sexual ethics constitute the historical cultural backdrop for law and policy making on women's rights, marriage, and abortion in Latin America. The Roman Catholic tradition provides a basic script for men's and women's proper roles, the function and nature of marriage and the family, and the significance of reproduction. Yet the Roman Catholic tradition has changed over time, particularly with respect to women's equal rights. From an initially patriarchal stance, the Church position evolved to endorse equality between spouses. The Church advocates an "essentialist difference feminism" in which women are equal to, but essentially different from, men. Women should not be discriminated against on the ground of sex, and deserve special rights and protections in virtue of their roles and aptitudes. This "essentialist difference feminism" has been an attractive ethic for many women in Latin America.

For most of the Church's history, however, Catholic thought held that women must be subordinate to male authority in the family. Women were considered less rational and less competent than men, and therefore unable

---

[1] Corporatism, according to Philippe Schmitter's well-known definition, is "a system of interest representation in which the constituent units are organized into a limited number of singular, compulsory, noncompetitive, hierarchically ordered and functionally differentiated categories, recognized or licensed (if not created) by the state and granted a deliberate representational monopoly within their respective categories in exchange for observing certain controls on their selection of leaders and articulation of demands and supports" (1979). G. W. F. Hegel also provided inspiration for corporatist arrangements. In the state model set out by Hegel in his *Philosophy of Right*, civil society is organized into functionally differentiated corporations (1991).

[2] Lynch, however, argues that Latin American Christian Democratic parties have departed significantly from classical Catholic social thought. Whereas the former have endorsed highly statist economic policies, classical thought is quite antistatist in its emphasis on independent social groups and their autonomy from the state (1993).

to exercise the same rights and assume the same obligations. Saint Thomas Aquinas maintained that husbands had exclusive authority over household decision making, and also stated that children should love their fathers more than their mothers because of their fathers' greater "excellence" (Archibald 1988: 141). In the encyclical *Rerum novarum* of 1891, Pope Leo XIII declared that "a family, no less than a State, is, as we have said, a true society, governed by a power within itself, that is to say, by a father" (Pope Leo XIII 1891:) Consequently, the Church opposed legal reforms to grant women greater power in family matters, such as in the control of marital property and in decision making related to children.

In the 1950s and the 1960s, Catholic doctrine changed. In *Peace on Earth* (1963), Pope John XXIII wrote of "equal rights and duties for man and woman" in the family. Pope John's statement foreshadowed the major doctrinal changes introduced by the Second Vatican Council (1962–5), which expressed a much greater awareness of women's importance to the Church and the mutuality of men and women in all spheres of life (Morrisey 1977). *Gaudium et spes*, the major document on the Church's relations with state and society, proposed that in marriage, man and woman "render mutual help and service to each other through an intimate union of their persons and their actions" (1965: 671) and claimed that "the unity of marriage will radiate from the equal personal dignity of wife and husband, a dignity acknowledged by mutual and total love" (1965: 673). In the late 1960s and 1970s, many bishops in Latin America, in line with Council doctrine, supported reforms to the civil code to grant women shared parental power and equal rights in the administration of marital property.[3] Nonetheless, some Latin American Catholics opposed family law reforms, not because they objected to women's equality, but because they felt that liberalizing changes would compromise the sanctity of the institution of marriage.[4]

Although the Church came to recognize women's independence and equality as persons, it insisted that this equality be rooted in women's proper nature. In 1974, Pope Paul VI praised women's demands for equal rights and dignity, but rejected a "false equality which would be in contradiction with women's proper role, which is of such capital importance, at the heart of the family as well as within society" (quoted in Foley 1997: 90). Women are distinct from men, and have a unique mission stemming from their reproductive capacity and their roles as mothers. As John Paul II puts it, *"a woman represents a particular value by the fact that she is a human person,*

---

[3] In a document released in 1975, for example, the Brazilian Bishops' Council declared its support for the "promotion of equality of the position of spouses within the family through the elimination of existing restrictions characteristic of a patriarchal society." *Jornal de Brasília*, March 21, 1975.

[4] As Chapter 4 discusses, Chilean conservatives opposed reforming the marital property regime and removing distinctions between legitimate and illegitimate children on the grounds that these changes would devalue the institution of marriage.

and, at the same time, this particular person, *by the fact of her femininity*"
(1988: 108). Roman Catholic "essentialist difference feminism" justifies gender equality from an essentialist standpoint. Complementary sex differences
are constitutive of equality.

Although the Church position changed on the issue of women's rights
in the family and in society at large, the Church has remained intractable
on the issues of divorce and abortion. The Church position against divorce
stems from its ideas about the nature of marriage. Marriage is not a personal
contract between the spouses, but an institution authored by God:

> The intimate partnership of married life and love has been established by the Creator
> and qualified by his laws. It is rooted in the conjugal covenant of irrevocable personal
> consent. Hence, by that human act whereby spouses mutually bestow and accept each
> other, a relationship arises which by divine will and in the eyes of society too is a
> lasting one. For the good of the spouses and their offspring as well as of society, the
> existence of this sacred bond no longer depends on human decisions alone. (*Gaudiem
> et spes* 1965: 670–1)

The Church praises the personal elements of marriage, such as conjugal
love, affection, and the "marital act." But marriage has public and social
objectives that are larger than the personal aims of the two spouses, and
a sacramental character that cannot be modified either by human will or
by public laws. The public and sacramental character of marriage makes it
distinct from civil contracts, and leads canonical scholars to refer to marriage
as an *institution*, not a contract (Hortal 1991: 21).[5] Marriage, moreover,
cannot be terminated except by the death of one spouse. As Canon 1141
proclaims: "Ratified and consummated marriage cannot be dissolved by any
human power or cause, except death" (ibid.: 176).

The Roman Catholic position on abortion today is clear: Abortion is the
murder of an innocent human life. Historically, however, the Church's ideas
about abortion were more nuanced. The Church always condemned abortion, but did not consider abortion to be homicide until the fetus had acquired
a soul. Until 1869, the Aristotelian notion that the fetus acquired a soul forty
to eighty days after conception largely prevailed. Although there was debate
over the distinction between the "ensouled" and "unensouled" fetus, most
Church canons accepted that homicide was committed only with the abortion of an ensouled fetus.[6] Scientific advances of the nineteenth century,

---

[5] Even in canon law, marriage resembles a contract more than an institution in some respects.
For example, marriage based on consent begins when the two spouses declare their consent at
a legitimate ceremony, and exists only as long as the two contracting spouses live. However,
the notion of marriage as a contract cannot capture (according to Catholic theologians) its
permanent and objective character, and the fact that marriage transcends the will and actions
of the married persons (Hortal 1991: 22–3).

[6] The compilation of ecclesiastical laws by Gratian (1140) and the decretals of Pope Gregory IX
(1234) sustained the distinction between the ensouled and unensouled fetus, and the papal bull

combined with developments in the doctrine of the Immaculate Conception (in 1854, the Pope declared that Mary was free from sin at the moment of her conception), prompted the Church to reject the distinction between the ensouled and unensouled fetus. In the 1869 *Apostolicace sedis*, the reference to the ensouled fetus was dropped in the abortion excommunication (Muraro 1989; Noonan 1970). As Posner puts it, "from the beginning, the Church took a hard line against abortion. Later it became even harder" (1992: 273).

Considerable ambiguity and debate surrounded the lawfulness of "therapeutic" abortion to avert a serious risk to the life of the mother. Much of the debate turned on the intention of the mother. If abortion is the indirect consequence of a medical procedure designed to save the mother, it may be morally valid, since the primary intention is to protect life, not to abort the fetus (Muraro 1989: 87; Noonan 1970: 28).[7] Many Church thinkers voiced support for therapeutic abortion until 1930, when the encyclical *Casti connubii* harshly condemned abortion, including therapeutic abortion. In "the strongest and most comprehensive denunciation of abortion by papal authority," Pope Pius XI asked, "What cause can ever avail to excuse in any way the killing of the innocent?" (Noonan 1970: 43–4). The hardening of the Church's position on abortion was accompanied by parallel changes in Church doctrine on contraception. The 1968 encyclical *Humanae vitae* declared that contraception violates the moral law and that "each and every marital act must of necessity retain its intrinsic relationship to the procreation of human life" (Pope Paul VI 1968). Still, debate about the beginning of life and the lawfulness of therapeutic abortion persisted among Catholic theologians, particularly those influenced by feminism. As late as 1974, the Vatican's Congregation for the Doctrine of the Faith released a declaration acknowledging that the personhood of the fetus was a theological question that could not be determined by science or medicine. Official statements claimed instead that the fetus must be treated *as if* it is a person. As Kissling points out, "this doubt about the condition of the fetus is critical to understand how one can be *Catholic* and support a woman's right to make a decision on whether or not to have an abortion" (Kissling 1989: 114).

Effraenatam (1588, revised in 1591) called for the penalties established by canon and secular law against homicide to be applied to the abortion of an ensouled fetus. For Saint Thomas Aquinas, the killing of an ensouled embryo was homicide, but ensoulment did not occur at conception. Finnis, however, argues that if Aquinas had the benefit of modern scientific discoveries, he would have concluded that insemination of the ovum is sufficient to establish the personhood (ensoulment) of the embryo (Finnis 1998: 196).

7 Aquinas had stated that the moral status of an act lies in its intention: "Moral acts are classified on the basis of what is intended, not what happened outside of our intention since that is incidental to it.... The action of defending oneself may produce two effects – one, of saving one's own life, and the other, killing the attacker. Now an action of this kind intended to save one's own life can not be characterized as illicit since it is natural for anyone to maintain himself in existence if he can" (1988: 70).

Seen from a liberal and a feminist perspective, Catholic ethics thwart individual aspirations for personal and reproductive freedom. But Catholic ethics are concerned with the valorization of femininity, motherhood, and the protection of women. Women's role in salvation and revelation means that women enjoy a special authority. As Pope John Paul II points out, "unless one looks to the Mother of God, it is impossible to understand the mystery of the Church, her reality, her essential vitality.... The Bible convinces us of the fact that one can have no adequate hermeneutic of man, of what is 'human,' without appropriate reference to what is 'feminine' " (1988: 84). The Church's regulation and promotion of companionate marriage, more-over, advanced women's interests.[8] Ecclesiastical courts, because they attempted to verify the free consent of each spouse to marriage, helped shield women from manipulation into marriage by their families (Dore 2000: 13). Church prohibitions on divorce gave women financial security (Posner 1992: 250). Early liberalism, by contrast, largely ignored women. There were few secular counterparts to the positive feminine identity scripts Catholic theology provided to women. Catholic ethics, moreover, implore men to be faithful to and respectful of their wives. As Aquinas stated, "[t]he intercourse of the male must be with a specific female and he should stay with her not for a little while but for a long period of time or even for a whole lifetime" (Aquinas 1988: 78). Men are forbidden to engage in promiscuous behav-ior, consort with concubines, or commit adultery. Moreover, by virtue of women's special part in shared parenthood, men must be aware that they owe "a special debt to the woman." John Paul II declared: "No programme of 'equal rights' between women and men is valid unless it takes this fact fully into account" (1988: 69).

Catholic ethics on gender, marriage, and reproduction are influential because the vast majority of Latin Americans are Catholics, and Roman Catholic bishops enjoy tremendous moral authority. Two components of the Catholic theory of the state further enhance the importance of Catholic ethics for public policy. The first is the idea that the state has a moral purpose, which is to realize the common good. Every action the state takes must be ori-ented toward and justified in light of this end. As Aquinas puts it, "law has as its first and foremost purpose the ordering of the common good" (1988: 45). In contrast to the liberal tradition, where the validity of laws derives from

---

[8] Companionate marriage "signifies marriage between at least approximate equals, based on mutual respect and affection, and involving close and continuous association in child rearing, household management, and other activities, rather than merely the occasional copulation that was the principal contact between spouses in the typical Greek marriage.... The idea of companionate marriage implies the injection of feeling and sentiment into a relationship dominated up to then by considerations of male sexual desire, financial arrangements, and heirship" (Posner 1992: 45). As Posner puts it, "if women are deemed simple breeders and drudges, uneduated and uneducable – they will not seem fit to participate with men in a relationship, such as companionate marriage, that is built on love and trust" (ibid.: 159).

the procedures through which laws are formulated, the common good provides a standard of legal legitimacy independent of procedures.[9] The second
important feature of the Catholic theory of the state is the idea that natural
law serves as the normative basis of law making. The legitimacy of human
laws rests on the extent to which they uphold the precepts of natural law,
"a single standard of truth and right for everyone" (Aquinas 1988: 50).
Several elements of Catholic ethics, such as the institution of marriage, the
prohibition of adultery, and the unlawfulness of killing, are rooted in natural
law. For strict Catholics, this means that such principles are eternal truths
and not subject to compromise.[10] In summary, two ideas at the center of
Catholic political thought – the notion that the state has a moral purpose
and that natural law guides and constrains civil laws – lend an urgency to
the Church's moral teachings on divorce and abortion. They imply that the
law cannot be neutral when it comes to gender, but must take a morally
principled stand.

Liberalism

Liberalism furnishes theoretical grounds for policy proposals opposed to
Church doctrine, particularly on divorce.[11] Three liberal principles – the

---

[9] Stepan points out that "this 'common good,' while by no means intrinsically anti-democratic,
lends itself to nonliberal legitimacy formulas for two basic reasons. First, it opens the possibility that, since the common good can be known by 'right reason,' there is no need for a
process whereby interest groups express their opinions and preferences in order for leaders
of the state to 'know' what the common good is. Second ... the pursuit of the common
good (rather than elections or representation by group interests) is the measure by which the
legitimacy of the state is evaluated" (1978: 31).

[10] As Aquinas pointed out, "every human law that is adopted has the quality of law to the
extent that it is derived from natural law. But if it disagrees in some respect from the natural
law, it is no longer a law but a corruption of law" (1988: 53). The proposition that the
indissolubility of marriage is rooted in the natural law, however, has generated debate among
Catholics. Many of the arguments against the legalization of divorce center on the claim that
according to natural law, marriage is indissoluble or else it is not marriage (Familias por la
Familia n.d.; Guzmán 1976). According to others, however, the indissolubility of marriage
forms part of what Aquinas called the "secondary precepts" of natural law, and therefore is
subject to change (Alywin and Walker 1996: 61). Aquinas admits that there are exceptions
to the application of these secondary precepts: "[A]s far as its general first principles are
concerned the natural law is the same for all, both as a standard of right action and as to
the possibility that it can be known. However as to more particular cases which are its
conclusions, as it were, from its general principles it is the same for everyone in most cases,
both as a standard of right action and as known (by all). However in particular instances
there can be exceptions both with regard to their rightness because of certain obstacles ...
and to their being known" (1988: 51).

[11] The diversity of the liberal tradition must be kept in mind. The differences in the legal framework of marriage, divorce, and abortion in the United States and Great Britain, on the one
hand, and continental Europe, on the other, are significant, although today all reflect a tension between "the symbolism of family cohesiveness and that of independent individualism"

separation of Church and state, the priority of principles of right over ideas of the good, and the defense of individual liberties – lend unequivocal support to legal divorce.[12] The conflict between Catholicism and liberalism over divorce touches at the core of the two traditions. According to most liberals, the state must be separate from religious institutions and not promote particular religious principles, As Locke's *Letter Concerning Toleration* argued, the jurisdiction of the state is confined only to "Civil Concernments," and in no way should be extended to the "Salvation of Souls."[13]

In line with these principles, liberals in Latin America always insisted on the firm separation of Church and state, and struggled to reduce ecclesiastical power and privileges during much of the nineteenth century. In Mexico, liberal reforms adopted under Benito Juarez in the 1850s secured a definitive separation between Church and state and provided full religious liberty (Mecham 1966: 364). During the Brazilian Empire, the Liberal Party advocated freedom of religion and state education free from religious control (Viotti da Costa 1985b). In 1890, Brazilian liberals and republicans established the equality of religions before the law, the separation of secular and religious education, the institution of secular marriage, the creation of a civil registry, and the secularization of cemeteries (Viotti da Costa 1985a). In the 1880s and 1890s, liberals in Argentina, Chile, and Uruguay implemented reforms that expanded state control over education and civil marriage, and reduced Church authority over the registry of births and deaths and over cemeteries (Mecham 1966). Uniting these reforms was the idea that

(Glendon 1989: 103). Still, the United States has gone further than other Western countries in articulating a constitutional right to marital privacy (and subsequent principle of nonstate regulation of marriage), permitting unilateral no-fault divorce on demand, and interpreting a woman's freedom of choice to have an abortion as a constitutional right (Glendon 1987, 1989). Continental European liberalism, which has historically reflected a more systematic effort to balance the claims of individual liberty and equality with the preservation of community norms than Anglo-American liberalism, is a more prominent reference point for liberal thought in Latin America.

[12] Though liberalism is unequivocal on divorce, there is considerable variation, among liberal states, on the conditions under which divorce should be granted. At one extreme is the United States, where marriage is terminable at the unilateral request of either party in eighteen states. The French divorce law, on the other hand, provides mixed grounds for divorce. Mutual-consent divorce is the centerpiece of the law, but other grounds for divorce such as divorce for prolonged separation or fault are contemplated and their procedures spelled out. See Glendon (1989), chap. 4.

[13] Church-state separation serves the interests of both parties. Locke maintained that the imposition of religion by the state is contrary to the true nature of faith, and therefore contemptuous of God. A proper Church has the right to make its own laws independently of the state's interference (Locke 1689). Around the time of the Second Vatican Council, the Roman Catholic Church embraced a similar argument by distinguishing between temporal and spiritual authority, thereby accepting the separation of Church and state. Nonetheless, conservative Latin American bishops failed to acknowledge this principle while arguing that the state should continue to uphold the Catholic principle of marital indissolubility.

principles of state decision making must conform to universal principles of
justice, not the ethics of any particular religious tradition. Only in this way
can the liberal state permit religious liberty as well as allow individuals and
groups to pursue their varied visions of the good life (Rawls 1971, 1993).
Particular ethical claims, such as the Catholic notion of the common good
and the natural law, cannot guide political decision making. As Dworkin puts
it, "political decisions must be, so far as possible, independent of any particular conception of the good life, or of what gives value to life" (Dworkin
1984: 64). Prohibitions on divorce violate the boundary between Church
and state and unjustly apply one religious doctrine to all citizens.[14] (Other
Christian denominations, as well as Islam and Judaism, admit divorce.)

Liberalism has had, in practice, more ambiguous implications for women's
equality in the family and for abortion. Though liberalism maintains that
citizens should enjoy equal rights, women's unequal treatment under liberal
regimes found justification within the theories of liberal thinkers. The early
liberalism of John Locke, for example, held that natural differences among
men could not justify the arbitrary rule of one over the other, but that natural differences between the sexes justified the subordination of women to
men (Pateman 1989: 121). As Okin points out, "both political rights and
the rights pertaining to the modern liberal conception of privacy and the
private have been claimed as rights of individuals; but these individuals were
assumed, and often explicitly stated, to be adult male heads of households"
(1991: 70). The unwillingness of traditional liberal thinkers to extend principles of public justice and equality to women derived from their belief that
women were inferior to men and naturally part of private or domestic life.
The domestic sphere was assumed to operate according to different, more
altruistic, principles than the public sphere of reason and justice. This assumption excluded the question of equality within the family from consideration in liberal theory. Thus, in spite of its universal pretensions, liberalism
has been historically blind to the concrete inequalities between husbands and
wives in family relations.[15] As we see in the next section, Latin American
liberal regimes were happy to uphold patriarchy in the family while insisting on equal rights for men in the public sphere. Even contemporary liberal
thinkers fail to apply theories of justice to the family, opting instead simply
to presume that the family is just (Okin 1989).

[14] The legalization of divorce was one of the first consequences of the application of principles
of Enlightenment liberalism to family law. Divorce was introduced in France in 1792 after
the French Revolution for a variety of causes, including mutual consent (Glendon 1989:
157–8).

[15] An important exception is John Stuart Mill, who, in *The Subjection of Women*, applied the
principles of liberalism to family life to argue that women should enjoy equal rights. Mill,
however, still assumed that women would freely choose to devote themselves to domestic
duties.

Around the world, people have used liberalism's ideas to arrive at different conclusions about abortion. On the one hand, liberalism offers grounds to permit abortion as an issue of personal privacy. As a majority of the U.S. Supreme Court ruled in *Eisenstadt v. Baird* (1972), if "the right of privacy means anything, it is the right of the individual, married or single, to be free from unwarranted government intrusion into matters so fundamentally affecting a person as the decision whether to bear or beget a child" (Tribe 1992: 94). One year later in *Roe v. Wade*, the Court held that the right to privacy established in U.S. constitutional jurisprudence was "broad enough to encompass a woman's decision whether or not to terminate her pregnancy." On the other hand, it has also been argued that fetuses merit equal protection of the law and that consequently, liberal states must protect fetal interests in being born by preventing abortions. In a decision that struck down a liberal 1974 abortion law,[16] the West German Constitutional Court ruled in 1976 that constitutional protections extend to "life developing in the womb." The court explicitly granted constitutional priority to the human life of the fetus over the right to privacy and self-determination of the pregnant woman (Glendon 1987: 26).[17] The position of Latin American liberals resembles the German court's interpretation more than the U.S. court's. Liberal parties and politicians in Latin America have almost never endorsed the decriminalization of abortion.

Feminism

Feminism is the belief that "women should not be disadvantaged by their sex, that they should be recognized as having human dignity equal to that of men, and that they should have the opportunity to live as fulfilling and as freely chosen lives as men can" (Okin 1999: 10). Though feminism was strongly influenced by liberalism, unlike classical liberalism it has clear implications for women's equality in the family and the legality of abortion. Feminism rejects the patriarchal family structure and maintains that spouses should enjoy equal rights and obligations. Beginning in the 1960s, feminism proposed that abortion be reconceptualized. The idea that abortion is a woman's choice has been one of feminism's unique contributions to debates on gender and the state. To be sure, there are multiple feminisms, and feminist thinkers

---

[16] As part of a larger reform to the criminal code, the 1974 law permitted "elective abortions" in the first twelve weeks of pregnancy.

[17] The Constitutional Court's decision did not lead to the prohibition of all abortions. Rather, the court's argument was that abortion regulations be proportionate to the supreme value of protecting human life and that they work toward the continuation of pregnancy. According to Glendon, "the 1974 statute violated the Constitution because ... it did not sufficiently register disapproval of abortion in principle" (Glendon 1987: 28).

hold distinct positions about these issues.[18] Rather than a seamless normative tradition, it may be more helpful to conceive of feminism as a *perspective*.
Applied to Roman Catholicism, liberalism, socialism, conservatism, Islam,
and the like, the feminist perspective offers diverse analyses and proposals
of the sources of and solutions to women's oppression.[19]

Feminism presents a profound challenge to way traditional liberalism has
excluded women and to Roman Catholicism's premise that women have
essential roles and natures. The concept of gender lies at the heart of this
challenge. "Gender," a term that refers to the social and cultural organization of sexual differences, implies that men and women's roles derive not
from their essential natures but from social structures and cultural norms.
Roman Catholicism and early liberalism, by contrast, rested on the belief
that women had distinctive natures that made it proper they be occupied
only with motherhood and domestic life. Once women's traditional roles
are seen as the product of social construction and not the essential order of
things, it becomes possible to imagine and propose ways to construct society
in a different, more egalitarian, manner. Feminism's concern with the state
derives from the recognition that the state plays a major role in the social
construction of gender (Brown 1995; Frug 1992; Molyneux 2000; Olsen
1993; Orloff 1993; Staudt 1997; Waylen 1998; Young 1997). Progress toward a just society thus entails reform of those features of the state that
injure women's dignity and thwart women's equal opportunities.

Opposition to patriarchal family laws is an obvious implication of feminist principles. Equality in family matters, including property, parenting, and
household decisions, has always been an element of feminist policy agendas
(Dore and Molyneux 2000; Lavrín 1995; Rhode 1989). Among the goals
of Argentina's Centro Feminista (Feminist Center), founded in 1905, was
reform of the civil code to grant women full juridical personality and eliminate their dependence on men (Lavrín 1995: 27). Delegates to the First

---

[18] The need to conceive of "feminisms" flows from recognition of the multiplicity and com-
plexity of female identity. Mouffe states: "Feminism, for me, is the struggle for the equality
of women. But this should not be understood as a struggle for realizing the equality of
a definable empirical group with a common essence and identity, women, but rather as
a struggle against the multiple forms in which the category of 'woman' is constructed in
subordination.... There are, therefore, by necessity, many feminisms and any attempt to
find the 'true form' of feminist politics should be abandoned" (1992: 382).

[19] The feminist perspective has offered a sustained critique of the dominant normative traditions
in the modern world. By illuminating the mechanisms of sex oppression in these traditions,
feminism offers contextually bound perspectives, not a universal, coherent doctrine (Fraser
and Nicholson 1990). Parekh's arguments about the multicultural challenge to liberalism
make a similar point. He writes: "For centuries liberal writers have claimed that theirs was
a transcultural and universally valid moral and political doctrine representing the only true
or rational way of organizing human life. A multiculturalism that rejects this extraordinary
claim is not so much a doctrine as a perspective" (1999: 73–4). For a particularly astute
analysis of what the feminist perspective offers, see Baer 1999.

International Feminine Congress, held in Buenos Aires in 1910, unanimously passed a resolution that proposed modifying the Argentine civil code to defend women's civil and property in marriage (Miller 1991: 75).

Feminism has been a bit more ambivalent about the question of divorce, however. To be sure, feminists in Latin America, Europe, and the United States almost always supported the legalization and liberalization of divorce to permit women to exit from abusive relationships and to promote the rights of female domestic partners. Though prohibitions on divorce rarely prevent couples from separating and forming new unions, the inability legally to terminate a previous marriage precludes the formalization of rights and responsibilities in a new union, leaving the weaker party vulnerable in the event of death or abandonment. Divorce has been necessary to ensure the legal rights of domestic partners (or companions) as well as to mitigate the social stigma attached to women in their second or third informal union.

Yet feminists have been concerned that excessively liberal and gender-neutral divorce laws end up hurting women and children. Weitzman's study of the sociological aftermath of California's divorce reform, for example, found that the living standards of women and children dropped precipitously after divorce, while men's welfare actually rose. The reform, which had introduced no-fault divorce and eliminated gender-specific entitlements and obligations in marriage laws, reduced the financial guarantees the old rules had previously guaranteed to women and children. Women's assets declined because they, far more often then men, devoted their half of family property to caring for children. And divorce settlements often failed to take into account the extent to which women, through marriage and childbirth, had jeopardized their own earning power in the labor market (Weitzman 1985: xi–xvii). By treating subjects equally who are in fact unequal, egalitarian marriage laws may end up reinforcing inequality. Easily available divorce must not grant men the right to relinquish responsibility toward former wives and children.

Feminism revolutionalized the way we think about abortion. Previously, abortion had been framed as an issue of medical discretion, criminal law, and public morality, and decision making on the issue was largely restricted to criminologists, doctors, and law makers. Political elites favoring reform of strict abortion laws were concerned about public health and the way the abortion black market fueled judicial corruption and undermined the rule of law, not about women's rights. Before the 1960s, few women, including feminist activists, participated in policy debates about abortion. Feminism's growing interest in abortion was provoked by structural changes in women's lives, particularly in the United States. As more women began not merely to enter the workplace, but to pursue careers resembling men's (i.e., careers central to self-definition, and not just careers that supplemented women's roles as mothers and homemakers), they found themselves discriminated against as mothers or potential mothers. U.S. feminists felt that access to abortion, by granting women full control over their fertility, was necessary for women to enjoy equal opportunities in society.

Feminist mobilization against restrictive abortion laws amounted to "an attack on a symbolic linchpin that held together a complicated set of assumptions about who women were, what their roles in life should be, what kinds of jobs they should take in the paid labor force, and how those jobs should be rewarded" (Luker 1984: 118). As Luker puts it,

When women accepted the definition that a woman's primary role was as wife and mother, control of one's own body meant little.... But when some groups of women began to think of themselves as having a different primary role in life, the brute facts of biology came to seem at odds with how they saw themselves. Once they had choices about life roles, they came to feel that they had *a right to use abortion in order to control their own lives*. (Ibid.: 118)

Linking the availability of abortion to women's opportunities in society prompted new ways to think about the abortion question. If women have the right freely to choose a life path that may or may not include motherhood, access to abortion is critical to freedom. U.S. feminists thus proposed that abortion be seen fundamentally as a question of personal choice and individual liberty.

Of course, not all feminists agree with this framing. MacKinnon criticizes the tendency of liberal feminists uncritically to accept the defense of abortion as a matter of personal privacy. She claims that under conditions of gender inequality, when women do not control access to their sexuality, liberal abortion merely frees women's heterosexual availability to men (1989: 190). Others have noted that the defense of abortion as an individual right is a strongly Western notion, and that "more research is needed to examine how a woman's right to make her own decisions regarding fertility and reproduction are construed in other cultural settings" (Corrêa 1994: 72). In Japan, for example, abortion is widely available, and has rarely been an issue of public debate. Abortion was legalized in the Eugenic Protection Law of 1948 with the stated rationale that a liberal abortion policy would help enhance the quality of the country's gene pool. The reform was also prompted by concerns with population growth, public health problems caused by illegal abortion, and the need for more forms of birth control (Gelb 1989: 120).

Rights dominated feminist discourse on abortion in the North (or developed world), but in the South (or developing world) abortion could be discussed as a health issue (Corrêa 1994: 69–71). Feminists point out that prohibitions on abortion serve only to push the practice underground, forcing millions of women to undergo the procedure at great risk. The mortality rate associated with abortion is hundreds of times greater in the South – where abortion laws tend to be more restrictive – than in the North (Alan Guttmacher Institute 1999: 35). Feminist activists and medical practitioners maintain that the legalization of abortion, by eliminating the need for women to resort to unsafe procedures, will reduce maternal mortality and morbidity and improve women's overall health.[20] As Corrêa points out: "The health rationale for legalizing abortion denounces such high rates of mortality, illness, disease and long-term consequences resulting from clandestine abortions as morally reprehensible.... Legalization of abortion on request ... is undoubtedly a necessary condition for the provision of safe services to all women who need them" (Corrêa 1994: 71). In this framework, access to abortion is a "critical marker" of a woman's right to health.

Southern feminists' focus on abortion as a health problem has considerable strategic value. In the United States, where abortion involves competing rights, the abortion debate has become a focus for large, polarizing questions of morality, life, and liberty (Luker 1984). Framing abortion as a question of health is less polarizing and expands the potential constituency supporting change. Legal abortion may cease to be seen as a threat to traditional family values and more as a necessary measure to avert a public health crisis. In this way, an absolutist issue may be recast as a technical concern.

Socialism

Socialism is the fourth normative tradition informing debates on gender rights in Latin America.[21] Socialist parties and politicians have always supported gender equality in the family and the legalization of divorce, though not all have endorsed the decriminalization of abortion. (Liberal abortion was common in communist countries, however.) In general, socialism has been more "feminist" than either Roman Catholicism or liberalism, and the majority of Latin American feminists have been associated with left-wing parties inspired by socialist principles. Yet the relationship between feminists and socialists has been fraught with tension, for socialist strategy tends to subordinate feminist objectives to economic development and social stability. Socialist regimes have rarely succeeded in eliminating gender inequality in society at large, and few socialist thinkers have questioned the sexual division

---

[20] Indeed, in many developing countries, feminist involvement with abortion grew as part of a broader effort to promote women's reproductive health. Feminists were concerned by coercive population control programs organized in much of the developing world, many of which goaded women into sterilization and contraception without adequate information about consequences and potential side effects (Corrêa 1994: 57). The feminist reproductive rights movement proposed that women be the subjects and not the objects of population and health policies, and that the programs of national and international development agencies adopt an integral perspective considering all of women's health needs, not merely their reproductive needs.

[21] Just as one need speak of "feminisms," internal variation within the socialist tradition – from the communist tradition of the former Soviet bloc to the social-democratic tradition of Western Europe – must be kept in mind. For the purposes of this brief analysis, I focus merely on those points of commonality among "socialisms."

of labor in the family or accepted feminist arguments about sexuality and domestic violence (Molyneux 1985: 49–52).

Socialist doctrine always denounced the legal subordination of women to their husbands. Marx and Engels held that male domination in the family was a linchpin of the capitalist system. As Engels put it: "The first class opposition that appears in history coincides with the development of that antagonism between man and woman in monogamous marriage, and the first class oppression coincides with that of the female sex by the male" (Engels 1884). In line with these founding principles and to further other goals such as expanding the size and improving the skills of the labor force, breaking up the preexisting social order, and promoting economic transformation, socialist regimes and social-democratic parties throughout the world have granted women equal rights in matters concerning family property and parenting, while abolishing men's privileges such as unilateral divorce and exclusive child custody (Molyneux 1985). The Cuban Family Code of 1975 established equal rights and duties for men and women, called on both spouses to participate in child rearing and the running of the household, granted husband and wife equal control over household property and equal rights of *patria potestad* over children, and permitted divorce by common agreement or on the request of either spouse (Domínguez 1978: 270–1). The idea of marriage as a cooperative partnership also prevailed under the Social Democrats in Germany, where the marriage and divorce law passed by the Social Democratic government in 1976 proclaimed that "the spouses [shall] conduct the running of the household by mutual agreement," and "both spouses have the right to be employed" (Glendon 1989: 93). Family laws adopted by revolutionary governments in China, South Yemen, and Afghanistan in 1949, 1967, and 1978, respectively, eliminated male prerogatives and granted women equal family rights (Molyneux 1985: 55). In the southern cone of South America, the programs of socialist parties have provided a historically consistent defense of sex equality in the family: In Argentina, Chile, and Uruguay, socialist politicians were among the earliest proponents of bills to grant married women equal rights (Lavrín 1995).

Socialism converges with liberalism over support for the legalization of divorce. Like liberals, socialists maintain that the Catholic Church (and other religious creeds) should have no influence on state policy making. Socialist and social-democratic governments have permitted divorce on very liberal grounds, and were often responsible for permitting women, as well as men, to request divorce (Molyneux 1985).[22] Yet unlike liberalism, which holds that the state must be neutral with respect to ethical traditions and views of the

---

[22] Nonetheless, some socialist regimes subsequently restricted liberal divorce laws in the interest of family stability (Molyneux 1985: 56). As in the case of abortion, socialist policy making has been guided by state leaders' perceptions of collective interests, not adherence to a basic rights framework.

good life, socialists believe that the state must assume ethical responsibilities. Whereas the liberal state upholds formal rights and procedures, the socialist state and its laws aim to cultivate virtues and to "prepare society for the ultimate demise of law." In a sense, socialism's belief that the state has a purpose resembles the Catholic view that the goal of the state is to advance the common good. For these reasons, some authors have referred to the "pseudo-religious" qualities of socialist legal systems (Glendon et al., 1982).

Socialism's statist and collectivist orientation is consequential for abortion. Socialism rejects any religious basis for the sanctity of the life of the fetus, and most socialist, communist, and social-democratic regimes have liberal abortion policies. Yet these policies are not grounded in a liberal rights framework, and some socialist and communist states have modified abortion policy according to state leaders' perceptions of the common interest. The Soviet Union's abortion decree of 1920 called legal abortion a necessary evil in order to minimize the public health risks of clandestine abortions and keep women in the labor force. Then, in 1936, Stalin outlawed abortion, calling on socialist women to fulfill their natural role and populate the country (Goldman 1991). The legalization of abortion following Stalin's death led to the decriminalization of abortion in other countries of the Soviet bloc. In most of these countries, however, the state permitted abortion to keep families small and women in the labor force, not because it recognized women's right to choose. In Latin America, socialists have not held a uniform position on abortion. Though abortion is legal in Cuba, socialist parties elsewhere in the region have been reluctant to endorse the decriminalization of abortion. Nonetheless, most of the bills presented in Latin American congresses to decriminalize abortion have been authored by representatives from socialist or social-democratic parties.[23]

What are the implications of the four traditions for policy making in the areas of gender equality in the family, divorce, and abortion in Latin America in the late twentieth century? By the time Church views changed in the 1950s and 1960s, sex equality in the family had largely ceased to be a matter of principled conflict. The impact of feminism and women's changing social roles produced a convergence among the Catholic tradition, the liberal tradition, and the socialist tradition on this issue. Yet the justification for sex equality in each tradition was unique: Catholics justified equality on the grounds of essentialism, liberals decided that sex was irrelevant to the equality of citizens, and socialists saw equality as a virtue to cultivate in preparation for socialist society. Divorce, on the other hand, continued to be an issue that

---

[23] In Brazil in the 1980s and 1990s, bills to liberalize the grounds for legal abortion were presented in Congress primarily by deputies from the leftist Workers' Party. In Argentina, centrist Radical Party legislators presented decriminalization bills. Historically, in Chile the few bills to liberalize abortion were presented by socialist or left legislators.

profoundly divided Catholics from liberals, feminists, and socialists. As a result, divorce debates tended to be framed in absolutist terms. Nonetheless, reformist coalitions of liberals, feminists, and socialists were able to defeat the Church at critical moments of Church-state conflict. With regard to abortion, feminism stood alone. Although liberalism and socialism in other parts of the world grew to endorse the legalization of abortion, Latin American liberals and socialists have not interpreted elective abortion to follow from the core principles of their normative tradition. Latin American Catholicism, liberalism, and socialism converge in condemning abortion. Beginning in the 1970s and the 1980s, the profound feminist challenge to these traditions produced bitter public debate, but feminists have thus far been unable to broaden the bases of support for change.

Historical Evolution of Gender Rights

Ideas from all four normative models of gender and the state inform contemporary debates on gender policy in Latin America. They have also mattered historically. During the colonial period, Latin American countries were governed by the centuries-old criminal laws of Spain and Portugal, which in turn were influenced by Roman and canon law. After independence, Latin American countries gradually adopted their own civil and criminal codes, using nineteenth- and twentieth-century continental European law – particularly the Napoleonic Code – as models. The legacy of gender policy in Argentina, Brazil, and Chile is constituted by these older legal codes.

Gender (In)equality in the Family

The civil power of male patriarchs was undisputed in colonial Latin America. As Dore points out, "men's gender privileges and obligations were regarded as natural law. It was taken to be self-evident that women were not equal to men" (2000: 11). After independence, Latin American countries began to formulate their own civil laws, though few changes were made to the status of women. Like their counterparts elsewhere in the Western world, Latin American laws were modeled after the 1804 Napoleonic Code. These codes contained detailed norms on what Glendon calls "the law of the ongoing family," largely a "nonsubject" in the Anglo-American world. These norms structured the personal and property relations between husband and wives and between parents and children, and contained descriptions of men and women's social roles and identities. Glendon points out that norms concerning family relations "are a strange kind of law," since "they tend to take the form of pronouncements of general models for behavior rather than specific rules of conduct with direct sanctions for violation" (Glendon 1989: 87).[24]

---

[24] Still, there is evidence that an individual's failure to live up to legally sanctioned norms of conduct sometimes served as grounds for formal complaints lodged in court (Guy 2000).

Following the Napoleonic Code, Latin American codes established two central concepts concerning the roles of men and women in marriage and the family: men's marital power (*puissance*) and women's incapacity (*incapacité*). Marital power meant that husbands had "extensive powers of command, control, and discipline with regard to the person and property of the wife," including the right to control and supervise her activities, choose the marital residence, and manage her property (Vogel 1998: 34). Women's incapacity precluded them from exercising rights or contracting obligations without the husband's authorization. The Chilean Civil Code of 1855, the Argentine Civil Code of 1871, and the Brazilian Civil Code of 1916 gave husbands the legal representation of the family, exclusive power to manage and dispose of family property, and power to determine and move the family residence at will. Married women could not work outside the home, open bank accounts, sign contracts, apply for passports, or serve as witnesses without their husband's authorization. Women were required to assume their husband's name upon marriage. As the Argentine Supreme Court put it in 1891, "as long as marriage lasts, women in general lack civil capacity and are under the tutelage and power of their husbands, forming in the eyes of the law a single juridical personality with them" (quoted in Lavrín 1995: 195–6). Marital power entailed rights as well as obligations: Men were legally required to support the family with the fruits of their labor. As Article 131 of the Chilean Civil Code stated: "The husband owes the wife protection, and the wife owes the husband obedience" (Gomes 1984; Grosman 1998; Gonzales Moya 1992; Tomasello Hart 1989; Verucci 1987; Zannoni 1998a).

Marital power had a second implication for the marital property regime (the set of laws referring to the management of the spouses' property and its relationship to third parties). In most of the original codes, there was one legal property regime that applied to all marriages. This community property system pooled together the mass of goods owned by both spouses. Marital power meant that these goods were managed by and held in the name of the husband. Women's incapacity was the reason they were unable to sell or trade such property without the husband's authorization.

The third implication of marital power had to do with the exercise of *patria potestad*, a concept derived from Roman law. In ancient societies, where the household was the central unit of production, the institution of *patria potestad* was the source of the male head of household's legitimate authority over his descendants, wife, and slaves. Since then, the powers granted to men by *patria potestad* have narrowed as economic production largely left the household, and the state usurped elements of the authority previously vested in male property owners. In the modern era, *patria potestad* is intended less to secure order in the "mini state" of the household than to regulate social reproduction. The institution of *patria potestad* structures the relationship between parents and children, referring specifically to "the set of rights and duties of parents over the person and property of minor children, as a means

TABLE 2.1. *Defining Concepts in Original Latin American Civil Codes*

Concept	Implications
Men's marital power	Legal representation of wife and family unit
	Right to select and move household residence
	Right to manage common household property and wife's property
Women's incapacity	Needed husband's authorization to pursue employment and business transactions outside the home, to appear in court, to manage common property
	Unable to make decisions about minor children
Patria potestad	The rights of parents over the person and property of minor children, exercised uniquely by the father

to fulfill their natural function of protecting and educating their offspring" (Zannoni 1998b: 682). In principle, both mothers and fathers hold *patria potestad*. But the law explicitly states that fathers are uniquely entitled to *exercise* the rights and responsibilities of *patria potestad*. Table 2.1 defines the various civil code concepts.

The position of women in the original Latin American civil codes mirrored social reality at the time of their crafting. Most women were financially dependent on their husbands, rarely received a formal education, and rarely entered into paid employment. Laws restricting women's liberties were based on a belief in women's inability to exercise rights, but also intended to ensure that women were adequately protected and cared for (Gomes 1984; Grosman 1998). In fact, guarantees of women's protection in Latin American laws were extensive in comparative perspective. Nineteenth-century Brazilian law, for example, granted women title to one-half of marital property in the event of the husband's death. Individuals had only limited testamentary freedom, for the law also required sons and daughters to inherit their parents' estates in equal proportions. In Great Britain, by contrast, men had full testamentary freedom, and the formulas calculating women's property rights upon a husband's death were considerably less favorable (Nazzari 1995: 788–91).

In the early twentieth century, economic growth, the expansion of women's education and employment opportunities, and feminist ideas about women's roles in modern society put pressure on old laws. The first International Feminine Congress, held in Buenos Aires in 1910, demanded full juridical equality for women (Molyneux 2000: 44). Liberal and socialist parties in Latin America began to advocate family law reform and woman suffrage to promote national development. As Molyneux notes: "The patriarchal basis of law was seen as out of step with the modern world that Latin America sought to join.... liberals and socialists alike had argued that family reform and women's emancipation from patriarchal absolutism

TABLE 2.2. *Early Twentieth-Century Modifications to Women's Position in the Civil Code*

Brazilian Civil Code of 1916	Earned income by married women considered to be "reserved asset"
	Established separation of property as an alternative marital property regime
Argentine Law on Women's Civil Rights (11.357) of 1926	Adult single, widowed, and separated women are fully capable of agency
	Earned income by married women considered to be "reserved asset"
	Principle of incapacity upheld, but exceptions are stipulated
	Right to exercise *patria potestad* over children of a previous union
Chilean Law 328 of 1925 (revised in 1934)	Earned income by married women considered to be "reserved asset"
	Established separation of property as an alternative marital property regime
	Right to exercise *patria potestad* upon the husband's death or incapacity

were an integral part of modernization and a necessary concomitant of economic growth" (2000: 47–51). Reformers succeeded in introducing the institution of *patrimonio reservado* (women's reserved property) to the new Brazilian Civil Code of 1916 and to civil law in Argentina and Chile in the 1920s (see Table 2.2). Under this new regime, women were granted full control of their independently earned income, which was kept separate from the stock of community property administered by the husband. The existence of *patrimonio reservado* made the continuation of other gender-based inequalities in family law more tolerable for upwardly mobile working women.[25] Nevertheless, *patrimonio reservado* did not lead to unconditional economic liberty for women, since men's formal authorization was often required or presumed when married women took up formal employment.

Besides creating *patrimonio reservado*, the 1926 Argentine Law on Women's Civil Rights granted adult single, widowed, and separated women equality with men. However, the law still denied married women full legal agency *in principle*, although numerous circumstances were stipulated

[25] In fact, *patrimonio reservado* privileged them relative to husbands in at least one way. In Argentina, for example, the law states that the consent of both spouses is required to dispose of *bienes inmuebles gananciales* (household property or real estate). However, if such household property is purchased by the wife with her income, the husband's consent is not necessary for her to do with the property what she pleases. See Zannoni (1998a: 398).

under which married women could act without marital authorization.[26] The Chilean reform of 1925 (refined in 1934) did not introduce as many exceptions to incapacity as the Argentine reform, but permitted couples to opt for a full separation of property (wherein each spouse administers their own goods and are not held responsible for debts or obligations contracted by the other). Separation of property, also included in the Brazilian Code, was primarily of interest to wealthy women unwilling to hand over inheritances to their husbands. These civil code reforms contributed to the momentum for woman suffrage, introduced in 1932 in Brazil, 1947 in Argentina, and 1949 in Chile (Lavrín 1995: 208). Though couples in Brazil and Chile could opt for a full separation of property, no alternative to community property existed in Argentina. In fact, as of 2002, there was still only one legal property regime in Argentina.

Marriage and Divorce

Throughout most of Latin American history, the Roman Catholic Church had exclusive responsibility over the formation of marriage, its effects, and its dissolution. The secular state seized control over marriage only in the late nineteenth century by adopting laws making civil marriage compulsory. Yet these laws did not represent a clean break with the Church. Although the state acquired the authority to regulate marriage and to maintain an official registry of citizens, the content of its marriage laws was broadly similar to the old policies of the Church. Civil law emulated canon law when it came to the conditions of marriage, causes for separation and annulment, and the principle of marital indissolubility. To understand the origins of contemporary civil law on marriage, we must trace the history of marriage in the Church.

In general, until the later Middle Ages, marriage was regarded in Europe as a purely personal and secular affair. Indeed, until the Roman Catholic Church claimed authority over marriage, there was very little systematic legal regulation of marriage on the entire European continent. Divorce, moreover, was widely accepted. Under the Roman Empire, marriage was an informal arrangement that could be dissolved at the will of either spouse, and divorce was admitted among Anglo-Saxon, Frank, and Germanic peoples. The assertion of Church control over marriage was fueled by doctrinal developments that viewed marriage as a sacrament. As Glendon notes:

The development of the doctrine of sacramental marriage furnished the theoretical basis for the assertion of ecclesiastical authority over an area of life which had

---

[26] Although some jurists believed that the 1926 law for all practical purposes recognized married women's agency (Zannoni 1998a), other jurists pointed out that the general rule was still incapacity, which characterized all situations not expressly stated in the law (Grosman 1976).

previously not been subject to any kind of official control. The acquisition of jurisdiction over marriage by the ecclesiastical courts and the application by these courts
of the various Church doctrines which eventually coalesced into a body of canon law
was something new in human history. (1989: 26)

At the Council of Trent (1563–81), the Church established the indissolubility
of marriage and held that marriages had to be performed by a Church official
in order to be considered valid. The indissolubility principle was not accepted
without debate among the bishops at the council, however. Many bishops
thought that adultery should serve as an exception to the general principle of
indissolubility (Zannoni 1998b: 27–9). Thus, the rule of indissolubility was
woven into Church rules at the same time that these rules came to be the first
comprehensive legal regulations on marriage in Europe. Still, as Rheinstein
points out, "full freedom to terminate a marriage was so firmly rooted in
the mores that it took centuries of Christian effort to replace it by the new
principle of indissolubility" (1972: 16).

The rule of indissolubility was mitigated in practice by the elaboration
of extensive causes for marital annulment, as well as by the requirement
that the original adoption of the marriage bond be rooted in the conscious,
voluntary, and free consent of both parties. The annulment of marriage did
not dissolve the marriage bond, but rather served as proof that the marriage
had never existed. This distinction is crucial to keep in mind. "The Church
does not annul marriages. If there was a marriage, this marriage exists until
death." Rather, "the only mission of the Church is to declare that effectively this marriage did not exist because there were causes that made it
impossible" (Tribunal Eclesiástico de Santiago n.d.). Grounds for annulment included consanguinial or affective relations between the spouses, age,
impotence, "precontract" (a prior engagement to another person), and lack
of consent (Phillips 1988: 8).[27] Canon law also provided for judicial separation, but only on the grounds of adultery, heresy, serious mistreatment, or
desertion.

Between the sixteenth and the eighteenth centuries, jurisdiction over marriage was gradually assumed by the secular state. In Protestant regions, the
thesis of the indissolubility of marriage was soundly rejected. Divorce was
permitted for adultery, abandonment, and other grounds, although it was
imagined as a punishment for grave marital misconduct, not as an individual
right (Rheinstein 1972: 22–3). Divorce was introduced in Catholic France
in 1792 following the Revolution for several causes, including mutual consent (Glendon 1989: 157–8). In Latin America, the separation of Church
and state was established later, through a gradual process that unfolded

---

[27] Lack of consent "could be formed through the use of duress, force, or abduction to compel
one party to marry or through a defect of intellect, such as insanity or simple ignorance of
what marriage entailed" (Phillips 1988: 8).

in most countries from the mid-nineteenth to early twentieth centuries.[28] For example, until the 1925 Constitution established a strict separation of Church and state, the official religion of Chile was Roman Catholicism; the public exercise of other religions was prohibited;[29] and the president was required to observe and defend the Catholic religion (Mecham 1966: 206). In Argentina, the Constitution of 1853 technically disestablished the Church, but still required that the president be Roman Catholic, declared that the federal government supports the Roman Catholic religion, and granted the state the right to exercise the *patronato*, or the nomination of bishops (ibid.: 234–5).

Official recognition of the Church was reflected in Latin American marriage legislation. In the original codes of Argentina (1871) and Chile (1857), the state recognized only religious marriages.[30] The Chilean Code acknowledged the authority of ecclesiastical courts to define the terms of legitimate marriage and to administer legal separation, and, in line with canonical principles, defined marriage as "a solemn and indissoluble contract by which a man and a woman unite today and forever, with the objective of a life in common, procreation, and mutual support" (Article 102 of the original Chilean Code; quoted in ibid.: 133). The Argentine Code likewise delegated decision making about the terms of marriage and the causes of separation and annulment to ecclesiastical authorities (Zannoni 1998b: 50).

Following the rise to power of liberal legal-positivist elites in the mid- to late nineteenth century, the terms of the original Church-state arrangement were recast. In Chile, the 1884 civil marriage law made a civil marriage ceremony compulsory. At around the same time, the law of lay cemeteries and the law of the civil registry were enacted, which deprived the Church of control over cemeteries (providing for their use by all denominations) and took away the registry of births, marriages, and deaths from the hands of parish priests (Mecham 1966: 213–4). The civil marriage law was a radical act that deprived the Church of its historic role in legally regulating the family. As Mecham notes, the clergy "protested, threatened, and even went to the extreme of attempting to prevent the marriage of anyone who voted for the measure. So much opposition was aroused by the clergy against this "sacrilegious law" that the country seemed to be on the verge of a revolution"

---

[28] See Gill (1998: 32) for a table with dates of effective religious disestablishment in many Latin American countries.

[29] In practice, "the constitutional exclusion of other cults was never completely enforced. . . . the constitutional phrase 'public exercise' was generally regarded as not prohibiting worship of non-Catholics *inside* buildings." Under a 1865 law, religious "dissidents" were also permitted to establish their own schools (Meacham 1966: 207).

[30] In Chile, however, a 1844 law (called the *Ley sobre Matrimonio de Disidentes*, or the Dissidents Marriage Law) withdrew the requirement that non-Catholics marry according to Catholic marriage rites (Mecham 1966: 208).

(ibid.: 213). In Argentina, the Civil Marriage Law was enacted in 1888; in Brazil, in 1890.

In spite of being "civil" marriage laws, however, all three laws preserved the canonical principle of marital indissolubility. The break with the Church was thus only partial. Still, when seen in the context of other Catholic countries, nineteenth-century Latin American mandatory civil marriage laws were radical. For example, until 1978 in Spain, Catholics were legally required to marry in the Church. Only non-Catholics were allowed to contract civil marriages. To qualify for a civil marriage, one had to provide documentary proof that one was not Catholic, or else make a sworn statement that one had not been baptized (Zannoni 1998b: 36–7). In one important respect, Brazil's civil marriage law was decisively more liberal than Argentina's or Chile's. All three countries admitted judicial separation, not full divorce, but only in Brazil was separation by mutual consent permitted by law (called *desquite amigável*). The 1916 Civil Code, in an innovation Verucci calls "a great liberality [*liberalidade*] of Brazilian law," allowed couples to separate after two years of marriage if both declared their consent (Verucci 1987). In Argentina and Chile, by contrast, judicial separation could be obtained only if the fault of one party was proven to the judge.

In summary, Latin American civil marriage laws reduced the Church's regulative authority over marriages, separations, and annulments. However, they preserved the principle of indissolubility and borrowed the canonical causes of annulment and separation, thus granting the Church an important measure of moral and cultural authority over marriage. The indissolubility of marriage symbolized the Roman Catholic cultural heritage, respect for the Church hierarchy, and the law's concern for public morality and the common good.

Abortion

Christianity was the first Western ethical system to equate abortion with homicide, and canon law was the first systematic body of legislation to criminalize abortion. In the pre-Christian era, abortion was relatively common and not punished. Abortion was common in ancient Greece, and advocated by Plato and by Aristotle for the purpose of population control. In the Roman Empire, abortion was widely practiced, although some laws permitted husbands to divorce their wives for having abortions without their consent, and punished citizens who provided fatal drugs to mothers with the intention of inducing an abortion (Noonan 1970). The New Testament and other teachings of early Christianity condemned abortion, and by the fourth century, formal rules had emerged to require penance from women who had undergone abortions. Early Christianity, however, made a distinction between the ensouled and unensouled fetus. As argued earlier, only the abortion of an ensouled fetus amounted to homicide.

Canon law strongly influenced the criminal legislation adopted in the territorialities of continental Europe and, by extension, in Latin American colonies.[31] Rules on abortion in the *Siete partidas*, one of the earliest codifications of Spanish law (1263), reflect Church teachings equating abortion with homicide. The law reads:

Where a pregnant woman knowingly takes drugs or anything else whatsoever to produce abortion, or gives herself blows in the abdomen, with her fist or with anything else, for that purpose, and by this means loses her child; we decree that, if the latter was living at the time of this, she must be put to death for the offense except where she acted under compulsion. . . . If the child was not living at the time, the woman cannot then be put to death on this account, but she shall be banished to some island for the term of five years. We decree that a man shall suffer the same penalty who knowingly strikes his wife while she is pregnant, so that she loses her child by reason of the blow. If a stranger should do this, he shall suffer the penalty of homicide if the child was living when it lost its life through his fault, and if it was not living at the time, he shall be banished to some island for the term of five years. (Scott 1931: 1346–7)

Prohibitions on abortion were maintained in the *Nueva recopilación*, a 1567 compilation of Spanish codes (including the *Partidas*). The *Nueva recopilación* was applied to Spain's colonies, and continued to serve as law in many countries even after the achievement of independence.

In Portugal, criminal law was codified in Book V of the Philippine Ordinances of 1603. The notoriously unjust[32] Ordinances represented the first legal codes to govern Brazil, and had a long life. Book V of the Ordinances remained in effect until 1830 in Brazil and 1852 in Portugal, when new criminal codes were promulgated (Thompson 1982). The Ordinances' rulings on abortion are vague, yet can be interpreted to prescribe the death penalty for a woman who provoked an abortion and for those who assisted her.[33] Laws in France, Austria, Tuscany, and Prussia also punished abortion as homicide. Medieval French law was the most severe, punishing abortion with the death penalty and failing to distinguish between the ensouled and unensouled fetus (Fontan Balestra 1983: 219–20). In line with laws in continental Europe, abortion was punishable by death in the colonial Latin America.

---

[31] Canon law was less influential elsewhere. In the common law of England and in Islamic law, for example, abortion was unlawful only if performed after the formation of the fetus. English law "did not recognize as criminal, or even class as contrary to morality, an operation performed to produce abortion when it took place with the consent of the woman, before the child was 'animated' or had 'quickened'." (Scott 1931: 1347, note 1).

[32] For example, death was the penalty applied for most crimes. There was no sense of proportion between the crime and the penalty, and torture was advocated. Husbands were granted permission to murder their adulterous wives and companions, and to bring along friends to help (Thompson 1982, chapter IX).

[33] Consultation of the original text of the Ordinances with Patricia Sobral, Professor of Portuguese, Harvard University, September, 1999.

In the nineteenth century, the development of modern science and modern legal science had two consequences for abortion laws in Europe and Latin America. In line with a global tendency toward a reduction in the severity of criminal penalties, abortion came to be more lightly punished than homicide, and even more lightly punished if performed by a woman to save her honor (Fontan Balestra 1983: 220; Fragoso 1987b: 108). On the other hand, scientific advances rendered untenable the Aristotelian proposition that ensoulment occurred forty to eighty days after conception, and Church doctrine changed tacitly to accept the automatic ensoulment of the fetus. As a result, criminal laws began to reject the distinction between the formed and unformed fetus (Noonan 1970: 38–9).

The first criminal code of independent Latin America was promulgated in Brazil in 1830. The code did not punish women for self-performed abortions, but stipulated punishments for women and abortion practitioners in the event of assisted abortions (one to five years in prison) and for the mere attempt to provoke an abortion (eight months to three years in prison). Doctors or surgeons found to have performed abortions would receive longer prison terms of four to twelve years. People who furnished women with abortive medications or devices would receive prison terms of two to six years (Código Criminal do Imperio do Brasil 1861). In the 1890 code, women who performed their own abortions would receive a one- to five-year prison term (Código Penal do Brasil 1913). The Chilean Criminal Code of 1875 (still in effect) dealt with abortion in its chapter on "crimes against family order and public morality." The code punished both women and abortion practitioners, and increased the penalties for licensed doctors who were caught performing abortions (Código Penal de la República de Chile 1889). Argentina's first national criminal code (1886) punished women for having abortions and practitioners for inducing abortions with penalties that ranged from one to three years in prison. Penalties were reduced if the abortion was aimed at protecting honor and reputation, and increased for practitioners if a woman did not consent to an abortion, if she suffered injuries, or if she died. Licensed doctors who performed an abortion would receive a three- to six-year prison term and have their licenses revoked for twice the length of their incarceration (Código Penal de la República Argentina 1887).

Although the criminal status of abortion has not changed since national criminal codes were adopted in the nineteenth century, in the 1920s and 1930s, legal changes in all three countries introduced a narrow range of circumstances under which abortion would go unpunished. The adoption of new criminal codes in Argentina in 1922 and in Brazil in 1940 introduced articles to exempt from criminal penalties abortions performed to save the mother's life or if the pregnancy resulted from rape. As I discuss in Chapter 6, these articles reflected vanguard ideas in the field of criminal law. In Chile, the national Health Code, adopted in 1931, exempted

TABLE 2.3. *Abortion Laws in Argentina, Brazil, and Chile*

Country	Status of abortion
Argentine Criminal Code (1922)	Identified as a "crime against life."
	Woman performing her own abortion or consenting to an abortion punished with one to four years in prison.
	Abortion practitioner punished with one to four years in prison (with woman's consent) or three to ten years (without consent). Penalties are doubled for doctors, surgeons, midwives, or pharmacists who abuse their profession to cause or cooperate in an abortion.[a]
	Abortion performed by a licensed doctor is not punished if (1) performed to avoid danger to the life or health of the mother, which cannot be averted by other means, or (2) if the pregnancy results from rape.
Brazilian Criminal Code (1940)	Identified as a "crime against life."
	Woman performing her own abortion or consenting to an abortion punished with one to three years in prison.
	Abortion practitioner punished with one to four years in prison (with woman's consent) or three to ten years (without consent).
	Abortion performed by a doctor is not punished if (1) there is no other way to save the life of the pregnant woman, or (2) if the pregnancy results from rape, and the woman consents to the abortion.
Chilean Criminal Code (1875)	Identified as a "crime against the family and public morality."
	Woman performing her own abortion or consenting to an abortion punished with three to five years in prison; if the abortion is performed to hide her dishonor, her sentence is reduced.
	Abortion practitioner punished with 541 days to three years in prison (with consent) or three to five years (without consent).
	Until 1989, the Health Code permitted doctors to interrupt a pregnancy for therapeutic reasons, with the written opinion of two surgeons.

[a] Penalties are also increased if the woman suffers injuries or death as a result of the abortion (this also holds in Brazil and Chile).

doctors performing abortions to save the mother's life from criminal liability (see Table 2.3). As the table shows, the laws in all three countries are today broadly similar, although Argentina and Brazil's laws are more liberal than Chile's. In Chile, therapeutic abortion (to save the mother's life) was permitted only until 1989, when the outgoing Pinochet government modified the Health Code, instructing doctors that they could not legally execute any measures with the intention of provoking an abortion.

In the original civil and criminal codes of Latin America, women were subservient to their husband's authority in marriage; the state recognized only religious marriages; and abortion was classified as a crime against life. In the nineteenth and early twentieth centuries, civil marriage was instituted and family law gradually recognized married women as subjects of rights, even if the equalization of rights and duties in the family took much longer, and in some countries was not completed even by the end of the twentieth century. Divorce was illegal in Brazil until the 1970s and in Argentina until the 1980s, and was still illegal in Chile in 2002. Abortion has been a crime historically in all three countries, though reforms of the early twentieth century introduced some narrow grounds for permissible abortion. These laws reflect ideas about gender that can be traced to the normative traditions of Roman Catholicism, Enlightenment liberalism, feminism, and socialism. By the middle of the twentieth century, social changes, international trends, and the emergence of feminist activism challenged the older normative traditions, contributing to mounting pressure for legal reform and producing greater tension between competing views of gender and state.

3

Reforming Women's Rights Under Military Dictatorships

In the 1960s and 1970s, military governments in Argentina, Brazil, and Chile launched efforts to modernize the civil law. In several cases, special commissions of experts debated and submitted proposals for reform on married women's civil status and property rights. Based on these expert recommendations, Argentina enacted major changes to women's civil and property rights under the military government of General Juan Carlos Onganía in 1968. Brazil, also under military rule, modified marital property law when a divorce law was approved in 1977. In Chile, experts working under the military government of Augusto Pinochet proposed similar changes, but the regime endorsed only a symbolic reform in 1989. By the late 1990s, Chile still had not implemented changes to the marital property regime introduced by the other two countries in 1968 and 1977. How could Latin American military governments, widely alleged to be patriarchal and conservative, make moves toward gender equality and democracy in the family? Why were many reforms achieved without pressure from feminist movements, the most conspicuous advocates of women's rights? Why has reform been so delayed in Chile, a country where women's literacy, incorporation into the labor force, and education levels have historically been the highest, or among the highest, in all of Latin America?

This chapter shows that the modernizing aspirations of military rulers opened a window of opportunity for small commissions of legal experts to craft liberal policy changes. Military leaders were motivated by the desire to modernize civil law as part of general projects of state reform, not improve women's status or make the family more egalitarian. In fact, most military governments espoused socially conservative policy preferences. Yet dictators were prepared to convene experts and accept their technical recommendations. For these experts, "modern" law reflected more egalitarian family relations. Despite the fact that senior military rulers often espoused socially conservative, patriarchal values, the closed-door decision-making institutions they established meant that their values, and those of the broader public, were effectively irrelevant to policy innovations in civil law.

This does not imply that code reform is possible only under authoritarian conditions. As Chapter 5 shows, civil law changes were also introduced under the democratic governments that assumed power in the 1980s and 1990s. Nonetheless, the military's "technical" approach to government decisions expedited reforms that expanded women's rights. When actors outside the small expert commissions were given a voice in policy, changes were delayed and even thwarted. Although the family law reforms explored in this chapter might eventually have occurred under democratic rule, it is likely that they would have taken longer. Reform is most expeditious when procedures exist that rapidly translate expert decisions into policy outcomes.[1] In Latin America, authoritarian regimes put such procedures in place.

This chapter deals with two different kinds of reforms: the largely symbolic reform granting married women full civil capacity and the more consequential reform of the marital property regime. First, I aim to show that reform in these areas was a technical issue. Politicians and the general public were interested in legal modernization, but lacked the technical knowledge and interest to participate in debates about how modern principles are manifest. I then trace the growth of ideas about modern family law by focusing on debates among experts at meetings of the Inter-American Bar Association (IABA). Beginning in the 1940s and 1950s, lawyers and legal scholars at international conferences deliberated reforms that would grant women more rights in marriage. A consensus began to form that women's property rights should be expanded, that parents should share responsibility for decision making about children, and that children born in and out of wedlock should be granted equal rights. The records of these meetings show that principles equality among family members were gradually assimilated into prevailing ideas of what constituted "modern" law.

The third section describes family law reforms under the Argentine, Brazilian, and Chilean military governments, respectively. In all three countries, small, closed-door commissions of experts deliberated for extended periods of time about legal modernization. In Argentina, the military government of Juan Carlos Onganía appointed several commissions of prominent jurists to modernize the country's legal codes after the coup of 1966. Major legal reform was called for to fulfill the military's announced goals of modernity, security, and stability. In Brazil, justice ministers working under the military government that seized power in 1964 made similar attempts to

---

[1] Another example of expeditious family law reform comes from the United States, where no-fault divorce was introduced in many states within a short period of time and with little controversy. Divorce reform was pioneered by legal experts, and was portrayed as a matter of routine, procedural decision making, thus escaping the attention of the general public (Jacob 1988).

modernize the civil law. Based on the recommendations of legal experts, family law reforms were adopted in 1977. The Chilean military government of Augusto Pinochet also appointed expert commissions to propose modernizing reforms. Yet in Chile, politics and ideology impeded the translation of technical ideas into state policy, precluding property rights reform not only under Pinochet but also after the democratic transition.

This chapter calls attention to previously neglected elements of military rule in Latin America. When most of us think of Latin America's military governments, we conjure up human rights abuses, the proscription of political parties, and the repression of leftist activists, labor unions, and student movements. We recall debates about the alleged trade-off between democracy, on the one hand, and the containment of communism, on the other, a trade-off that justified for the U.S. government its support for many military dictators in the region from the 1960s through the 1980s. We may also think of industrial deepening and the rationale that military rule ensures the political stability needed to attract investment. Yet ironically, the modernizing motives that drove military rulers to promote economic growth and political order at the expense of political liberty opened a window to modernizing reforms of the civil law, including women's civil and property rights.

Married Women's Civil and Property Rights

After the achievement of women's suffrage in the 1930s, 1940s, and 1950s, the next major obstacle to women's achievement of equality before the law was the unequal civil status of married women. The wife's unequal civil status and the husband's control over marital property prevented married women from exercising effective property rights or acting as legal agents in the public realm. Within the structure of Latin America's civil law systems, married women's inability to exercise property rights resulted from two types of legal norms. The first were explicit provisions labeling married women as incapable and investing husbands with legal representation over their wives and with authority over activities such as establishing the family residence. The second was the marital property regime (the set of rules governing property relations between the two spouses and their relationship to third parties). Eradicating the explicit rules endorsing male privilege turned out to be easier than modifying the marital property regime. Yet for married women to enjoy effective property rights, the marital property regime had to be changed.

Women's Civil Status: From Relative Incapacity to Equality

According to the laws in place in Argentina and Brazil until the 1960s and in Chile until the 1980s, the civil status of women altered dramatically upon marriage. As long as they remained single, women enjoyed equal civil rights, including the right to establish businesses and make money, seek professional employment, travel abroad, and serve as litigants or witnesses in judicial proceedings. Once married, however, a woman's legal personhood was subordinated to her status as wife and mother. Women's agency was curtailed so that the husband could enjoy unquestioned authority within the family and so that the family could represent itself to the outside world with one voice. To erase any doubt about women's subordinate status, the codes labeled married women as citizens who were unable autonomously to exercise rights or contract obligations. The Brazilian Civil Code of 1916 declared that married women, along with minors, spendthrifts, and "forest dwellers" (a reference to Indians) were "incapable with respect to certain acts or the manner of exercising them." Without their husband's authorization, women could not be employed outside the home, could not be issued a passport or travel outside the country, could not accept or refuse inheritances, enter into contracts, or purchase or sell goods. The codes also established a host of male privileges referred to by legal scholars as the institution of "marital power." The Chilean Civil Code, in force since 1857, was the most explicit in this respect. Article 132 defined marital power as "the set of rights that the laws concede to husbands over the person and property of their wives." These rights included the right of the husband to oblige his wife to live with him and to follow wherever he decides to establish residence; the right to manage the wife's property; the right to prevent the wife from appearing in court or initiating a civil suit; and the right to prevent the wife from entering into contracts or breaking them, from paying a debt, from accepting or rejecting a gift or inheritance, from acquiring property, or from serving as guardian or administrator (Klimpel 1962).

Latin American civil laws were not the world's only legal systems to deny married women equal civil rights. The Anglo-American counterpart to the civil law's institutions of relative incapacity and marital power was called "coverture." The idea behind coverture, famously captured by British legal scholar William Blackstone, was that by marriage, the husband and wife "are one person in law: that is, the very being or legal existence of the woman is suspended during marriage, or at least incorporated and consolidated into that of the husband under whose wing, protection and cover she performs every thing" (quoted in Glendon 1989: 94). The common law doctrine of coverture was adopted by the North American colonies and survived unchanged during the Revolutionary War. According to Tapping Reeves's widely used nineteenth-century treatise on the "law of domestic relations," husbands had complete authority over the bodies, property, and activities of their wives (Kerber 1998: 13–15). Coverture was weakened when married women's property acts were adopted by many states in the mid- to late nineteenth century, but the desire to uphold male prerogatives in marriage colored many Supreme Court decisions into the late twentieth century. In fact, Kerber argues that coverture was definitively eradicated only in 1992 when the Court ruled in *Planned Parenthood v. Casey* that "women do not lose their constitutionally protected liberty when they marry" (1998: 380, fn. 6).

Labeling women "relatively incapable" and preserving the prerogatives of marital power upheld norms of gender inequality in the private sphere. Yet in practice, many women were working and freely disposing of the earnings of their work according to provisions of the married women's property acts adopted in Brazil in 1916, in Chile in 1925, and in Argentina in 1926. These acts granted married women who worked outside the home the right to manage their income and property purchased with that income. Nonetheless, husbands still controlled the common marital property as well as real estate or other "immovable property" purchased with the wife's income. Furthermore, husbands could theoretically prevent their wives from working and earning income in the first place. By recognizing women's full civil capacity, the reforms promoted by the lawyers analyzed in this chapter (see the next section) would deny husbands the right to prevent their wives from working, traveling outside the country, and engaging in routine financial transactions. But until the marital property regime changed, the scope of women's freedom remained limited to the income earned from their extrahousehold employment, a freedom already largely recognized under the terms of married women's property acts. Even when women attained full civil capacity, authority to manage and dispose of common household property rested exclusively in the husband's hands. For these reasons, legal scholars have argued that without a simultaneous modification of the marital property regime, reforms to grant women full civil capacity are primarily symbolic (Dolinger 1966; Tomasello Hart 1989).

The Marital Property Regime

According to most legal scholars, the structure of the marital property regime lies at the core of women's ability to exercise property rights. Under the "full community property" regime used in most Western countries until the mid-twentieth century, spousal property was pooled and administered by the husband. This implied that only the husband could make binding financial decisions related to investments, mortgages, loans, inheritances, and the like. Out of concern for women's vulnerable position in such a situation, most countries required both spouses' consent when the husband attempted to sell or mortgage the family home, car, or other household property. Women would assume authority over family property in the event of the husband's disappearance or incarceration. Moreover, the reserved income earned by women who worked outside the home was kept separate from the community property managed by the husband. Yet a woman's other assets – such as the property she owned upon contracting the marriage and returns on it, as well as gifts and inheritances received during marriage – would be subject to the husband's administration.

Since the vast majority of women did not earn income outside the home (in 1990, women's economic activity rates in Latin America were still less than 30 percent), the continuation of the full community property system left women at the mercy of their husband's financial decisions and the social and emotional leverage this entailed. Recognizing the severe inequality and skewed power relations engendered by such a situation, many European countries in the early to mid-twentieth century began to introduce new property regimes that substantially altered the relative financial empowerment of husband and wife. Under these "deferred community property" systems, each spouse continued to administer his or her property after the marriage. Rather than entering the husband's sphere of administration, the wife's property remained under her control. Upon the termination of the marriage, both spouses' property was pooled together and divided equally (hence the notion of a "deferred" community). The even division of household assets at divorce or separation implied recognition of the contribution of unpaid household labor to family assets.

Egalitarian reform of the marital property regime is necessary for women to enjoy effective civil capacity. As long as women are not granted the ability to manage their own property, society will not see them as legitimate business partners or financial actors. Symbolic recognition of women's full civil capacity is necessary but not sufficient to women's citizenship. For Latin American legal experts committed to the modernization of their countries' legal institutions, reform of the marital property regime was an urgent task.

Expert Issue Networks and Family Law

Latin American reformers could draw on new sources of thinking and activism in their efforts to promote reform. Debates in international lawyers' conferences, demonstration effects produced by reforms in other countries, particularly France, and international treaties endorsing gender equality all contributed to the spread of reformist sentiments and new interpretations of the elements of a modern legal system. New ideas were put forward by "issue networks" of legal experts who transmitted international ideas into domestic politics. By calling attention to their prominent role in civil code reform, I seek to make two theoretical points. The first is that many actors, not merely actors within women's movements, have an interest and a stake in gender policy changes. The second point is that international trends influence domestic policy changes, but not in an automatic way. The international system generates ideas and normative standards that are made salient in local politics by individuals and groups. Experts deliberated reforms to various legal systems at international meetings, helping to consolidate expectations about "modern" legal systems. These norms inspired legislators to present bills for civil code reform and enlarged the pool of ideas available to those seeking to modernize domestic legal and political institutions.

The process is similar to the way in which countries have increasingly incorporated human rights protections in reformed constitutions and domestic legislation. International human rights treaties create norms about the proper behavior of liberal democratic states. Transnational advocacy networks pressure national governments to adapt to these norms. Those governments desiring to be perceived as participants in the international society of "civilized states" tend to internalize these human rights norms, even if they conform to them initially for purely strategic reasons (Risse and Sikkink 1999).

The founding of the Inter-American Bar Association (IABA) in 1940 created an institutional context where civil law experts from different countries could meet regularly to debate innovations to family law. The IABA was composed of national and regional legal professional associations from all over the Americas who sent delegates to the meetings where, over the course of several days, working groups considered various aspects of the law. Beginning in the early 1940s, conference delegates participating in the committee on civil law discussed monographs on issues such as reform of the marital property regime, requirements for marriage and divorce, the recognition of foreign divorces, women's legal equality, adoption, and stable unions.[2] IABA debates generated ideas that reformers carried to local contexts and helped forge norms about what constituted modern law.

Over the course of the 1940s and 1950s, IABA delegates approved various resolutions on the legal equality of married women. Following the recommendations of Cuban feminist lawyer Isabel Siero Pérez, the fourth IABA conference, held in Santiago in 1945, issued a resolution calling on all American nations to "work actively to obtain the passage of laws providing for the abolition of all civil and political discriminations [sic] between the sexes" (IABA 1945: 44). Married women's rights were also discussed at the seventh IABA conference, held in Detroit in 1949. Rosemary Scott of the United States presented an extensively documented paper on statutes governing married women's capacity to contract in both the common and civil law systems of the Western hemisphere (Scott 1949). Isabel Siero Pérez of Cuba presented a second paper, which concluded that "the capacity of married women to contract depends upon the administration of marital property, as well as the reciprocal relations with third parties, which varies under the laws of the different countries" (Siero 1949).

Debates about married women's civil capacity at the 1949 Detroit conference directly motivated reformers in Brazil to demand legal equality and greater property rights for married women. After attending the Detroit meeting, Brazilian feminist lawyer Romy Medeiros da Fonseca proposed

---

[2] Records of IABA meetings from 1941 through the 1970s are available at the International Legal Studies Library at Harvard University.

that the Institute of Brazilian Lawyers conduct a study of married women's civil status and then request that Congress act to eliminate the incapacity of married women.[3] Following Romy's initiative, several legislators presented bills in Congress seeking to alter the legal status of married women. The supporter of one bill, Deputy Nelson Carneiro from Rio de Janeiro, pointed to the legal changes already under way in Europe, and rhetorically asked: "Why should Brazil be one of the last of civilized countries to erase the label of incapacity imposed on married women and to regulate her civil rights as her husband's collaborator in the defense of the home and the education of children?" (Carneiro 1985a: 48).[4] Although Romy Medeiros and Nelson Carneiro proposed not only that women gain full civil capacity but also that the marital property regime be reformed to make that civil capacity effective, the Married Women's Statute, a reform approved in 1962, left the full community property regime intact. Although some prominent jurists recognized the need to change the marital property regime,[5] many others insisted on retaining the husband as the executor of marital property (*chefe da sociedade conjugal*). This made eradication of incapacity primarily a symbolic achievement (Dolinger 1966; Verucci 1987).

IABA delegates also debated reforms to the marital property regime, a subject more contentious than the formal civil capacity of married women. The deliberations among lawyers in the 1940s established the parameters of competing arguments that have characterized family law debates into the 1990s. Whereas some delegates argued that reforming the marital property regime was necessary to guarantee women's rights, others claimed that introducing egalitarian property relations into marriage would undermine family unity and violate each country's traditional culture and customs. At the second IABA conference held in Rio de Janeiro in 1943, the civil law committee entertained a vigorous debate about a Chilean delegate's proposal that all American countries modify their civil codes to establish "deferred community property" as the default marital property regime in order to guarantee women's rights and financial security within marriage. Under deferred community property, husband and wife would administer their assets

---

[3] Unless otherwise noted, information about Romy Medeiros's campaign for civil code reform comes from two interviews conducted by the author with Romy in Rio de Janeiro, June 28 and December 12, 1997.

[4] In 1938 and 1942, France's laws were modified to reduce marital power and expand women's liberties to pursue work outside the home; Italy followed suit in 1942 (Zannoni 1998a: 398–9). The fact that Vichy France and Mussolini's Italy, on the one hand, and Latin America's military governments, on the other, expanded women's property rights shows that there is no straightforward relationship between the form of political regime and gender policy.

[5] Orlando Gomes argued that granting married women more rights would imply modifications of the marital property regime, but recognized that such modifications would be radical and sure to incite controversy (*Correio da Manhã*, August 13, 1961).

separately during the marriage. To justify his proposal, Fernando Cerda Varas noted:

Since the first years of the twentieth century, a renovating spirit has invaded the legal field as modern legislators have granted women the same civil rights enjoyed by men to liberate women from the shackles and straps reflected in the precepts of ancient law ... precepts that might have been just and appropriate with the traditions of the era of their crafting, but today ... must disappear. (Cerda Varas 1943: 31)

Cerda argued that a new default marital property regime would "avoid placing women's assets in the dangerous situation of being under the administration of profligate husbands of poor economic judgment" (ibid.: 35). In anticipation of the debates provoked by Chilean legislators' proposals to establish the deferred community property regime fifty years later in the 1990s, Cerda argued that it was not enough to establish deferred community property as an optional property regime. Women would never express a preference for it openly, since this would imply mistrust for their husbands' financial acumen. If the regime were the default regime, however, no spouse would feel wounded and the harmony of marriage would be secured (ibid.).

Due to objections raised by Argentine and Brazilian delegates, the civil law committee eventually voted against Cerda's proposal. These delegates argued that it would be inappropriate for the IABA to recommend a uniform marital property regime for all of the Americas, since family law was closely related to the particular traditions, culture, and religious beliefs of each society. Although American countries could probably agree to unify their laws on obligations and contracts, it would be almost impossible to unify family law. One Argentine delegate insisted that marriage had a "moral and ethical basis" and that "everything that permits the division of the community or moral unity could be the germ of [the family's] dissolution" (IABA 1943).

It is interesting to observe the positions taken by delegates from Argentina, Brazil, and Chile in the 1943 civil law debates. The Chilean delegates submitted a progressive proposal calling for the radical modification of family law to advance women's rights, and Argentine and Brazilian delegates joined to defeat it. Yet it was Argentina (in 1968) and Brazil (in 1977) that first reformed their laws to approximate the Chilean lawyer Cerda's 1943 proposal. In contrast, by 2002 Chile still had not reformed its default marital property regime to establish equality between the spouses. Meanwhile, many countries around the world had already or were in the process of introducing the deferred community property regime: Sweden in 1920, accompanied by other Scandinavian countries; Colombia in 1932; and Germany in 1957. Israel, Costa Rica, Quebec, Switzerland, and the Netherlands also adopted the deferred community property regime (Glendon 1989: ch. 3).

Lawyers' debates at the IABA meetings point to two conclusions about married women's civil capacity. First, it was fairly easy to reach consensus that gender equality required that laws labeling women as "relatively incapable" and granting husbands "marital power" over their wives be reformed. These symbolic reforms were endorsed by the IABA in the 1940s, the Bogotá Convention of 1948, and the United Nations Declaration on Human Rights of 1948. However, experts in the 1940s and 1950s did not agree on how or whether married women's property rights should be made effective through a reform of the marital property regime. The technical details involved in these reforms and the allegedly nefarious implications of women's property rights for family unity kept the IABA from adopting a strong stand on the issue. The demonstration effects produced when more and more countries around the world abandoned old community property systems for partial community property, combined with evolution in Roman Catholic doctrine to endorse women's equality in marriage, turned the tide in favor of property rights reformists by the 1960s.

Military Governments and the Drive for Legal Modernization

The desire to reorder state and society that characterized the "bureaucratic authoritarian" military governments of Latin America produced unexpected consequences for married women's civil property rights. Dictators did not intend to grant women more rights. In fact, military governments in all three countries aimed to usher in a return to traditional family values. In Argentina, President Juan Carlos Onganía and many of his close associates were conservative Catholics. The president and several top civilians in his government were known to have participated in the "*cursillos de cristiandad*" workshops prior to taking power. Modeled on the *cursillos* held during Franco's rule in Spain, these workshops "constituted a sort of Catholic 'moral rearmament' designed to nourish the believer and endow him with a doubtless, faultless faith" (Potash 1996: 198, fn. 9; Rouquié 1984: 259). Many officials in the administration believed that public policies to reinforce the moral order would help to resist communist influences. Municipal ordinances were issued in Buenos Aires that prevented couples from kissing in public, women from wearing miniskirts, and men from growing their hair long, and banning muted lighting in bars (Rouquié 1984). In 1969, Onganía dedicated the country to the "protection and intercession of the Immaculate Heart of Mary" (Klaiber 1998: 72).

In Brazil, the military coup of 1964 was preceded by the widespread mobilization of conservative women who called for the ouster of leftist president João Goulart (Simões 1985). The military responded by deploying "traditional symbols of female piety, spiritual superiority, and motherhood" in an attempt to legitimize its authoritarian political project. As Alvarez notes, "Brazilian coup makers established a new modal pattern for reactionary gender politics in the Southern Cone" (1990: 6). Later, however, the orientation of the Brazilian military government changed. By the late 1970s, Brazilian president General Ernesto Geisel affirmed the right to family planning without coercion. In the early 1980s, the military government organized a women's health program under consultation with feminist advisors.

In Chile, the imposition of military rule was preceded by demonstrations by women who pleaded with military officers to save their families from Marxism. In the most dramatic incident, tens of thousands of women, empty cooking pots in hand, marched through downtown Santiago declaring that the Allende regime had destroyed their livelihoods and demanding its overthrow (Crummett 1977). Once in power, the Pinochet government deployed a discourse of traditional motherhood, which upheld women as the moral guardians of society and the "trustees of national traditions" (Munizaga and Letelier 1988). Between 1975 and 1983, some 430,000 women were members of state-sponsored mothers' centers, and the National Women's Secretariat involved over two million women as participants in seminars and courses (ibid.: 336).

Yet the decision-making process established by military dictators reduced the impact of their personal conservative convictions on policy outcomes. To modernize, military rulers in Argentina, Brazil, and Chile convened special commissions of experts to study and propose reforms to each country's civil, commercial, and criminal laws. Small commissions of expert lawyers, not dictators and their cronies, deliberated over family law, opening a window of opportunity for liberalizing reforms. Expert reformist commissions in Argentina, Brazil, and Chile debated reforms that were implemented most rapidly when they were seen as purely technical, with minimal interference from military leaders and other regime elites.

Argentina

Advances in married women's property rights in Argentina came about in 1968 as part of a massive reform of the country's civil, commercial, and criminal codes. Shortly after seizing power in 1966, the government of General Juan Carlos Onganía (the self-declared government of the "Argentine Revolution") launched a major effort to modernize the country's civil, criminal, and commercial codes, code of civil procedure, and various laws concerning capital markets, aviation, and labor. Onganía's minister of justice, Conrado Etchebarne, held that legal reform was necessary to further the objectives of modernization, peace, and security that guided the government as a whole. The legal reforms implemented under his leadership were the first major changes made to Argentine civil law since the promulgation of the codes in the nineteenth century. Jurists also argued that reform was necessary because social and economic changes had rendered the old codes out of date.

In a speech before the IABA, which held its sixteenth meeting in Buenos Aires in 1967, Minister of Justice Conrado Etchebarne laid out the motivations behind the legal reform:

After achieving order, the necessary precondition for peace, the government of the Argentine Revolution, in line with its objectives, finds itself embarked on the task of revising the national legislation to keep it updated in accordance with principles of justice, solidarity, and freedom.

The function of the judiciary is emphasized amidst revolutionary processes. Every change must be institutionalized in a reform of the legal order. De Tocqueville, with his characteristic insight, said that "There is no revolution without change in civil legislation," and the moment the Republic now lives in is no exception to this judgment.

The time has come, gentlemen, for Argentina to modernize her judicial institutions, to renew them, to put them at the "spirit of the age." It is the law of humanity that new interests and productive ideas triumph in the end over aged traditions, unsound practices, and conformist attitudes.

Reform imposes itself, neither for a simple desire to innovate nor for an aspiration to scientific perfection, but rather from the needs deriving from a mismatch between laws and reality and the evolution of our ways. This has been affirmed by university faculties, scientific conferences, organizations of entrepreneurs, and professional associations. (Etchebarne 1967: 5)

The social changes experienced by Argentine society in the postwar period required changes in laws affecting women and family relations. As in other countries, World War II heightened the demand for labor, and women flooded into the workplace in unprecedented numbers. The Argentine census of 1947 revealed that in the city of Buenos Aires, 47 percent of women between the ages of eighteen and twenty-nine worked outside the home (Germani 1955). As women became increasingly important economic actors, the need to secure their financial security and property rights became more acute. Customs in Argentina were also profoundly influenced by changes in the United States. The liberalization of gender relations following World War II was captured in Hollywood cinema images that provoked new debates about women's political and civil rights. By the 1960s, dramatic changes in social structure had altered "the daily life of women and men of various social classes; customs were transformed, and new legitimacies were constructed.... Women, especially those of the middle class ... apparently achieved an autonomy unthinkable even a generation before; they went out alone, returned late, enjoyed greater sexual freedom, used contraceptives, and more effectively controlled the number of children they bore (Feijoó and Nari 1996). These social changes had a direct effect on the ideas of lawyers. As former minister of justice Conrado Etchebarne recalled:

There was a general consensus in Argentine society, and among experts in the science of law, that a reform was necessary to update the codes that had been in effect for almost one hundred years without modification. These old codes were out of touch with the economic and social reality of a century later.[6]

The need to change laws in light of social evolution was amply debated among lawyers at national conferences. According to former interior minister Guillermo Borda: "The reform was fundamentally based in what had already been demanded by various conferences of civil law . . . the reform was already in the air."[7]

Minister Etchebarne organized 100 prominent jurists into commissions to propose changes to the old codes. According to Etchebarne, it was the only time in the history of Argentina that the 100 most important jurists in the country had been convened to reform the country's laws.[8] The commission charged with reforming the civil code was composed of three prominent civil jurists, who met for about a year. The first issue faced by the commission was whether to propose partial reforms to the existing civil code or formulate an entirely new code. The commission decided on the adoption of partial reforms in order to preserve continuity with past civil law jurisprudence and legal doctrine. The maintenance of the old civil code, they argued, "is the greatest honor that can be bestowed on it and on [its author] Vélez Sarfield who, in an era of limited means succeeded in drafting a code that fixed the destiny of a country ruled by diverse economic and social circumstances, by virtue of having the good judgment to craft institutions respectful of fundamental rights and order them with prudence and wisdom" (Bidau, Fleitas, and Ruiz 1968: 1811). In the eyes of Argentina's most prominent civil jurists, the civil code was far more than a set of mere rules and regulations. By upholding the social and moral norms binding people together, it embodied the country's sense of self. In forwarding its recommendations to the minister of justice, the commission explained that its proposals amounted to "prudent reforms that were appropriate to prevailing legal doctrine. . . . This Commission gave particular weight to bills already submitted in Congress and the decisions reached by conferences and workshops of prominent jurists promoting modifications to the civil code" (ibid.: 1811–12). The commission added: "[T]he protection of the family . . . deserved special consideration, with provisions for the defense of community property, especially the protection of women's property . . ." (ibid.).

The fact that no Congress functioned during the Onganía regime undoubtedly expedited the reforms. According to Etchebarne, past civil code bills had been introduced in Congress only to suffer from politically motivated criticisms and die. He remarked: "[L]egal science is not always in agreement with politicians."[9] Indeed, the lawyers perceived their work as technical,

---

[6] Interview with Conrado Etchebarne, Buenos Aires, July 16, 1998.
[7] Interview with Guillermo Borda, Buenos Aires, July 15, 1998.
[8] Interview.
[9] Interview.

apolitical, and virtually invisible. Etchebarne noted at the time that "the immense task of lawyers in elaborating proposals for legal reform tends to go unnoticed by the public, that many times is unaware of the long toils and sacrifices that lead to the acquisition of the knowledge and experience necessary to responsibly undertake a task of such magnitude" (1967: 9).

The civil code commission submitted its recommendations of draft articles to Minister of Justice Etchebarne and Minister of the Interior Guillermo Borda.[10] Etchebarne and Borda introduced one small change[11] to the draft and then forwarded the articles to president Onganía to sign into law. In their note to the president, Etchebarne and Borda noted:

The reform is the result of a deeply held aspiration expressed through conferences, seminars, and publications. It not only seeks to update civil law to the present times, which is what is important, but also resolve the numerous problems that had led to debates and uncertainties. We consider, Mr. President, that the proposed reform will have a positive impact on the progress of our law, and the improvement of our institutions. (Borda and Etchebarne 1968: 1810–11)

Onganía then rubber-stamped the recommendations of his civilian ministers and the expert commission. Etchebarne and Borda sent the president the civil code articles on April 22, 1968; on April 26, 1968, the new law was published in the *Boletín Oficial*.

The civil code changes enacted under the Onganía administration expanded women's property rights and liberalized family law. Law 17.711 labeled married women as "fully capable" citizens and significantly modified the marital property regime. Both husband and wife were granted free administration over property earned or inherited during marriage. The law required the consent of both spouses for the alienation of household property and real estate. The reform also introduced the possibility for couples to obtain a legal separation by mutual consent. Previously, judicial separations were granted only when spouses could prove that grounds existed for divorce due to the fault of one party. In summary, though a consensus among lawyers had been developing since the 1950s, it was only during the military government of Juan Carlos Onganía that the drive for modernization opened a policy window permitting the civil code to be reformed in line with prevailing ideas in domestic and international legal circles.

---

[10] Guillermo Borda had originally participated in the commission as an expert, but was subsequently appointed minister of the interior. Although the new post prevented him from officially serving on the commission, he continued to advise its deliberations and, together with Etchebarne, forwarded the recommendations to President Onganía.

[11] The small change (which is discussed in Chapter 5) modified Article 67 bis to add the requirement that couples applying for a judicial separation undergo a waiting period and second judicial hearing.

Brazil

Like its Argentine counterpart, the Brazilian military government that seized power in 1964 sought to restructure state and society. The government accelerated state-led industrial development; reorganized the political system to create two, rather than multiple, political parties; and suppressed labor movements and the Communist Party. As in Argentina, the drive for modernization that produced repressive and reprehensible consequences in other areas led to unexpected policy outcomes for women's rights. Since legal reform was viewed as part of the modernization of the state, ministers of justice working under the Brazilian military government appointed commissions of law professors to prepare recommendations for reforms of the civil code. In 1969, Justice Minister Luiz Antonio Gama e Silva appointed a commission of jurists to update the civil code of 1916.[12] The commission was supposed to preserve the "spirit" of the old civil code as much as possible but produce a new code that reflected the evolution of Brazilian society and "advances in legal science" (Moreira Alves: 1992 116). In contrast to the Argentine case, the Brazilians aimed to replace the original 1916 code with an entirely new document. The commission presented its work to the ministry in 1971, where technical changes were made to the draft. Without introducing any of his own modifications, President Geisel sent the bill to the Chamber of Deputies in 1975, where a special commission was created to consider it.

The government's draft civil code bill proposed establishing "partial community property" as the default marital property regime. Under this regime, each spouse would continue to administer his or her own assets after the marriage, although the husband would remain in charge of the common goods acquired by the couple during marriage. The new property regime would expand women's property rights by recognizing their agency not merely over the products of their own labor but over the assets and investments they brought into the marriage.

Because of the sweeping nature of the reforms envisioned in Brazil and the larger number of actors participating in deliberations, however, the process

---

[12] The reform built on two prior attempts to reform Brazil's 1916 code. In 1940, the government appointed a three-member commission to revise the civil code. The commission's work, which focused on the law of obligations and not family law, was not completed. In 1961, the Ministry of Justice again appointed a small commission headed by prominent civil jurist Orlando Gomes to draft reforms to the civil code. Gomes's proposals, published in 1963, would have implemented full juridical equality between the spouses in relation to one another and to their children. Each spouse would continue to administer his or her own property upon marriage in a partial or deferred community property system (Moreira Alves 1992: 113–15). In 1965, the new military government (which seized power in 1964) forwarded Gomes's draft to Congress. The justice minister said at the time, "It would be impossible, at this time of rapid change, to keep the Brazilian codes as they are, without reformulation" (quoted in Carneiro 1991). However, the proposals came under serious criticism and the government decided to withdraw the drafts and initiate another cycle of deliberations (Moreira Alves 1992: 116).

was much slower than in Argentina. The commission's proposals were sent by the military executive to Congress in 1975, yet received the approval of the Chamber of Deputies only in 1984 and the Senate in 1997 (after which the Senate's version was sent back to the Chamber for final approval). However, the divorce law separately approved by Congress in 1977 incorporated one suggestion from the government's 1975 civil code proposals. Law 6515 established partial community property as the default marriage regime, thereby advancing women's property rights.[13] (The divorce law, which followed a constitutional amendment, had an altogether different logic from property rights reform and is the subject of Chapter 4.) As a result, women's property rights, which had been partially recognized with the 1962 Married Women's Statute, were definitively advanced through the back door with the sanction of the divorce law in 1977. The 1962 and the 1977 reforms together amounted to the functional equivalent of Argentina's 1968 reform. However, as Chapter 5 shows, debates about additional reforms to the civil code to secure women's full juridical equality continued throughout the military administration and after the 1985 transition to civilian rule. The democratic transition generated momentum for advances in women's rights in the Brazilian Constitution, but produced little momentum for the speedy enactment of changes to the civil law.

Chile

Like military governments in Argentina and Brazil, the Pinochet government that seized power in 1973 was interested in legal modernization. The government appointed several commissions to study and propose policy changes, including the Constituent Commission organized by Pinochet in 1976 to draft a new constitution and a group of several prominent law professors and judges convened by the minister of justice in 1975 to draft reforms to the civil code.

They aimed to address the fact that in the 1970s, Chilean women enjoyed fewer legal rights than women in Argentina and Brazil. For example, the Chilean Civil Code stated that "the husband has the right to oblige his wife to live with him and follow him wherever he moves his residence," and that "the husband is the chief of the conjugal society, and as such may freely administer his property and that of his wife" (Articles 133 and 134). The commission deliberated the "urgent issues" of women's civil capacity and the marital property regime during 146 formal sessions and "innumerable" working group meetings that took place over a four-year period (Philippi 1979: 239–40).[14]

---

[13] Article 50 of Law 6515 of 1977, modifying Article 258 of the civil code.

[14] The military coup in Chile initiated a new round of attempts at legal modernization. However, modernization efforts had already commenced during the ousted socialist government of Salvador Allende, in power from 1970 to 1973. Officials in the Allende administration wanted to expand women's property rights within marriage. A bill presented to Congress in

In 1979, the commission published its draft, which proposed to grant married women full civil capacity and eradicate the institution of "marital power" that had granted husbands the power of legal representation over their wives, the ability to command their wives to follow them wherever they moved, and the authority to prevent their wives from working outside the home. However, the commission decided not to change the default marital property regime to a system of deferred community property or "participation in earnings." The solution agreed upon by experts in the Philippi Commission was not as liberal as the reforms proposed in Argentina and Brazil (where expert commissions sought to install partial community property regimes that granted women more authority). The Chilean commission's chair, Julio Philippi, explained: "After considering the advantages and disadvantages of different property regimes, the Commission decided that the most appropriate for our country, considering its social development, traditions and customs, is to maintain for the present the regime of conjugal society [or full community property], notwithstanding the full juridical capacity we grant married women under this regime" (Philippi 1979: 239).

The proposal was leaked to the press and generated excitement among the public about the possibility of expanding women's rights. Yet social conservatives within the regime, including the First Lady and representatives from the national network of Mothers' Centers, declared their opposition to the reforms. As Sara Navas said: "It would be better, instead of granting women equality, to highlight their dignity and different roles in the family" (Brito 1997: 74). Some of the resistance stemmed from those who believed that the traditional patriarchal family constituted a bulwark against Marxism. Diminishing the father's authority to create democracy in the family would open the door to Marxist influence on society (Valenzuela 1987: 49–50). Unlike in Argentina and Brazil, where military governments translated expert ideas into state policy, Chilean ideologues stepped in to block the reform. Debate about the proposal was aborted, and the minister of justice released a statement saying that the government would offer an initiative to reconcile women's rights with the family at an opportune time (Brito 1997: 76–7).

The reasons why the Pinochet government aborted the reform are unclear. Nor is it clear who leaked the proposal before it landed on the president's desk. The general secrecy of the Pinochet regime makes it difficult to find record of the policy process. In his study of the Constitution of 1980, for

1970, based on the work of a commission composed of various law professors and judges, proposed granting married women full civil capacity and establishing deferred community property as the default marriage regime (Tomasello Hart 1989: 25; for a declaration of the government's support for the bill, see comments by Davor Harasic in Instituto de Docencia y Investigación Jurídica 1973). The 1973 military coup interrupted the bill's treatment by the democratically elected Congress.

example, Barros found very few documents that detailed the sequence of events, noting that many of the key discussions leading up to the decision to enact a new constitution took place in "private encounters for which there are most likely no complete records" (1997: 137). The "non-public nature of dictatorial deliberation and decision makes it extremely difficult" to ascertain motives and procedures with certainty (ibid.: 136). Nevertheless, we can speculate that since a vast governmental apparatus existed to deal with "women's issues," someone thought it important to take into account their views on women's rights initiatives. The Pinochet government relied heavily on gendered imagery to defend its legitimacy and sought to cultivate support among women in particular. Pinochet created a women's ministry and supported a national network of 10,000 Mothers' Centers (originally created under the Christian Democratic government of the 1960s). It could also be the case that the government suppressed the civil code reform to avoid polarizing the public in the period leading up to the national plebiscite to ratify the new constitution, held in 1980. (In the vote, 68 percent of the population voted in favor of the new constitution, that is, in favor of continuing Pinochet's rule.)

In 1985, the government renewed its efforts at civil code reform. Pinochet issued a presidential degree convening a new commission to debate and propose a bill to improve the legal situation of women. Several experts served on the committee, which considered proposals from government agencies and from university faculty. The rector of Gabriela Mistral University, Alicia Romo, and Enrique Barros, director of the private law faculty at the University of Chile, submitted proposals that strongly resembled a 1970 bill introduced under the Allende government. Both proposals aimed to grant married women full civil capacity and to install a version of the German family property regime in which each spouse administers her own property during marriage, and when the marriage is terminated, the property is lumped together and split down the middle. Romo and Barros's proposals provoked fierce opposition from conservatives, who claimed that an egalitarian property regime was contrary to natural law and that the man had to be the unique source of authority in the family.[15] This time, however, the Pinochet government agreed to implement a partial reform. The law, which was adopted in 1989 on the eve of the democratic transition, resembled Philippi's 1979 proposal: It granted married women full agency and eradicated marital power in principle, but left intact the property regime that was administered by the husband.

In Chile, the military dictatorship advanced women's rights in rhetoric but not in practice. Women's full civil capacity and the suppression of male control in marriage was a rhetorical gesture. Barros argues that "the central objective [of the law] was to grant married women capacity, to demonstrate

[15] Interview with Enrique Barros, Santiago, April 22, 1998.

a political achievement, but without really doing anything.... The reform was more symbolic than practical."[16] The reform failed to produce concrete effects, since husbands retained the authority to administer their wives' assets. As Tomasello Hart claims, "it is highly doubtful that husbands ceased to be, in practical terms, the legal representatives of their wives. Similarly, it is highly doubtful that women married under the conjugal society have ceased to be relatively incapable" (1989: 138). Chile's 1989 reform of women's property rights strongly resembled Brazil's 1962 reform. Both were primarily symbolic, but the same symbols produced dramatically different effects in 1962 and in 1989. Several Brazilian legal scholars recalled that in the early 1960s, the legal recognition of women's full equality represented a "cultural breakthrough" and a "watershed in women's rights." Although husbands rarely initiated judicial proceedings to prevent their wives from working, the inferior legal status of married women reinforced cultural practices that discriminated against women.[17] When the law changed, such cultural practices fell into disrepute and were no longer legitimized by the legal order. In Chile, on the other hand, the recognition of women's full civil capacity, delayed until 1989, marked less of a cultural change. Since society had in many respects already incorporated the language of women's equality, the legal reform was nice but inconsequential. Because of its tardiness, the 1989 reform "had no real effect on Chilean society."[18]

Conclusion

The desire for legal modernization inspired military governments in all three countries to appoint special commissions to draft reforms to family law and women's property rights. The subordinate position of women with respect to men was seen as a vestige of a past that impeded social and economic development. As Argentine minister of justice Conrado Etchebarne proclaimed in 1967, "it is the way of humanity that new interests and fertile ideas triumph in the end over aged traditions, faulty practices, and conformist attitudes" (1967: 5). The policy process in all three countries was similar. Small committees of experts, unaccountable to anyone except for government elites and having to uphold their own reputations only in professional circles, deliberated extensively about principles of law, developments in other countries, and the existing needs of their societies. Except for Chile, dictators rubber-stamped the recommendations submitted by these expert commissions. As a result, married women's property rights advanced significantly

---

[16] Interview.
[17] Interview with Leilah Borges, Rio de Janeiro, October 17, 1997; Desembargador Wilson Marques, Rio de Janeiro, December 10, 1997; Desembargador Silvio Capanema de Souza, Rio de Janeiro, December 11, 1997.
[18] Interview with Enrique Barros.

under military rule in Argentina and Brazil. In Chile, the legal reform eventually enacted under the Pinochet government was largely symbolic. Women gained full legal agency in name but not in practice. The more limited extent of Chile's reform in comparison to the other two countries did not reflect public opinion, Church pressure, or social movement demands. Rather, the exposure of expert decisions about reform to the press led to the involvement of more actors in the policy debate and provided them with veto possibilities. Conservative elites curtailed reforms that would have translated women's actual gains in the Chilean economy and society into the legal recognition of their rights to marital property.

4

Church and State in the Struggle for Divorce

Divorce's legal status is profoundly consequential for private lives and relationships. Divorce provokes intense conflicts within public institutions. These dual aspects of divorce were acutely evident in late twentieth-century Latin America, when the struggle to legalize divorce threatened to unravel the historic bargains forged between Church and state over the terms of marriage and its dissolution. Insisting that the social problems created by lack of divorce demanded resolution and that Roman Catholic ethics should be absent from public decision making, the partisans of divorce mobilized throughout political and civil society. In defense of Catholic doctrine, bishops and principled believers dug in their heels to defend the sanctity of the institution of marriage. Debates between the partisans and opponents of divorce centered not just on evolving social practices, such as rates of separation, consensual union, and illegitimacy, but also on the public status of the Roman Catholic Church. Family values figured prominently in deliberations on divorce, but so did competing claims about the civil or divine nature of marriage, the separation between Church and state, and the origins and purposes of the civil law.

This chapter's comparative historical analysis of Brazil, Argentina, and Chile illustrates the personal and ethical dilemmas provoked by the issue of divorce and theorizes the political conditions that make legal divorce possible. The three countries faced similar social problems created by growing rates of marital breakdown and illegitimacy, but patterns of policy change on divorce were dramatically different. Divorce was legalized during military authoritarian rule in Brazil and a few years after the democratic transition in Argentina. By the end of 2002, divorce remained illegal in democratic Chile despite numerous attempts to change the law. Why did a military government sanction a divorce law in Brazil, but not in the other two countries? Why did democratization bring about the legalization of divorce in Argentina but not in Chile? Why was Chile unable to legalize divorce over the course of twelve years of democratic rule?

78

As Chapter 2 described in detail, the Roman Catholic Church's prominent role in politics, society, and culture has been reflected in rules on marriage and divorce. The Church had exclusive responsibility over marriage in Argentina, Brazil, and Chile until the end of the nineteenth century. At that time, liberal governments reduced ecclesiastical power and privileges by appropriating the official registry of citizens' births, marriages, and deaths; assuming control of cemeteries, hospitals, and schools; and making civil marriage compulsory. Yet even the "civil" marriage laws preserved the canonical principle of marital indissolubility. Retention of the indissolubility principle meant that Church doctrine continued to be a valid source of public policy. This legacy makes the Church a central actor in debates on marriage and divorce.

Historically, political and institutional collaboration between national governments and Roman Catholic bishops posed a barrier to the legalization of divorce. Given the Church's social power and influence, few governments were willing to confront it over divorce, even when changes in social practice, culture, and public opinion made divorce an obvious solution to social problems. This chapter shows that the bishops' veto power over marriage laws was curtailed only when crises destabilized the relationship between Church and state. Though the Latin American Church was historically an ally of the conservative oligarchy, the Church experienced a profound reorientation following the Second Vatican Council (1962–5), the Latin American bishops' meeting in Medellín (1968), and the emergence of liberation theology. The Church changed its doctrine and organizational practices, putting greater emphasis on lay participation and on actions to benefit the poorest and most marginalized sectors of the population, also known as exercising a "preferential option for the poor." As a result, some national churches came into increasing conflict with military governments who abused human rights and whose economic programs increased economic inequality. In other countries, the Church neglected to criticize military rulers, generating discontent among democratic forces, which put pressure on the Church-state relationship after the transition had been completed. In these various ways, changes in the Church interacted with the politics of military rule and democratic transition in Latin America to crack the Church-state alliance. Conflicts between bishops and state officials over human rights, education, and economic affairs opened a window of opportunity for prodivorce coalitions. For divorce to be legalized, the government had to be willing to confront the Roman Catholic bishops over issues other than divorce.

Church-state conflict in military Brazil and democratic Argentina opened a window of opportunity for reformers organized around divorce. In the 1960s and 1970s, the Brazilian government grew more repressive as the Church grew more radical, provoking confrontations over human rights, economic policy, and authoritarian rule. In this context, the government had an incentive tacitly to support the legalization of divorce to strike at the

Church in the hopes of undermining its legitimacy in society and opposition to the government. In Argentina, Church-state conflict broke out *after* the transition to democracy. When the military left power in 1983, reformers organized in favor of divorce under the auspices of the liberal Radical Party government, which aimed to reduce ecclesiastical influence over education and politics. At the same time, the failure of the Church more actively to condemn abuses under the previous military government reduced its ability to veto a new divorce law.

Divorce remains illegal in democratic Chile. Besides Malta, Chile is the only country in the world where divorce is not legal. Chile's failure to legalize divorce during twelve years of democratic rule is puzzling in light of strong public support for divorce (over 80 percent of Chileans say they want a divorce law) and the country's high level of economic development. Chile has enjoyed the most rapid economic growth in Latin America and one of the highest levels of human development. The rationality and efficiency of Chile's financial institutions are models for the rest of the region. The fact that Chile clings to the principle of marital indissolubility, a concept originating in canon law, contradicts the country's embrace of liberal norms in other spheres of life. To solve the puzzle, we must look at the position of the Church. By serving as a powerbroker in the Chilean transition to democracy, the Church hierarchy acquired political legitimacy and developed close relations with the politicians who later took control of the national government. In the 1990s, the Church spent the political capital gained during the struggle against the dictatorship to oppose divorce, and politicians have been reluctant to confront it because of the Church's importance to democratic consolidation and defense of human rights. Meanwhile, the bishops found common ground with socially conservative politicians from the Chilean Right, who fought the Church over Pinochet but agreed with it on divorce.

The Roman Catholic Church and Divorce

As an institution, the Roman Catholic Church has structured politics in most countries of the Western world. In their seminal work on the origins of the Western European party system, Lipset and Rokkan argued that the "decisive battle" that forged the defining social cleavages in the countries of Europe was fought between the nation-state and the Church (1967: 102). In Latin America, conflicts over the role of the Church have been equally influential in shaping the political landscape. Battles over Church privileges and the moral order during the nineteenth century shaped the original cleavages of the Chilean and Colombian party systems (Meacham 1966; Scully 1992). In other countries, the Church has played a pivotal role in the collapse or consolidation of different governments. In Venezuela, Church outrage over secularizing education policies helped to provoke the military overthrow of the government of the Acción Democrática Party in 1948 (Levine 1973).

Support from Roman Catholic bishops was decisive for the consolidation of the government and the dictatorship of Getulio Vargas in Brazil in the 1930s (Serbin 1996; Todaro Williams 1976).

The Church's power in society leads governments to take its position seriously. The bishops exert influence over networks of institutions and organizations in civil society, including Catholic Action programs, Catholic workers' groups, youth groups, student groups, and women's groups (Fleet and Smith 1997; Mainwaring 1986; Smith 1982). Pastoral strategies directed at civil society accelerated after the Second Vatican Council: in Brazil, Ecclesiastical Base Communities (CEBs) involved more than two million people in the early 1980s (Mainwaring and Viola 1984). These Church networks are a source of potentially enormous political leverage. The bishops also have influence over Catholic schools and those educated in them. In Argentina in 1980, some 30 percent of students at the secondary level and 18 percent at the primary level were enrolled in private schools, the vast majority of which are run by the Church (Krotsch 1988). In Chile in the 1990s, 55 percent of children in Santiago were enrolled in private schools (Gauri 1998). Church schools account for a large portion of these, particularly the highly prestigious schools for children of Chile's ruling classes as well as the national Catholic University.

Church authority also derives from its role as a moral umpire. In contrast to the cycles of authoritarianism, constitutional change, and military coups that have destabilized the secular state in Latin America, the Church has been a relatively stable institution. The Church speaks on social and political problems with more authority than the officials of the secular state. Latinobarómetro surveys taken between 1996 and 2000 show, for example, that many more Latin Americans confide in the Church than in the armed forces, judiciary, the president, the police, Congress, political parties, or the media (see Table 4.1).

Church opposition to divorce and the bishops' ability to mobilize public opinion against policy change suggests that to explain the legalization of divorce, it is necessary to examine the structural and conjunctural relationship between Church and state. Structurally, there has been a history of cooperation between Latin American governments and Roman Catholic bishops. In Argentina, the Roman Catholic Church retained the character of a "public institution" until the constitutional reform of 1994. The Argentine federal government continues to furnish a (largely symbolic) public subsidy to the Church, and there is evidence that municipal governments allocate a certain amount of the public budget for the support of local churches.[1] In

---

[1] Interview with Emilio Mignone, Buenos Aires, August 6, 1998. Another Argentine recalled that when he worked in the provincial government of Buenos Aires in the 1970s, municipalities allocated public funds to the Church disguised in the budget as "miscellaneous contributions" (interview, August 3, 1998).

TABLE 4.1. *Latin American Confidence^a (percentage)*

Person or group respondents claimed to have "a lot" of confidence in	1996	1997	1998	2000
Church	49	52	54	52
Armed forces	16	19	14	15
Judiciary	8	12	9	8
President	–	15	12	12
Police	8	12	8	9
National Congress	5	10	6	6
Political parties	3	7	4	4
Television	13	15	12	10

^{a} The results reported are aggregate data collected in seventeen Latin American countries by Latinobarómetro. The *N* varies between 17,000 and 19,000 each year. The question asked of respondents was: "Please look at this card and tell me how much confidence you have in each of the following groups, institutions or persons mentioned on the list: a lot, some, a little or no confidence?" The table reports only the percentage answering "a lot of confidence."

Source: Lagos (forthcoming).

Chile, the 1925 Constitution officially separated Church and state, but public monies continue to flow to the Church through state subsidies to dioceses and to Catholic schools (Fleet and Smith 1997; Smith 1982). Even though the Brazilian Church was severed from the state in 1891, bishops retained close ties to political leaders and lobbied to expand Church influence, particularly during the reign of Getulio Vargas (1930–45). Under Vargas, Church privileges lost in the late nineteenth century were reinstated: The Church received state subsidies for its schools, religious teaching was instituted in public schools, and a constitutional provision declaring the indissolubility of marriage was adopted (Todaro Williams 1976).

During the 1960s and 1970s, the Church-state relationship experienced deep shocks. The Latin American Church had historically been considered the ally of the oligarchy and establishment. Yet in the wake of theological and organizational changes stemming from the Second Vatican Council (1962–5) and the Latin American Bishops' Conference in Medellín (1968), progressive Latin American churches introduced new participatory structures such as ecclesiastical base communities, supported the formation of neighborhood movements, and allied with labor unions and human rights groups (Drogus 1997; Gilfeather 1979; Levine and Mainwaring 1989; Mainwaring and Wilde 1989; Moreira Alves 1984; Smith 1982). This concern with social justice brought bishops into conflict with military regimes. In many countries, but above all in Brazil and Chile, the Church hierarchy formally opposed the military government and even served as the hub of networks of social movement organizations struggling to bring about an end to authoritarian rule (Mainwaring 1986; Smith 1982).

The response of national churches to the challenges of the 1960s shaped the future course of Church-state relations. Following military coups in 1964 and 1973, Roman Catholic bishops in Brazil and Chile stopped using their moral authority to support state power and demanded an end to military rule.[2] The Argentine Church hierarchy, on the other hand, failed to challenge the legitimacy of the two military governments (1966–73, 1976–83). One of the most convincing explanations for the variation in Church response to military authoritarianism focuses on pressure from religious competitors, particularly Protestant evangelicals. Gill, for example, claims that the Argentine Church's reluctance to oppose the military was a function of the low levels of Protestant competition in the country. Whereas religious competition (measured as the number of people adhering to non-Catholic Christian religions) had grown around 15 percent in Brazil and Chile between 1900 and 1970, in Argentina these numbers had increased by only 2.7 percent (Gill 1998: 107). These conservative estimates of Protestant growth over time should be supplemented by current statistics on the percentage of the population of each country that is Protestant. In Chile, 25 percent of the population is Protestant, compared with 18 percent in Brazil and 7 percent in Argentina.[3] Faced with high levels of competition from Protestant sects, national bishops' councils in Brazil and Chile sought actively to maintain the loyalty of parishioners by advocating for the poor in national politics and organizing Church-based popular groups. To retain the allegiance of these constituencies, the Brazilian and Chilean Churches opposed military governments that threatened social justice and equitable development. In Argentina, on the other hand, the Protestant "threat" was minimal, giving the Church hierarchy little incentive to oppose the military regime (ibid.).

The return to democratic rule in the 1980s changed Church-state relations again. In Brazil and Chile, the Church moved from being an opponent of the government to being an ally of the government as many of the Church's former collaborators in the struggle against authoritarian rule assumed control of the state. In Argentina, the Church turned from an ally of the military state to an opponent of the new democratic government led by Radical

---

[2] In both Brazil and Chile, however, some institutional collaboration persisted between Church and state in spite of the Church hierarchy's formal condemnation of military rule. The Church continued to accept state subsidies for religious schools and other Church-run institutions in health and social services.

[3] Data presented by Anthony Gill, "The Economics of Evangelization," lecture at the David Rockefeller Center for Latin American Studies, Harvard University, November 8, 1999. Data on religious affiliation in Latin America are inconsistent, however. According to another study, a mere 15 percent of Chileans are Protestant, including 14 percent of urban and 25 percent of rural residents (Centro de Estudios Públicos 1995).

TABLE 4.2. *Stages of Conflict and Cooperation between Church and Government*

	Church allied with government	Political conflict between Church and government
Argentina	1966–73 (Onganía) 1976–83 (Proceso)	1983–9 (democracy with Alfonsín)
Brazil	1985 to present (democracy)	1970–85 (military rule)[a]
Chile	1990 to present (democracy)	1976–90 (Pinochet)[b]

[a] The Brazilian military government ruled from 1964 to 1985. Significant conflict between the bishops and the government started around 1970.
[b] The Chilean military government ruled from 1973 to 1990. Significant conflict between the bishops and government started around 1975.

TABLE 4.3. *Explaining Divorce Legislation*

		Political conflict between the government and Catholic bishops	
		Yes	No
Reformist coalitions favoring divorce in Congress	Yes	Brazil 1970s Argentina post–1983 Divorce	Chile 1990s No divorce
	No	Chile 1970s–1980s No divorce	Argentina 1976–83 No divorce

Party leader Raul Alfonsín (see Table 4.2). The shifting relationships between Church and state were consequential for debates on divorce. During periods of general Church-state cooperation, state leaders realized benefits from the Church's political support and were unwilling to make moves to incur Episcopal wrath. When the Church turned generally against the state, however, reformers had more room to maneuver.

The two factors accounting for the legalization of divorce are the presence of reformist coalitions in Congress and antecedent political conflict between Church and state (see Table 4.3). Divorce was legalized in Brazil in the 1970s and Argentina after 1983 due to the presence of reformist coalitions favoring divorce and antecedent political conflict between the bishops and the government. In Chile of the 1990s, by contrast, reformers demanded divorce, but amicable relations between the Catholic bishops and the government blocked the approval of divorce. Church and state clashed in Chile in the 1970s and 1980s, but political repression and the closure of Congress precluded the mobilization of reformers around divorce. In Argentina before 1976, Church-state cooperation and political repression meant that there was neither a governmental incentive to approve divorce nor a coalition demanding it.

Church-State Conflict and Divorce: Brazil and Argentina

In Brazil and Argentina, divorce was legalized in different political contexts: The military ruled Brazil, and Argentina had recently completed a transition to democracy. Both cases shared two features: a large congressional coalition that favored divorce and a government that clashed with Catholic bishops over human rights, economic policy, and education. In Brazil, the imposition and consolidation of military rule brought progressive bishops into conflict with a government that abused human rights and persecuted Church officials. In Argentina, a Roman Catholic hierarchy that had failed forcefully to condemn a repressive military government clashed with its democratic successor over a secular agenda that aimed to reduce the influence of the Church over national politics.

Brazil

The struggle for divorce in Brazil is as old as the Republic itself. In debates about the first Republican constitution (promulgated in 1890), some delegates proposed the legalization of divorce, and several other bills were presented around the turn of the century. In 1896, a Senate commission approved a divorce law, though it was later defeated in the Chamber of Deputies. Again in 1900, a divorce law achieved a majority in one round of voting in the national Senate, but was later defeated. These early deliberations established the contours of Brazilian divorce debates:

On one side, there were those that portrayed the problem from a philosophical and religious angle. On the other, those who considered it from a legal perspective. For the first [side], all Catholics, marriage had to be analyzed as a sacred institution, unalterable by human will. For the rest, the problem was legal and should be treated as such. (Carneiro 1985b: 124)

Issue networks of lawyers continued to express their support for divorce. In 1908, the first Brazilian Juridical Congress met in Rio de Janeiro and issued a statement in favor of divorce. All subsequent national meetings of the Brazilian Bar Association and other legal conferences have done likewise (ibid.; Fonseca 1958).

In 1934, the movement toward divorce suffered a major setback. The Liga Eleitoral Católica (Catholic Electoral League, or LEC, a group organized by Cardinal Leme of Rio de Janeiro to revive the Church's position as a major powerbroker in national politics) had helped elect politicians to the 1933 Brazilian Constituent Assembly in exchange for a promise to defend Church interests in the new Constitution (including a constitutional prohibition on divorce). The LEC screened candidates according to their commitment to Catholic principles, and urged voters to support only those who promised to remain loyal to the Church (Todaro Williams 1976: 450). All of the LEC's demands were included in the 1934 Constitution, including the indissolubility of marriage, religious education in public schools, the right to vote for clerics, and public subsidies for the Church (ibid.). As a result, after 1934, divorce faced a constitutional hurdle in Brazil, a unique situation in all of Latin America.

The marriage indissolubility clause did not enter into the Constitution without fierce opposition, however. One delegate to the constitutional convention protested:

When designing civil law, especially while implementing the organizing principles of the people, it is an error and a shame to impose a religious nature on the idea of citizenship.... Let us not forget that we are elaborating a Constitution for men, for free citizens, and not for followers of one or another religion. The act of making divorce legal does not place any impositions on Catholics. To outlaw divorce, however, creates obstacles for others, for it contradicts the people's general consensus and the demands of a society that wishes to be both independent and carefree. (Acúrcio Torres, quoted in Carneiro 1976: 157–8)

The indissolubility principle was upheld in subsequent constitutional reforms, though liberals fiercely opposed it. After the Constitution of 1946 was approved, one commentator remarked that "the disposition was maintained for love and hypocrisy. No one who voted for it denied that the norm is arbitrary and incapable of deterring what is apparent in Brazilian society: *de facto* divorces and resulting *de facto* marriages.... To be consistent ... they should have created an article in the Constitution ... prohibiting drought in the Northeast or an increase in the cost of living" (Alcino Pinto Falcão, quoted in ibid.: 159).

By the mid-twentieth century, Nelson Carneiro, a legislator from Rio de Janeiro, had assumed a position at the center of the divorce reform movement in Brazil. Shortly after entering Congress in 1947, Carneiro began to submit bills regulating marital breakups and expanding the rights of women and children. Carneiro had practiced family law in Rio de Janeiro, where he gained first-hand experience with the social problems, particularly for women and children, caused by the prohibition on divorce (Tabak 1989). Carneiro saw many couples who, unable legally to divorce from their first partners, lived in unregulated stable unions. He also saw how women separated from their first husbands lived with a permanent social stigma: Either they renounced romance and sexual activity altogether or they entered into new relationships without the possibility of marriage and unable to assume their partner's name (Carneiro 1973). Carneiro believed that a divorce law was necessary to advance women's rights so that

a divorced woman can legally remarry. She will be a wife. She will no longer bear the cross of her ex-husband's sins. And she will have the protection that the law grants to wives in the event of abandonment or death. Divorce does not impede a woman from passing herself from man to man, but neither does it thrust her into such misfortune. (Ibid.: 17)

A divorce law would also advance children's rights:

The children of divorcees . . . are legitimate children. The children of separated people, born from a second union, are illegitimate. The man that marries a separated woman is her husband. The man that shares a bed with a separated woman is her lover. Children know this well, and many suffer for it. (Ibid.: 18)

In 1951 and again in 1964, Carneiro submitted proposals to amend the constitution to permit divorce, both of which were defeated, largely due to the fierce opposition of the Church. As the Archbishop of São Paulo wrote at the time in reference to Carneiro's "criminal" divorce campaign:

If pro-divorce campaigners are the biggest destroyers of our land, domestic enemies, which are the worst enemies according to the words of the Divine Master – it is clear that those who defend the indissolubility and the sanctity of the family are the biggest and most necessary friends of the Church and the nation. (Sales Brasil 1953)

Carneiro also introduced bills to expand the grounds for civil marriage annulment as a way of sneaking divorce into civil legislation without challenging the constitution. One of these bills would have permitted annulment if it could be shown that one of the spouses had erred in her judgment of the personal qualities of the other spouse (bill no. 3099/1953), another was based on a misjudgment of the moral qualities of the other spouse (bill no. 6/1971).[4]

Carneiro's proposals built on a growing consensus among many lawyers, judges, sociologists, and public officials that a divorce law was needed to accommodate changes in Brazilian social and family structure. Official statistics on marital breakups showed a steady increase since the 1950s: the number of separations per 1,000 married women was 0.08 in 1950, 0.17 in 1960, 0.61 in 1970, and 1.3 in 1985 (Goode 1993: 193). Other data show that between 1966 and 1971 (a decade before the legalization of divorce), the number of marriages contracted in Rio de Janeiro increased by 30 percent, but the number of separations grew by 90 percent (Carneiro 1973: 14). These data underestimate the real rate of marital breakdown, since civil registry statistics reflect only the number of separations processed through the courts, when the vast majority of separations are de facto (with property arrangements and child visitation rights established informally). Meanwhile, the percentage of Brazilians living in consensual unions increased: It has been estimated that in the 1960s, around 19 percent of Brazilians living in a stable union were not formally married (Kogut 1976). Data from the 1980 census, when the government first asked a direct question about consensual unions, reveal that 12 percent of Brazilians claimed to be living in consensual unions; the

---

[4] Some of these qualities included incurable alcoholism, homosexuality, sexual perversity, morbid jealousy, or other defects, prior knowledge of which would have prevented one spouse from consenting to the marriage and later revelation of which made life in common intolerable.

1984 household survey gave a total of 15 percent (Petrocelli 1994). As in the case of marital breakdown, these figures tend to underestimate the number of consensual unions, since many people consider and represent themselves as married, regardless of whether they are formally married or not (Goode 1993: 194).

Over the course of the twentieth century, networks of lawyers succeeded in enacting laws to accommodate marital breakdowns and new unions. These "partners' laws" granted female companions equal status with wives and gradually erased distinctions between children born in and out of wedlock.[5] Laws passed beginning in the 1930s permitted male workers to designate their domestic partners as beneficiaries of social security pensions, women to use their partners' names, and men to claim their partners as dependents on tax returns (Carneiro 1991: 121–2). Judges also attempted to contend with one of the largest problems posed by consensual unions: the allocation of common property upon the breakdown of the union. To avoid a situation where women who had worked for the maintenance of the household and the care of children were left with nothing, lawyers and judges considered that the couple's life in common had created a de facto community of goods (*uma sociedade de fato*), whose partition could be regulated by the same rules governing corporations and small businesses. Jurisprudence crystallized into a Supreme Court ruling (*súmula 380*), which held that if a stable relationship could be demonstrated, the property generated through "common effort" would be divided between the two partners. To permit men to grab their property and run would amount to "illicit enrichment," which was prohibited by Brazilian civil law.[6] In this way, a body of law deemed "companions' rights" (*direitos das companheiras*) grew out of provisions in ordinary legislation and through innovative sentences issued by judges.

Meanwhile, the circumstances of a child's birth became irrelevant for rights to inheritance and child support. The Constitution promulgated by dictator Getulio Vargas in 1937 declared that "natural" children recognized by both parents have the same rights as legitimate children born from a formalized marriage. In 1949, Congress approved a law that granted equal rights to children born of adulterous or incestuous relations. The law also permitted married men to recognize their mistresses' children in closed testimony (Tabak 1989: 64). However, the terms "legitimate" and "illegitimate" continued to exist in the law until the 1988 Constitution declared them to be invalid.

The middle and upper classes created a wide range of extralegal means to circumvent the absence of a divorce law. Couples would travel abroad to Uruguay and Mexico to obtain divorces and to remarry. These marriages were not recognized by Brazilian law but served to legitimize the union in the

[5] Interview with Norma Kyriakos, São Paulo, December 4, 1997.
[6] Interview with Desembargador Silvio Capanema, Rio de Janeiro, December 11, 1997.

eyes of friends, family, and colleagues. Another tactic was the formulation of a "prenuptial" civil contract to regulate the allocation of common property in the event of a "marital" breakup. Finally, there were renegade priests who would grant second unions a blessing, a practice highly condemned by the Church, but for which families felt very grateful.[7] In the northeastern state of Pernambuco, one entrepreneurial lawyer performed a ceremony and regulated the effects of a "love compact" between people unable to be married formally.[8]

Unlike the incremental growth of partners' laws, proposals to legalize divorce openly confronted fundamental questions of public philosophy and the moral order. As Carneiro recalled: "It is impossible to relive the intensity, the enthusiasm, the emotions, the highs and lows of the discussion that impassioned, and still impassions public opinion" (Carneiro 1985b: 129). The opponents of divorce, led in Congress by deputies who were also ordained clerics,[9] portrayed it as a blow to the Brazilian family, and a welcome mat to free love and even communism (ibid.: 128; see also Sales Brasil 1953). Other arguments against divorce stemmed from principles of natural law. One federal deputy claimed: "It is an undeniable fact that marriage is founded in natural law. As a consequence of this linkage, marriage has two properties: it is unitary, and indissoluble" (Furtado 1975). Some opponents anticipated that divorced mothers and their children would place a heavy burden on the social welfare system, and feared that the Brazilian state would be unable to cope with all of the social atomization that divorce would produce.[10]

In the eyes of Carneiro and other divorce supporters, the fact that the Constitution opined on the indissolubility of marriage amounted to a violation of the principles of separation of Church and state and freedom of conscience. As stated in the justification for one of the several constitutional amendment proposals facilitating divorce:

It is imperative to recognize that the law is a rational science that should not be mixed with dogmas of faith and sacraments. Human reason must bow to the principles of the law.... One cannot extend the dogmatic rigidity of the sacramental character of marriage to the civil plane ... mixing the spiritual and temporal powers in a country like ours where the union of Church and state no longer exists. (Carneiro 1976: 154)

With arguments about society's need for divorce, the separation of Church and state, and the advancement of women and children's rights, Carneiro and others took the struggle for divorce outside Congress to the entire Brazilian

---

[7] Interview with Moema Toscano, Rio de Janeiro, October 10, 1997.

[8] *Jornal do Brasil*, June 11, 1978.

[9] Among the deputy-priests who fiercely opposed Carneiro's bills were Monsignor Arruda Câmara of Pernambuco and Father Nobre of Minas Gerais.

[10] Interview with Celio Borja, Rio de Janeiro, September 10, 1997.

population. Carneiro recalled:

The principal [initiative] was always to attack, from all flanks, the legal stubbornness, in a battle without rest or shelter. This was done, not only in the halls of Congress, but in thousands of lectures, debates in law schools, clubs, radios and television, in interviews with the press from all over the country and abroad, through personal contacts, and even through a play whose sole intention was to popularize the idea [of divorce] on the stage of various cities. (Carneiro 1985b: 130)

In the 1970s, a young deputy from Rio de Janeiro joined Carneiro's struggle. Rubem Dourado had been a popular young law professor before getting elected to the state legislature and then to the national Chamber of Deputies. He remarked, "[T]he more I studied the law, the more interested I became in the issue of divorce." Dourado then made the legalization of divorce the principal theme of his congressional campaign.[11]

The liberalization of divorce laws in other Western countries influenced Brazilian divorce reformers. Lawyer Gelson Fonseca argued, "We cannot deny that the spirit of the age accepts divorce" (1958: 199). Beginning in the late 1960s, states in Western Europe and North America introduced radical modifications to marriage laws. Several European Catholic countries, including France, Italy, Spain, and Portugal, legalized divorce. Some of these laws marked a major public defeat for the Church. In Italy, for example, Catholic movements and parties collected 1.3 million signatures on a petition to oblige Congress to subject a 1970 divorce law to a popular referendum. In the referendum, held in 1974, an overwhelming majority of the Italian electorate voted in favor of divorce.[12] In other countries where divorce had been legal, changes in the 1960s and 1970s recognized or expanded no-fault grounds for divorce, or simplified procedures for obtaining a divorce by mutual consent (Glendon 1989: chapter 4).

Civil society organizations in Brazil rallied around the issue of divorce. Zizi Leon, former wife of the Brazilian Ambassador to Greece, founded one prodivorce organization, called the "Movement Against Desquite and in Favor of Divorce," in 1942. The "Pro-Divorce Movement" headed by Maria Lucia D'Avila presented a manifesto with 60,000 signatures to the National Congress in 1977. The manifesto affirmed: "[D]ivorce does not destroy the family.... divorce constructs the family, the legality of *de facto* families." Members of the movement traveled to Brasília to accompany Senator Carneiro on his pilgrimage seeking support from members of Congress for the constitutional amendment.[13] Public opinion polls in the 1970s demonstrated strong support for the legalization of divorce. A 1974 survey conducted in Rio de Janeiro and São Paulo found that 67 percent of

---

[11] Interview with Rubem Dourado, Rio de Janeiro, October 10, 1997.
[12] *Jornal do Brasil*, May 12 and 14, 1974.
[13] *Jornal de Brasília*, June 15, 1977.

respondents were favorable to divorce.[14] Support for divorce had grown over time. In 1967, a mere 44 percent of São Paulo residents polled had declared themselves favorable to divorce, but by 1975, this had grown to 64 percent. Young people, women, nonreligious people, and wealthier people were more favorably inclined toward divorce.[15]

As the 1970s progressed, Carneiro convinced more legislators to join the divorce coalition. But these reformers faced an obstacle unique in Latin America. As mentioned earlier, the Brazilian Constitution upheld the principle of the indissolubility of marriage, effectively giving the Church a veto over a divorce law for four decades. The indissolubility principle made it quite difficult to introduce divorce in Brazil. Amending the constitution required endorsement by a two-thirds' supermajority of both the Chamber and Senate in two votes spaced one week apart. When an amendment proposal to remove the indissolubility principle was brought to the floor for a vote in 1975, some 222 legislators voted in favor and 145 against, a majority, but not two-thirds of both Chambers. Of those who voted against the amendment, many were motivated purely by fear of the Church.[16] The two-thirds' hurdle seemed as if it would serve as an obstacle to divorce until congressional opinion shifted massively or until the rules governing constitutional amendments were modified. As conflict grew between the government and the hierarchy of the Roman Catholic Church, the military president lowered the vote threshold required for a constitutional amendment from two-thirds to one-half of Congress, effectively permitting divorce to be legalized. The reasons behind the president's actions require tracing a bit of the history of Church-state relations under military rule.

The Catholic hierarchy and the Brazilian military government had cooperated in the initial stages of the military regime. The bishops had welcomed the 1964 military coup against leftist president Goulart as necessary to eliminate a communist threat. During the governments of Castelo Branco (1964–7) and Costa e Silva (1967–9), there were frequent meetings between military rulers and the hierarchy of the bishops' conference, called the National Council of Brazilian Bishops (CNBB). The government tried to gain the support of the Church by sponsoring public religious processions, sending senior officials to attend religious ceremonies, and funding the construction of the cathedral of Brasília and other Church works. The

---

[14] *Manchete*, June 1, 1974.

[15] *O Globo*, February 26, 1975.

[16] A 1975 survey of a sample of legislators, for example, revealed a discrepancy between the number of legislators who were personally in favor of divorce and those who intended to vote in favor of divorce (*O Globo*, February 27, 1975). My interviewees in Brazil also provided anecdotal evidence of individual legislators from both the MDB and ARENA who voted against their conscience out of fear of the Church. One ARENA legislator told Jarbas Passarinho that he was personally in favor of divorce, but if he voted as such, the Church in his state would liquidate him (interview with Jarbas Passarinho, September 26, 1997).

president reportedly sent a telegram to the Vatican to proclaim Brazilian support for the principles elaborated in *Humanae vitae*, the papal encyclical declaring ecclesiastical opposition to birth control. Conservative bishops gained control of the CNBB and the CNBB's periodic public statements made no mention of military repression or economic policies. The bishops served as intermediaries between the government and regional elites, collaborated on various governmental initiatives, and muted the criticism coming from lower ranks of the Church (Mainwaring 1986: 83; Moreira Alves 1979: 201–2).

Toward the late 1960s and into the early 1970s, however, relations between the CNBB and the government soured as military repression accelerated and the Church grew more radical. The implementation of Institutional Act No. 5 in 1968 (AI-5) granted the president extraordinary powers to suspend the rule of law in the interests of national security. Congress was dissolved, the Supreme Court purged, and many legislators were deprived of their political rights. Censorship increased, and leftist faculty (including Fernando Henrique Cardoso, president of Brazil from 1994 to 2002) were expelled from public universities (Skidmore 1988). Meanwhile, the Second Vatican Council (1962–5) and the Latin American bishops' conference held in Medellín, Colombia, introduced significant doctrinal and institutional changes into the Latin American Church. The documents of Vatican II and Medellín expressed the Church's commitment to the defense of human rights, the promotion of social justice, and the modification of authority structures within the Church itself to allow for greater lay participation (Mainwaring and Wilde 1989: 10). Given the country's severe social inequalities and injustices, these shifts in Church doctrine at the international level were welcome among Brazilian priests and bishops. These opposite trajectories of Church and state set the stage for a collision in the late 1960s and 1970s.

One of the first conflicts emerged in the Amazon region. The government sought to promote development by furnishing subsidies for large-scale agriculture and investing in infrastructure such as the Trans-Amazon highway, which gave incentives to landowners to evict peasant squatters en masse. State and landowner violence against the peasants, combined with the lack of schools and hospitals in the Amazon region, provoked the Church to speak out in protest. In 1970, bishops and priests from the Amazon issued statements denouncing government policies and landowner violence. In response to these and other protests, members of the armed forces detained and tortured priests and Catholic lay leaders and placed a bishop from Mato Grosso under house arrest. Government repression of the Church generated unity within the hierarchy. Rather than denouncing the Amazonian Church, as the military had expected, officials from the CNBB supported their radical counterparts (Mainwaring 1986: 84–94). In subsequent years, progressive priests and bishops gained more power in the Brazilian Church.

In the state of São Paulo, for example, Archbishop Dom Paulo Evaristo Arns made human rights, the rights of the poor, and the development of ecclesiastical base communities priority areas for Church action. During the worst years of military repression in São Paulo, the Church "was the only institution that retained sufficient autonomy to defend human rights.... As Dom Paulo stated, 'The society needed a voice, and because of the repression, no other institution could provide that voice. The Church became the voice of all those sectors that had no voice.'" The archbishop's denunciations of torture by the security forces gained international attention, and he "quickly became the nationwide leader – inside and outside the Church – of the campaign to protect human rights" (Mainwaring 1986: 105–6). Military repression pushed the Church hierarchy as a whole into opposition. Throughout the 1970s, various bishops criticized the military government, denouncing the doctrine of national security and the persecution of priests and layworkers. In response, the government cracked down on the Church. Soldiers and paramilitary units tortured and assassinated several priests in 1976, and a bishop was kidnapped (ibid.: 152–6).[17]

In the context of this conflict between Church and the state, the government had an incentive to support, rather than suppress, a campaign for divorce. Moreover, Brazil's president had little personal commitment to Roman Catholic principles. General Ernesto Geisel, president of Brazil from 1974 to 1979, was a Lutheran, the first non-Catholic president in the country's history. In fact, the Lutheran Church in Brazil released an official statement in 1975 that declared its support for divorce.[18] Although Geisel never publicly endorsed divorce, his close associates report that he was personally in favor. As Celio Borja recalled, Geisel "thought that Brazil should accept divorce." His position was explicit, but discreet. He never discussed divorce in public speeches or in interviews with the press, but "in private conversations, he made his point of view clear."[19]

Geisel could seize upon divorce as a weapon against the Church and also use it as a wedge to divide the Catholic bishops and the opposition political party. In contrast to the other countries of South America, national elections were held and Congress continued to function during military rule in Brazil. The basic electoral rules were established between 1964 and 1968, though the government continued to change these rules well into the 1980s in order to structure the vote to its advantage.[20] One significant change was the replacement of the country's multiplicity of parties with only two. The

---

[17] After 1978, political liberalization accelerated and state repression decreased, leading to a gradual improvement in relations between the bishops and the government. Later, the consolidation of conservatives within the international Church generated pressure to silence progressive Brazilian bishops.

[18] *Jornal do Brasil*, April 11, 1975.

[19] Interview with Celio Borja.

[20] For a comprehensive discussion of changes in Brazil's electoral rules, see Fleischer (1995).

ARENA party allied with the government, and the Movimento Democratico Brasileiro (MDB) served as an umbrella grouping of the various parties and factions opposed to the government.

Few of the elections held during military rule were free and fair. Nevertheless, starting with the national elections held in 1974, the MDB began to make gains at the ballot box. That year, the MDB won 50 percent of the popular vote in the Senate elections (against 35 percent for ARENA), and 38 percent of the House vote (against 41 percent for ARENA) (Fleischer 1995: 47). Although the government retained an absolute majority in Congress, it lost its two-thirds' majority and thus its ability to amend the Constitution. In April 1977, as part of a broader package of constitutional reforms intended to assure continued electoral victories for ARENA, Geisel unilaterally lowered the quorum required for a constitutional amendment from two-thirds to a simple majority (ibid.).

The official rationale presented for the quorum reduction was Geisel's desire to reform the judiciary. Yet Brazilian observers maintain that facilitating divorce was the real motive, since it would further the president's political objectives in several ways. The first was to strike a blow to the Church. Celio Borja explained: "The Church was in political opposition. It criticized the government's policies toward the poor, which embarrassed the government.... The divorce law served as an instrument in this fight. It was understood as such by both sides: by the President, and by the Church."[21] By promulgating legislation that was popular with the public at large yet opposed by the Church, the government could usurp some of the Church's social authority and undercut its opposition to the regime. Second, by legalizing divorce, Geisel could pit the two principal opponents to military rule – the MDB political party and the Church – against one another. MDB politicians were the main proponents of the divorce law. Priests and bishops had vowed to defeat, in the 1978 elections, those legislators who had voted in favor of divorce. Geisel's hope could have been that, by making it easier for MDB politicians to pass a divorce law, the Church's revenge on prodivorce legislators would weaken the electoral position of the MDB.[22] Several MDB politicians criticized Nelson Carneiro and other divorce supporters for playing into this strategy.[23]

---

[21] Interview with Celio Borja, Rio de Janeiro.

[22] Indeed, following the approval of the divorce law, the National Bishops' Council criticized the MDB, accusing legislators of opportunism and "dishonorable haste" for having taken advantage of an illegitimate modification of the constitutional quorum in order to pass a divorce law. The Secretary General of the CNBB also stated that he didn't recognize the "moral authority of the MDB to talk about national problems" after the passage of the constitutional amendment permitting divorce.

[23] The second vice-president of the Lower House, Deputy Ademar Santillo, declared that divorce "is a disservice that Senator Nelson Carneiro is doing to the nation by diverting the attention of the people away from the April package and toward the [divorce] reform."

The weeks surrounding the 1977 vote on divorce were filled with tension and drama. The hard-line bishops intensified their campaign. Threatening letters were left on senators' benches in the plenary, and a priest from Porto Alegre delivered 75 kilograms of antidivorce petitions to legislators. As part of the Corpus Cristi celebrations, the Church mobilized 100,000 people in Belo Horizonte to demonstrate against divorce. In Rio de Janeiro, 10,000 people marched through the city carrying banners with antidivorce slogans such as "What God united Man can't separate," "Family United, People Happy," and "No to the divorce threat!"[24] Bishops threatened to excommunicate prodivorce legislators, and compiled an index of legislators who voted in favor of the divorce law in order to campaign against them in the next elections.[25] For the two joint sessions of Congress where votes were taken to amend the Constitution and permit divorce, the galleries were filled to capacity with citizens waving banners for and against the law. The final vote was 226 in favor; 159 against the amendment. Six months later, a bill regulating the causes of divorce and its effects for property and child custody was passed. The law was strict: Divorce was permitted only after five years of de facto separation or three years of judicial separation, and individuals were allowed to obtain only one divorce in their lifetime. As one legislator explained, restricting divorce in this way was a necessary compromise to get the law passed.[26]

Argentina

Argentina has a long history of divorce mobilization. In the late nineteenth century, "liberals of various shades campaigned for divorce as part of an anticlerical and secularizing program; anarchists advocated free unions with no religious mediation and detested the church; socialists, strong supporters of the family, favored it because they were anti-clerical, regarded divorce as a break with bourgeois social structures, and favored women's liberation

---

Correio Braziliense, April 26, 1977. Santillo said that although he would vote in favor of divorce, the moment was "inopportune," because Brazil should instead be debating the return to civilian rule and the distribution of wealth. *O Globo*, April 29, 1977. Prominent opposition leader Francisco Montoro, senator from São Paulo, also criticized the divorce initiatives. He claimed that the divorce debate was "highly prejudicial" to democratization, and that the Congress should instead debate the problems that most affect Brazilian society instead of losing time in a discussion about divorce. He argued that the divorce issue served only to divide a Congress that should be concerned with more urgent national problems. *Jornal do Brasil*, March 18, 1975. This controversy in the MDB highlights the importance of Geisel's role in getting divorce approved.

[24] *O Estado de São Paulo*, June 10, 1977.

[25] See charges made by Deputy Cantídio Sampaio in *O Globo*, June 12, 1977. The secretary general of the Brazilian Bishops' Council, Dom Ivo Lorscheiter, denied that the Church would persecute legislators, but admitted that the Church was compiling a list of prodivorce politicians "to use at the opportune moment." *O Estado de São Paulo*, June 21, 1977.

[26] Interview with Rubem Dourado.

from church influence. Feminists adopted it as part of the process of achieving female equality before the law and as a solution to the age-old problems plaguing gender relations" (Lavrín 1995: 228–9). Between 1888 and 1932, divorce was debated in Congress seventeen times and always defeated (ibid.). In 1932, the Chamber of Deputies approved a divorce bill, but it later died in the Senate because President Hipólito Yrigoyen was unwilling to confront the Roman Catholic bishops. In 1954, President Juan Perón legalized divorce, but soon after was overthrown by a military coup that later repealed the law. Although several bills were presented during democratic intervals in the 1950s, 1960s, and between 1973 and 1976, none were formally debated (Lagomarsino and Uriarte 1991: 74). Divorce was made legal in Argentina only after the country returned to democracy in 1983. The return to democratic conditions enabled the partisans of divorce to mobilize in civil society and in Congress, and the eruption of conflict between the Roman Catholic bishops and the government opened a window of opportunity for reformers to enact the new law.

Unlike Brazil, where a functioning Congress provided an institutional location for the mobilization of prodivorce coalitions under military rule, the closure of Congress and severe state repression under Argentina's military government (1976–83) precluded the articulation of any demand for divorce. As lawyer Eduardo Zannoni recalled, "there was no doubt that we felt the need for divorce. But the issue was whether one could express this, debate it, and speak in public. In law schools, one could talk about divorce. But the issue was never raised before public opinion, where it was virtually censored."[27] In fact, the government forbade people from uttering the word "divorce" on television. Supreme Court Justice Gustavo Bossert recalled that he was invited to a popular television talk show to discuss the problems encountered by children following a marital breakup. The host of the show took Bossert aside and asked that he not say "divorce," "divorcee," or "divorced" during the show, since the host had received a notice from the government prohibiting the word "divorce" from being spoken.[28]

The return to democracy in 1983 thus gave rise to debate that had been festering for years due to social changes, public opinion, and the desire of Argentine elites to emulate international trends toward divorce. The percentage of Argentines over fourteen years of age living in nonmarital stable unions had increased from 4 percent in 1960 to 7 percent in 1980. The percentage of legal separations among the population had grown from 0.6 percent in 1960 to 2.1 percent in 1980 (Wainerman and Geldstein 1994: 191). As in Brazil, these figures underestimate rates of stable union and the rate of marital breakup, since many people tell census enumerators that they are married, and many separations are never processed through the courts. The

[27] Interview with Eduardo Zannoni, Buenos Aires, August 6, 1998.
[28] Interview with Gustavo Bossert, August 11, 1998.

high percentage of children born out of wedlock suggests that the number of Argentines living in families not constituted by formal marriages was quite high. In the 1980s, the proportion of children born to parents not legally married was over 50 percent (an increase from 40 percent in 1960). In the city of Buenos Aires, the rate was around 40 percent (from 26 percent in 1960), and in some of the provinces, as high as 80 and 90 percent (FLACSO 1993: 28). Public opinion polls taken after the democratic transition showed broad public support for a divorce law. One survey taken in 1984 revealed that 62 percent of those surveyed favored divorce, including 51 percent of respondents who reported attending mass regularly (Osnajanski and Llano 1985).

To compensate for the absence of a divorce law, Argentines had for decades resorted to a multiplicity of odd social institutions. Since they could not obtain a legal divorce from their first spouse, couples in second or third unions in Argentina, as in Brazil, traveled to Mexico and Uruguay to get remarried. Argentine lawyers then took these foreign marriage certificates to local offices of the civil registry to obtain a local marriage certificate. These local certificates were important socially, not legally (since no court would recognize them), for they demonstrated to peers and colleagues that even though Argentine law did not permit it, the stable union had been converted into marriage somewhere.[29] As in Brazil, jurisprudential solutions emerged to protect women and children in consensual unions and in illegal foreign marriages. In the 1960s and 1970s, some courts ruled that women partners could receive a man's social security pension as a wife (Lagomarsino and Uriarte 1991: 76–7). Courts also gave a very liberal interpretation to the causes of civil marriage annulment, permitting in some cases a de facto consensual divorce (ibid.: 78). Thus, even though the formal law did not admit it, one observer recalled that "the reality of divorce was already installed in social life."[30] International trends also contributed to pressures for divorce. Since divorce was legal in most other countries, a host of practical and jurisdictional problems emerged when Argentines married abroad or when Argentines married foreigners. At the same time, the liberalization of divorce laws in the United States and Europe produced a "legislative contamination," or pressure on Argentina to change its laws so that they were more in harmony with the norm in other countries (ibid.).

Beginning in 1984, lawyers, feminists, and legislators began to circulate proposals for divorce. A vigorous debate ensued in the press, in Congress, in universities, and in women's groups about reforming the law to accommodate social changes. A new current in legal doctrine began to dominate legal journals and magazines, conferences and seminars of jurists, and legal

[29] Interview with Cecilia Grosman, Buenos Aires, July 26, 1998.
[30] Interview with Emilio Mignone.

professional organizations.[31] A total of twenty-three divorce bills were presented in Congress in the early 1980s (ibid.: 85–9). Bossert recalled: "Everything changed with democracy. When the authoritarian government left the scene, censorship and self-censorship ended."[32]

Opposition from the Roman Catholic bishops still posed a potentially devastating obstacle, however. In public, the Argentine Church took a firm and united stand against divorce. In 1984, the Bishops' Conference issued a statement to remind Argentines of the Church's position. It read, in part, that:

marriage ... is not a mere contract dependent on the will of the contractors; it is a natural institution, strictly linked to the very being of man, with its own laws and ends. Those who marry are free to grant their love to one another, but the consent they give is irrevocable, because they cannot unsay nor undo what they themselves did not found or establish and that, by consequence, is out of their power. (Conferencia Episcopal Argentina 1984c)

Argentine bishops offered principled philosophical and doctrinal arguments against divorce. Some priests criticized the Church hierarchy's rigid position, arguing that by opposing the law in principle, the Church lost the ability to affect its content. Had it adopted a more conciliatory position, the Church might have been able to participate in divorce debates and help make an eventual law more restrictive, much as the bishops had done when legal separation for mutual consent was introduced in 1968 by the Onganía administration.[33] The Church backed up its words with public action. On July 5, 1986, a bishop led an estimated 50,000 Catholic faithful on a march from the suburbs to the Plaza de Mayo in the center of Buenos Aires to protest the divorce bill (Burdick 1995). Bishops sent letters to legislators,

---

[31] Interviews with Eduardo Zannoni, Gustavo Bossert, and Cecilia Grosman; interview with Haydee Birgin, Buenos Aires, July 28, 1998.

[32] Interview with Gustavo Bossert.

[33] Interview, Buenos Aires, July 13, 1998. Legal separation for mutual consent was introduced as part of the bigger package of civil law reforms discussed in Chapter 3. Promulgation of the mutual consent provision followed a series of discussions between the government and the Church. After the initial reform proposals arrived on President Onganía's desk, he received a letter from the Archbishop of Buenos Aires stating that the Church was not in agreement with aspects of the reform and wanted its position to be taken into account. The Minister of the Interior, Guillermo Borda, then met with a group of bishops several times in order to convince them of the need to drop fault grounds from the law regulating marital separations. The bishops suggested that the new law require that two audiences with a judge be held before the separation could be granted. As Borda recalled, the Church's concern was that "the marital bond not be left completely to the discretion of the two spouses, because then marriage would cease to be an institution defending the public order and become something dependent on the mere will of the parties involved." The Church's suggestions were incorporated into the final law signed by the president. Interview with Guillermo Borda, Buenos Aires, July 15, 1998.

Church officials held private meetings with legislators to express their views, and priests made pleas from the pulpit to mobilize the public against the divorce bill.[34]

Yet the Church's association with Argentina's authoritarian past reduced its authority and legitimacy, and the government's willingness to confront the bishops over human rights and education made it clear that fear of the Church would not get in the way of approving a divorce law. Public beliefs in the bishops' complicity with Argentina's military government tarnished the Church's image. The repression suffered by the Argentine people during the Proceso de Reorganización Nacional (the military government that ruled from 1976 to 1983) had been the most severe in the country's history. With the purported aim of rooting out and eliminating the Montonero guerillas, the armed forces detained, interrogated, tortured, and caused the disappearance of thousands of people. Even so, the Roman Catholic hierarchy failed to take a firm and united stance in condemning the military. In fact, the largest group of bishops agreed with the government's goal of eliminating leftist subversion. Though this group disagreed with the military's methods, it was unwilling to criticize the regime in public or break relations with the government. Only a minority of moderate bishops voiced muted protests against the regime, and about six progressive bishops (out of a total of eighty in Argentina) took a clear and public stand for human rights (Klaiber 1998: 77; Mignone 1988).

The Church was rewarded for its silence. The hierarchy obtained a state salary for each bishop, special retirement packages, and a grant to build a new house for the Archbishop of Buenos Aires. The government banned Jehovah's Witnesses from the country (Gill 1998: 165) and transferred 6,000 schools from federal to provincial jurisdiction, thereby removing them from the range of the Lay School Law (1420) that had banned religious education in federal schools (Leonard 1989: 281). Whereas the Chilean and Brazilian churches emerged from the period of military rule with broad support and legitimacy among former opponents of the regime, the Argentine Church's failure to condemn the military's attack on human rights more actively reduced its political influence, particularly among the political opposition, human rights activists, and neighborhood organizations that were the core of the Church's popular base in Brazil and Chile. As one Argentine observer remarked, "the Church was on the defensive. It was on the side of those who lost."[35]

The Radical Party headed Argentina's democratic government, which assumed power in 1983. The government had a secular agenda and sought

---

[34] One observer recalled that a priest delivered a sermon calling prodivorce federal deputies "more barbarious than Attila the Hun." Interview with Nelson Perl, Buenos Aires, August 7, 1998.

[35] Interview, Buenos Aires, July 1998.

to reduce the scope of Church power and prerogatives. The Radicals prosecuted top military rulers for human rights violations rather than heeding the bishops' calls for reconciliation, proposed the constitutional separation of Church and state, and convened a pedagogical congress to secularize the educational system (Burdick 1995; Ghio 1996; Krotsch 1988). More tension arose when the Alfonsín administration vetoed the Church hierarchy's candidate for the Archbishop of Buenos Aires. The government rejected Cardinal Quarracino (a theological conservative), and the post remained vacant for a few years while the Vatican waited until the end of the Alfonsín administration to appoint him.[36] Though some individual bishops maintained close relations with some Radical Party leaders, the government's policies severely strained Church-state relations. The Episcopal conference protested that the Church was being unfairly portrayed and attacked, and that the government was proposing educational reforms that threatened to undermine national culture (Conferencia Episcopal Argentina 1984a, b). The bishops were particularly irritated by a statement President Raul Alfonsín made in response to a reporter's question about divorce: "I am in favor of divorce; but I would never get a divorce myself as long as my mother lives."[37]

In the end, the Roman Catholic bishops exerted little influence over the terms of the divorce debate in Argentina in the 1980s. Unlike the situation in Brazil and Chile, where legislators opposed to divorce made frequent references to Church principles and Church doctrine in their pronouncements on the floor, very few Argentine divorce opponents invoked religion in the justification for their votes. Most legislators who opposed divorce claimed that the law would weaken the family and hurt children, and one referred to Hegel's rejection of the idea of marriage as a contract (Antecedentes Parlamentarios 1998: 1428).[38] In fact, some deputies used Church doctrine to show how it supported the legalization of divorce. In an influential speech, Peronist deputy Antonio Cafiero claimed that divorce would ratify Vatican II's principle of the autonomy of earthly life from the spiritual domain. The Church itself, he argued, emphasized the primary importance of freedom of conscience, citing statements by bishops in Spain and France that the Church's ethical principles needed to be interpreted in light of social reality (ibid.: 1617–20). Privately, the Church assured legislators that although it would publicly declare its opposition, it would not initiate any serious campaign

---

[36] Although the *patronato* (a tradition granting the state the right to appoint Church officials) had officially been curtailed in Argentina, the government still customarily gave its seal of approval to the various candidates presented for consideration to the Vatican. Interview with José María Ghio, Buenos Aires, August 1998.

[37] *La Nación*, July 10, 1994.

[38] The serious alternative to the divorce law was a bill proposed by Christian Democratic Deputy Carlos Auyero. The bill would have significantly expanded the grounds for annulment of marriage, created a range of public policies destined to promote the family, and created family courts (Antecedentes Parlamentarios 1998: 1295–304).

against deputies who held a position on divorce that the Church did not agree with.[39]

When divorce was brought to a vote in the Chamber of Deputies, an overwhelming majority of Radical Party deputies voted in favor (108 for, 3 against, and 17 absences). The Peronists were more divided: 52 voted in favor and 26 against, with 23 absences.[40] Most of those absent were probably in favor, but feared Church reprisals.[41] All three legislators from the small right-wing UcéDé party voted in favor of divorce. The vote of UcéDé legislators contrasts to the position of the Chilean right, the vast majority of whose members support classically liberal positions on economic issues but oppose divorce. In the Senate, however, the divorce bill encountered more resistance, as a majority of the commissions on general legislation and families and minorities voted to recommend that the full Senate reject the divorce bill. While the bill was blocked in the Senate, a blockbuster Supreme Court ruling dramatically shifted the terms of the divorce debate.

On November 27, 1986, the Supreme Court, all of whose members had been appointed by President Alfonsín, declared Argentina's hundred-year-old civil marriage law unconstitutional. The ruling, a response to a petition by an Argentine doctor seeking to remarry, declared that by prohibiting divorce, the civil marriage law imposed one religious doctrine on the whole country, violated the right of citizens freely to follow their personal life plan, and amounted to an unjust invasion of privacy (República Argentina 1986). In theory, the ruling created divorce in Argentina, regardless of what happened in Congress. The sentence permitted all Argentines who had been legally separated to appear in court and request that their capacity to remarry (*aptitud nupcial*) be recognized. Even if lower courts refused to honor the Supreme Court's ruling, couples could appeal again and again until their right to remarry was eventually recognized by a higher court. Of course, a new civil marriage law was preferable to a situation of repeated appeals and court rulings, but with the Supreme Court's sentence of 1986, divorce became possible in Argentina.[42] The ruling generated momentum to convince skeptics in the Senate. In fact, the ruling was timed almost perfectly to influence the Senate vote, as if to show recalcitrant senators the futility of trying to block divorce. The new civil marriage law was sanctioned by Congress

---

[39] The positions of the Peronist legislators and the Church hierarchy were clarified at a private meeting between Cardinal Aramburu and Deputy Nelson Perl. Interview with Nelson Perl.

[40] *La Nación*, August 21, 1986.

[41] Interview with Eduardo Zannoni. Apparently, some deputies called him to ask for advice about the law before the vote. He assured them that divorce would not lead to a deeper crisis of the family, and that they should vote in favor. One deputy who had agreed to vote in favor, however, was conspicuously absent from the floor vote.

[42] Off the record interview, Buenos Aires, August 12, 1998. See also *Clarín*, November 28, 1986.

and promulgated in June 1987. The specifics of the new law were broadly egalitarian: Husbands no longer had the right to fix the place of marital residence, married women could retain their maiden names, spouses owed mutual assistance to one another, and divorce could be obtained through mutual consent, rather than by proving the guilt of one spouse.[43]

Church-State Cooperation and No Divorce: Chile

As mentioned earlier, Chile is virtually the only country in the world where divorce is not legal. Two of Chile's southern cone neighbors, Argentina and Paraguay, admitted divorce shortly after the democratic transition (in 1987 and 1991, respectively). Colombia, which had also prevented divorce, approved a divorce law in 1991. Chile's failure to legalize divorce during twelve years of democratic rule is puzzling for various reasons, not least of which is the country's relatively high level of economic development and its embrace of liberal principles in other areas of public administration. How can we explain this situation? Though the return to democracy in 1990 permitted divorce reformers to organize in civil society and in Congress, amicable relations between the bishops and the government created an obstacle to a divorce law. Under the Pinochet regime, the Church had sheltered dissidents, provided services to the poor, and then served as a powerbroker in the democratic transition. In this process, the Church gained tremendous moral authority and built alliances with politicians from the left and Christian Democratic political parties. When these parties gained control of the state in the first democratic election, they felt indebted to the Church and were therefore reluctant to endorse divorce legislation. Meanwhile, parties of the right, though they had clashed with the Church during the Pinochet government, found common ground with the bishops on issues such as divorce and abortion.

In one important respect, the sociology of divorce is dramatically different in Chile than in Argentina or Brazil. In Chile, it is common practice for the middle and upper classes to have their failed marriages legally annulled using a loophole in the civil code. The 1884 Civil Marriage Act made civil marriages compulsory, and required that marriages be performed by a "competent" official of the civil registry and before two able witnesses. Yet civil registry officials are competent to perform marriages only between people who live within their territorial jurisdiction. The grounds for competency come from canon law, the rationale being that it is easier for priests to avoid marrying people twice when they know the neighborhood well (Corral 1997: 170–1). The legal basis for the practice of fraudulent annulments originated in Supreme Court decisions issued in 1925 and 1932. In these judgments, the Chilean Supreme Court first declared that witness testimony could serve

---

[43] See Ley 23.515, *Boletín Oficial*, June 12, 1987.

as proof of residence, and then that witness testimony in an annulment suit sufficed to demonstrate the incompetence of the civil registry official and thereby the invalidity of the marriage (Alessandri Rodríguez 1932). To have a marriage annulled in Chile today, one must convince two friends to swear in court that the place one claimed to reside in at the time of marriage was false.

The Church vigorously opposed the practice of fraudulent annulments. In 1946, the Chilean bishops' council met in Santiago and issued a document in which they declared that everyone participating in fraudulent annulments had committed a sin and was excommunicated from the Church. The declaration read:

We declare that, for all of the ecclesiastical provinces of Chile, initiating or continuing, with malicious intent, a legal action to obtain the nullity of a civil contract when this coexists with a valid religious marriage, is a sin *latae sententiae* reserved to the official of the area, as this crime is pernicious to Christian marriage, leads to divorce, and causes social immorality. (Primero Concilio Plenario Chileno 1946: 171)

Deemed to have sinned were not only the two spouses, but also the lawyers who defended the suit, the witnesses who presented false testimony, the judge, and anyone else who cooperated in the suit (ibid.). The fact that excommunication was *latae sententiae* meant that priests could apply the sentence automatically, without following a formal procedure. According to one Chilean cleric I interviewed, he and other colleagues applied the sentence many times when people admitted to having contracted fraudulent annulments in the confessional.[44] The penalty of excommunication remained in force until 1983, when the new code of canon law was promulgated.[45]

These loose annulment rules mean that in practice, divorce by mutual consent exists for Chileans who have the resources to hire lawyers for expensive suits. Many people admit that without the annulment system, social pressure for divorce would be unstoppable. In the 1990s, courts granted almost 7,000 marriage annulments per year (Alywin and Walker 1996: 121). But annulments are an unsatisfactory solution for the problem of marital breakups, as they afford no protection for weaker family members and enforce no rules on the distribution of marital property. Moreover, divorce via annulment is beyond the reach of those Chileans without access to legal services and without the time to sit through the months of processing that annulment suits require. The desire to end the fraud associated with annulments has been an extra motivating factor for Chilean divorce reformers.

[44] Interview, Santiago, April 1998.
[45] The new code did not include fraudulent civil annulments among the grounds for excommunication, and rescinded laws and declarations issued by particular churches that contradicted the provisions of the new code. Interview with Monseñor Bernardo Herrera, Santiago, April 24, 1998.

Like the partisans of no-fault divorce and elective abortion in the United States, many of whom wanted to put an end to divorce fraud and the black market for illegal abortions, Chilean reformers were concerned about the deleterious effects the annulment market has had on judicial corruption and public respect for the rule of law (Alywin and Walker 1996; Jacob 1988; Luker 1984).

The movement for divorce began shortly after Chile's first civilian president assumed power in March 1990, after seventeen years of military rule. Two feminist politicians, one from the Humanist Party and one from the PPD Party, presented divorce bills in Congress. Due to insufficient support, both were archived before reaching the floor for discussion. Yet the bills, particularly the Humanist Party proposal, which built on focus group discussions, seminars, and conferences held throughout Chile, sparked public debate about divorce and forced the topic into the media. Journalists questioned politicians about their views, forcing them to opine on the issue. As Mariana Alywin put it, "we saw [these early bills] as a sign that the issue was coming."[46]

As in Brazil and Argentina, growing rates of family breakup and public opinion supported divorce. In the 1970 census, 5 percent of women declared themselves to be separated. In 1983, a study carried out in the Santiago metropolitan area found that 12 percent of those surveyed had been separated from their previous marriage (Reyes 1992: 66). Another study estimated the breakup rate using the number of court suits based on guardianship or child support (as indicators of failed marriages) and calculated that the number of breakups was almost half of the number of marriages in 1988 (Gacitúa 1991: 33–4). In a 1991 survey, 74 percent of survey respondents declared that the law should permit divorce in some cases (Centro de Estudios Públicos 1991c). By the end of 1996, support for a divorce law had grown such that 85 percent of Chileans believed that the country should have a divorce law (Cousiño Valdés 1997: 69).[47]

In 1994 and 1995, a multiparty group of legal experts and legislators organized around divorce. They recognized that, in light of opposition from the Church and most of the parties of the right, the only way a divorce law could be approved was through the achievement of broad consensus among a wide group of people. The group, which included legislators from the Christian Democratic, Democratic (PPD), and Socialist parties, as well as three socially liberal legislators from the right, met every week for one year to deliberate over the content of a new civil marriage bill. One of the group's participants recalled: "We worked together with people from different parties.... we

---

[46] Interview with Marina Alywin, Santiago, April 23, 1998.
[47] Thirty-eight percent of respondents declared that the law should permit divorce in general, 46 percent said divorce should be permitted in some cases, and 15 percent said that divorce should not be permitted under any circumstance (Cousiño Valdés 1997: 69).

discussed the bill that we would present, we did not start from a completed bill. This was our success: we first achieved consensus and agreement among a very diverse group."[48]

Discussions in the group reflected the ideological tensions between the Christian Democrats and the liberal parties of the governing coalition. The Christian Democrats saw divorce not as a right or a consequence of the civil contract of marriage, but as a lesser evil to Chile's corrupt annulment system, high rates of illegitimacy, and single-parent households. For them, divorce should be legal so that people can remarry, but should be available only if grounds are proven in court, so that the law upholds the importance of family stability. Christian Democrats argued that in light of the corrupt annulment regime, a new civil marriage law in Chile would actually make divorce more difficult to obtain (Alywin and Walker 1996). The other legislators and lawyers of the group did not share these Catholic convictions. They believed that a future divorce law should accept divorce on the grounds of mutual consent, but they needed to cede ground to the Christian Democrats in order to keep the coalition together. The bill ultimately proposed by the group permits divorce for reasons that must be proven in court and after four or five years of separation.[49] According to PPD deputy Maria Antoinetta Saa, "We had to make many compromises.... It ended up being a very conservative bill."[50]

By 1997, the group had mobilized considerable support for divorce in the Chamber of Deputies, albeit amidst tremendous controversy and debate. In January, the Chamber voted in favor of the idea of legislating a new civil marriage law (53 in favor, 40 against). The Chamber approved the actual law, which regulated the grounds for divorce, separation, annulment, and their effects, on September 8, 1997.[51] In 2002, however, the civil marriage bill was stalled in the Senate and divorce was still not legal in Chile. To understand why, we need to explore the course of Church-state relations.

Church-state relations in democratic Chile were significantly different than in Argentina. The Argentine Church had failed to condemn, and even defended in some cases, the outgoing military regime. The Chilean Church's role under the military was quite different. Through organizations such as

---

[48] Interview with Maria Antoinetta Saa, Santiago, April 23, 1998.
[49] Divorce can be obtained two years after judicial separation (itself obtainable after two years of de facto separation), or after the impossibility of living together has been demonstrated after five years of separation.
[50] Interview with Maria Antoinetta Saa.
[51] Oddly, the approval of the divorce bill by the Chamber of Deputies in September received very little coverage by the media. When I visited Chile in 1998, very few Chileans, including academics and activists, were aware of it. Most knew only that in January 1997, the chamber had voted to approve the idea of legislating. The lack of celebration surrounding this victory is probably representative of the overall climate suppressing discussion of controversial issues in Chile.

the Vicaría de Solidaridad, created by Cardinal Silva, the Archbishop of Santiago, the Church provided legal assistance to people accused of political offenses, helped reconstitute labor unions, produced a monthly newspaper that kept track of human rights violations, and organized community groups in poor neighborhoods. Church programs "constituted public spaces in which people could come together and develop feelings of solidarity with one another. They became vehicles of organizational, social, and political development for the duration of the period of military rule" (Fleet and Smith 1997: 67). The bishops became increasingly critical of the regime after 1975, when it became clear that Pinochet had no intention of leaving power in the short term, that his economic policies were producing greater impoverishment, and that repression of opposition politicians, human rights activists, and Church personnel was increasing. The bishops issued public statements calling for amnesty for political exiles, and denounced the government's repression of Church personnel and refusal to provide information on people arrested or disappeared (ibid.: 63–4). In a 1975 letter to Pinochet, Cardinal Silva said, "The fact that a significant number of priests have been and continue to be arrested in virtue of behavior directly linked to their charity work is considered by international public opinion as an sign of animosity, and even persecution, of the Catholic Church." Silva told the president that it was in Chile's best interests for the government to relax its practice of arrest and detention.[52]

After Pinochet began to lift restrictions on political party activity and social movements in the early 1980s, the new Archbishop of Santiago (who replaced Silva when he retired), Juan Francisco Fresno, organized a series of meetings between representatives of the Pinochet government and members of the political opposition, and also tried to bring opposition groups together to present a united statement to the Pinochet government. The latter meetings culminated in the National Accord on the Transition to Full Democracy, which was the first in a series of agreements that eventually led to Pinochet's defeat in the 1988 plebiscite on continuation of his rule. As Fleet and Smith point out, "the mediating influence of Fresno and his advisors was substantial, if not decisive. Fresno was able to convince people who otherwise would not have met with one another.... the Church's auspices, Fresno's presence, and the sequence of bilateral sessions followed by group all made it easier for the participants to speak their minds, acknowledge common ground, and make concessions without appearing to do so" (ibid.: 124).

Not all Chilean bishops were opposed to the military government, however, and Pinochet's Catholic supporters strongly objected to the Church's involvement in opposition politics. A public statement signed by eight prominent Catholics in 1978, for example, argued that bishops should not try to

---

[52] Letter from Raul Cardinal Silva Henríquez to President Augusto Pinochet, December 10, 1975, Archives of the Fundación Jaime Guzmán.

shape the political opinions or behavior of the Catholic faithful. In their view, the hierarchy's public declarations had contaminated moral teachings with appeals to Catholics to take political actions, thereby violating the Catholic principle of freedom of conscience.[53] Chileans from the right particularly objected to statements such as the one made in 1980 by the Episcopal conference that called on all Catholics to contribute to the return of democracy.[54] The Vatican reinforced the position of conservative bishops and Catholics on the right. After the election of John Paul II as Pope, the Vatican launched an effort to eradicate the influence of liberation theology from Latin American churches and redirect the bishops' attention to moral and spiritual concerns. The Vatican reassigned bishops and appointed conservatives to top posts in Chile: Seven of the ten top Chilean Church officials appointed between 1980 and 1983 were conservatives (ibid.: 116). In the late 1980s, the Vatican appointed three more conservative bishops, including the former head of the Opus Dei, and two conservatives as auxiliary bishops (Meacham 1994).

The growing conservatism of the Chilean Church was consequential for debates about divorce after the return to democracy, since a more progressive Church might have ceded some autonomy to civil authorities to legislate on the issue. In an ironic twist, conservative Chilean bishops lobbying against divorce in the 1990s were able to cash in on the capital accumulated by their more progressive counterparts during the struggle against authoritarian rule in the 1970s and 1980s. As Haas notes:

In its encounter with representatives of the Left who had been persecuted by the military government, Church lobbyists made particular reference to the protection the Church had given the democratic opposition during this time. Many representatives characterized this approach as the Church's attempt to "collect on the bill" from its pro–human rights work under the dictatorship. In many instances, those bishops at the forefront of the divorce debate are not the same bishops who fought for human rights under the dictatorship. (2000: 185)

The Church adopted fierce lobbying tactics to prevent divorce. The hierarchy issued statements claiming that the indissolubility of marriage derives from natural law, and that legalizing divorce "is contrary to the Law of God and to the common good of the nation."[55] The bishop of Valparaíso, Jorge Medina, took an even harder line, maintaining that since the Church had already adopted a clear position, divorce was no longer open for free discussion

---

[53] "Ante un deber de conciencia," December 15, 1978, Archives of the Fundación Jaime Guzmán.

[54] Declaration of the Permanent Committee of the Episcopal Conference of Chile, Santiago, April 12, 1980, Archives of the Fundación Jaime Guzmán.

[55] See, e.g., "Por el bien de las familias de Chile," Conferencia Episcopal de Chile, ref. no. 254/94, Archives of Mariana Alywin.

among Catholics.[56] Bishops insisted that Catholic legislators not support bills that contradict Church teaching and declared public opinion, as well as statistics on separations and annulments, irrelevant because "morality is not based on statistics" (ibid.: 184).

The position of Chilean bishops was reinforced by pressure from the Vatican. The Archbishop of Santiago requested that Cardinal Joseph Ratzinger, head of the Congregation for the Doctrine of the Faith, help Chilean bishops address the argument that a divorce law was a lesser evil than the practice of fraudulent marriage annulments. Ratzinger's reply was forwarded by the Santiago Archbishop to Christian Democratic deputies, and read, in part:

Legalizing an abusive practice with the end of limiting its growth does not solve the problem but on the contrary creates another far more grave that violates a principle contained in natural law. The enactment of a law of civil divorce ignores the indissoluble character of matrimonial union that between Christians is sacramental. Such a sanction is an immoral act that ... produces an unjust law, and therefore an illegitimate one, that undermines the basis of the social fabric and gravely violates a key principle of the moral order revealed by Christ.[57]

Pressure from the Vatican silenced Chilean bishops who might have otherwise supported a divorce law. Only one bishop from Punta Arenas publicly supported a revision of the civil marriage law. Other priests and bishops were sympathetic to divorce, but only in private. Mariana Alywin recalled, "We knew that there were some bishops who were in favor [of divorce] ... there were many who wanted to adopt a more conciliatory attitude with us and could not, because the Vatican imprisoned them."[58]

As the hierarchy's stance hardened against divorce, close relations established between leaders of the governing coalition and the Church hierarchy during the period of military rule made the former reluctant to jeopardize their relationship with the latter by advocating for a divorce law. Immediately after the transition, ruling elites wanted above all to consolidate democracy in Chile, and therefore avoided raising issues liable to provoke conflict. As PPD senator Sergio Bitar said:

What you have to avoid at the beginning [of the transition] is the accumulation of factors provoking polarization.... For us, the first fundamental task was the struggle to strengthen democracy, to confront the dictatorship, to combat the archaic

[56] "Considera Obispo Medina: Divorcio no es Tema Libremente Discutible," *El Mercurio*, n.d., Archives of Mariana Alywin.

[57] The personal letter, signed by Carlos Cardinal Oviedo Cavada, Archbishop of Santiago, President of the Bishops' Conference and Javier Prado Aránguiz, Bishop of Rancagua, Secretary-General of the Bishops' Conference, is dated October 15, 1996, Archives of Mariana Alywin.

[58] Interview. Senator Sergio Bitar also said in an interview that he believes one of the obstacles to a divorce law in Chile stems from a deliberate Vatican policy to use Chile as an "example" for the future. Interview, Santiago, June 12, 1998.

institutions of designated and lifelong senators, to launch a big effort in the area of human rights ... this generated a degree of national unity that was very important, including an important linkage to the Catholic Church.[59]

Moreover, because of Chile's loose annulment regime, some politicians on the left believed it to be an easily expendable issue: "Divorce is always an issue of conflict, *but useless conflict* ... because a divorce law exists in Chile but it has another name: annulments. And it's a permissive law."[60]

Church pressure was particularly effective on the Christian Democratic politicians of the governing coalition. Though several Christian Democratic legislators participated in the coalition that introduced the divorce law to Congress, the party as a whole was deeply divided on the issue. When prodivorce deputies Mariana Alywin and Ignacio Walker initiated a debate about divorce and the family within the party, their proposals encountered some support but also firm opposition:

The resistance came from two sides: one from conviction, from people who felt that [divorce] was terrible and that we were violating a fundamental principle of Christian Democracy. Others [were motivated by an] electoral calculus, people who said: let's not get involved in this issue because this will produce only costs for the Christian Democrats, because we will not be united and because we will seem to be against the Catholic Church.[61]

In an effort to preempt Church criticism, Alywin and Walker consulted with priests and bishops, wrote to Church officials about their divorce bill, invited Church officials to seminars and conferences, and sent letters to all bishops asking for support. Some responded favorably, but others firmly opposed the idea of legislating divorce. Alywin recalled: "We always felt like traitors.... I was afraid of going to mass and being refused communion. They sent us crucifixes, they sent us little statues of saints, they sent us people's letters saying, 'We are praying for you so that you don't make a mistake; don't make the wrong decision.' It was tough."[62] Eventually, the Christian Democratic party's discussions about divorce produced an official document that affirmed the state's role in sustaining conditions for family happiness and harmony and the party's commitment to defending and promoting the family. It acknowledged the need to revise the conditions of marriage annulment and to terminate the fraudulent annulment system, and endorsed a number of policy measures designed to strengthen the family, such as the creation of family courts, flextime at work, sex education, and support for retirees. But the document stopped short of endorsing a divorce law, reflecting the inability of the party to come to consensus on the issue (PDC 1994).

[59] Interview with Sergio Bitar.
[60] Interview with Senator José Antonio Viera-Gallo, Santiago, June 15, 1998.
[61] Interview with Mariana Alywin.
[62] Interview with Mariana Alywin.

Politicians from the parties of the right joined the Church in opposing divorce. Both claimed that legalizing divorce would threaten the institution of marriage and weaken the family. The right think tank Freedom and Development argued:

Divorce in the law brings divorce in practice and degrades marriage. By eliminating its permanent character, marriage is tantamount to cohabitation and ... divorce becomes a normal situation. The easier divorce is, the more likely couples with difficulties will resort to it (who earlier broke up their marriages only in extreme circumstances), and the more legitimate its use becomes. ... There are more children of divorced couples, which raises the divorce rate even more, because half of these children repeat the conduct of their parents. Divorce feeds back on itself over time, and marriage loses importance as an institution. (Libertad y Desarollo 1997b: 23)

By furthering the disintegration of the family, a divorce law would produce greater poverty and nefarious consequences for children, including drug addiction, school drop-out rates, suicide, and delinquency (ibid.: 25–6). Divorce was seen to be bad for women, by increasing their economic insecurity and violating their dignity (Familias por la Familia n.d.). Finally, divorce was held to contradict principles of natural law and to violate the individual right to commit herself for life to another person (ibid.). The right's hard line on divorce was influenced by cultural trends among Chilean elites. During military rule, the Chilean right grew increasingly socially conservative. Catholic social movements such as the Opus Dei and the Legionnaries of Christ spread among the upper classes, which reinforced conservative values among adults and ensured the transmission of those values in elite Catholic schools.[63]

The Chilean case illustrates a phenomenon we might call the "dilemma of the democratic Church." In the 1980s, the progressive and popular Chilean Church played a crucial role in bringing about the fact of political democratization. In the 1990s, the bishops took advantage of the moral authority and political clout gained during the military government to veto legislative change on divorce. The same democratic Church that helped opposition political parties, human rights groups, and women's movements bring about the fact of political democratization served as a brake on consolidation of democratic liberties. By contrast, it was in Argentina, where an authoritarian Church helped legitimize military rule, that the liberalization of divorce was easiest after the return to democratization.

[63] According to Spanish journalist Rafael Otano, who has studied the Opus Dei, the success of the organization in Chile stems from the way it has been perceived by middle- and upper-class Chileans as a "rapid means of social ascension," as a way to "become part of a nobility." The Opus Dei's growth has contributed to the strength of conservative values in Chile. Otano argues that Opus Dei "monopolizes the moral common sense" of the Chilean upper classes. Interview, Santiago, June 16, 1998.

Conclusion

Argentina and Brazil's prohibitions on divorce until the last quarter of the twentieth century, and Chile's continuing ban on divorce, even in the early twenty-first century, testifies to the continued influence of Roman Catholic ideas on politics in Latin America. This influence, while not consistent across all policy areas, has been particularly acute on matters of marriage, the family, and reproduction. Yet under certain conditions, even the Roman Catholic bishops can be defeated. This chapter showed that when Church-state relations deteriorated due to conflicts over human rights, economic policy, and education, a window of opportunity opened to approve a divorce law. In Brazil, the break between Church and state came during the military government, when the bishops' conference opposed the military's human rights and economic policies. In Argentina, Church-state relations soured after the transition to democracy as the bishops' image was tainted by their failure more vocally to condemn the military's human rights abuses and the Radical Party government pursued policies to reduce ecclesiastical influence. In Chile, by contrast, amicable relations between the bishops and the government since the return to civilian rule in 1990 have constituted a major obstacle to the legalization of divorce.

Historically, prohibitions on divorce reflected a disturbing reality: a marked failure of the state effectively to extend its authority over an important area of social life. A central purpose of the state is to uphold a legal system that offers texture and predictability to social relationships. In this sense, the gap between law and practice on divorce (and, we see in the next chapter, on abortion) exposes the state's weakness. The lack of legal divorce in no way serves as a deterrent to marital breakdown; family crises occur regardless of what the law says (Barros 2002). Rather, their inability to remarry leaves men and women, and their children, in a legal limbo, powerless formally to regulate property arrangements or to seek protection in the event of death or abandonment. When divorce is illegal, family life thus can be included in one of Guillermo O'Donnell's "brown" areas of minimal state penetration or regulation (O'Donnell 1999a). The more "brown" areas (both functional and territorial) there are, the harder it is to consolidate a democratic, constitutional regime and the greater the risk that politics and society will be dominated by arbitrary, capricious, and privatized power. Without access to legal divorce, family members are particularly vulnerable to such risks.

The gap between law and practice is glaringly evident in Chile. At the end of 2002, divorce was still illegal, but courts were granting over 6,000 (mostly fraudulent) marital annulments per year; 47 percent of children were born out of wedlock; and the vast majority of Chileans favored the introduction of a divorce law. Though the Chamber of Deputies approved a compromise bill in 1997, the bill sat in the Senate without any movement until early 2002, at which time the constitutional committee began to discuss it. The assumption by Ricardo Lagos, a socialist, of Chile's presidency in 2000 changed the divorce outlook somewhat. Chile's first two democratic presidents (who ruled from 1990 to 2000) were Christian Democrats and shared their party's historic commitment to the Church. While continuing to rule in coalition with the Christian Democrats, some officials in the Lagos government expressed support for the legalization of divorce and introduced to Congress a more liberal version of the divorce law for the Senate to consider.[64] Though leaders of the left were unwilling to confront the Church in the early 1990s because of their desire to consolidate democracy, the sturdiness of Chile's democratic institutions after 2000 has reduced the need for such caution. Even with this renewed political will, however, the struggle for divorce, particularly a mutual-consent divorce, will be bloody.

---

[64] The version submitted by the Lagos government would permit divorce after two years of judicial separation or three years of de facto separation, provided both spouses agree. At the same time, Christian Democratic senators have proposed that divorce be granted only if one spouse is found gravely to have violated the obligations of marriage, while senators from the right suggest that instead of a real divorce law, the grounds for marital annulment be amplified (*La Tercera*, March 23, 2002).

5

Completing the Agenda

Family Equality and Democratic Politics

In the 1980s and early 1990s, civilian governments in Argentina, Brazil, and Chile assumed power and pledged to consolidate democracy in state and society. At the time, all three countries had laws on the books that granted fathers full parental rights over children, denying mothers the ability to make decisions about their children's welfare. Chilean law invested men with rights to administer common marital property, and Brazilian law still recognized the husband as the head of the household. Motivated by egalitarian ideals, changes in other countries, and feminist principles, networks of activists mobilized in all three countries to demand legal reform. Their successes varied. Argentina's civil law was reformed to grant women equal parental rights and erase distinctions between legitimate and illegitimate children. Brazil's new democratic Constitution advanced women's rights, but discrimination in the civil code continued through 2001.[1] In Chile, conservative opposition delayed and derailed the government's plans to promulgate legal reforms to expand women's parental and property rights.

Why were family equality reforms advanced in some countries but delayed and prevented in others? The transition to democracy permitted issue networks of feminists, lawyers, and sympathetic government officials advocating family equality to organize and advance proposals for change. Like their predecessors who worked to expand women's rights under military dictatorships, these "specialized subcultures of highly knowledgeable policy watchers" (Heclo 1978) were inspired by international agreements and changes in other countries. The difference in the 1980s and 1990s was that

---

[1] The Brazilian Congress approved a new civil code in August 2001. The new code granted men and women equality in marriage, rendered children equal in rights and obligations regardless of the circumstances of their birth, and eliminated the term "paternal power" (*patrio poder*). The reform also eliminated some archaic aspects of the old code, such as a rule enabling husbands to annul marriages on the grounds that the wife was not a virgin, and parents to abandon daughters of "dishonest" behavior.

they were also backed by a feminist movement with a mass base and high visibility. As we see below, the varied success of issue networks in promoting policy change was shaped by several features of democratic institutional politics, including an authoritarian legacy, coalitional politics, and the commitment of actors in the Executive, Congress, and political parties.

Chile's problems with reform stemmed in large part from the authoritarian legacy. This legacy included nine appointed, or "institutional," senators, whose presence denied the government a majority in the Congress and overrepresented conservative views. The continuing power of the military, moreover, made the achievement of democracy seem fragile, and generated a sense of urgency to preserve the unity of the governing coalition. Gender issues – including divorce, the equality of children, the marital property regime, and the criminalization of adultery – provoked conflict between the Christian Democratic and left, secular parties of the government and between the government and the right opposition. As a result, Chilean politicians treated gender issues with more caution than did their counterparts in Brazil and Argentina. Rather than lobby fiercely for change, they sought to build consensus and forge compromises, a posture that delayed reform of parental rights and children's equality and thwarted a real change to the marital property regime.[2]

In Brazil and Argentina, the authoritarian legacy was less relevant for policy making on family equality. To be sure, Brazil's military remained powerful after the transition and was able to block some reforms it disliked in the constitutional convention. But military power in Brazil waned in the late 1980s (Hunter 1995), and, unlike in Chile, the military was not socially conservative on gender issues.[3] In Argentina, the return to democracy produced a clean slate. Following Argentina's defeat to Great Britain in the Falklands War, the governing military junta broke apart. The military could not impose conditions on the next government in exchange for the transition. After their surrender to the British, "the military were not seen as a reliable or competent ally by any major section of Argentine civil or political society and internal military dissension, recriminations, and lack of discipline reached such unprecedented levels that some officers worried about intramilitary armed conflict and the dissolution of the military as an

---

[2] As will become clear below, the government's proposal to introduce a system of deferred community property as the default marriage regime was defeated. The reform that was approved allowed couples to opt for deferred community property at the time of marriage. Unless specified otherwise, however, the old marital property regime that granted most decision-making power to the husband would apply.

[3] In Brazil, appeals to traditional motherhood and family values were made at the time of the initial coup, but then disappeared from public military discourse (Simões 1985). In the later stages of the regime, the military government proved to be rather neutral on gender issues and even endorsed some liberal policies such as a divorce law and a Women's Health Program designed by feminists (Alvarez 1990; Pitanguy 1994).

organization" (Linz and Stepan 1996: 191). Rather than negotiate pacts with the military, the political parties eventually agreed to return to the terms set by the 1853 Constitution.

In Brazil, it was a lack of executive interest and weak parties in Congress that delayed family equality reforms. Provisions to grant women equal rights in marriage formed part of a larger bill to overhaul the civil code that had been sitting in Congress since 1975; few deemed its approval an urgent priority. In the first few years after the transition, activists and legislators worried more about crafting a new constitution. Feminists in civil society and the state labored to make sure that this constitution was sensitive to gender equality, and they succeeded. Even after the Constitution was promulgated in 1988, however, the civil code lacked prominence. The National Council on Women's Rights, the state agency responsible for promoting gender equality, was gutted in the late 1980s, and has remained weak ever since. Nor did other executive actors demonstrate a strong commitment to gender equity, and political parties and members of Congress were unwilling to champion the issue. Parties of the left, including the Workers' Party (PT), are an exception, but these parties hold only a small minority of legislative seats. In Brazil's "inchoate" or weakly institutionalized party system, the vast majority of parties are undisciplined, catch-all parties without strong policy positions, and, on its own accord, Congress rarely legislates on issues of national importance (Ames 1995a, b; Mainwaring 1999).

In Argentina, issue networks of feminists and lawyers were more successful in influencing the institutions of the state and political society. In the first elections held after the military left power, the governing party's campaign platform called for reform on parental rights. State officials began to study the issue in the early 1980s; lawyers affiliated with opposition politicians drafted family equality reform bills; and feminist activists organized workshops and petition drives to mobilize support for reform. Partisans of change organized a multiparty coalition in Congress and faced little opposition to their proposals. In contrast to Brazil, Argentine issue networks were not distracted by the challenge and labor of reforming the Constitution, and their interests converged with those of the executive and parties in Congress. Unlike in Chile, no authoritarian legacy stood in the way of the government legislating a liberal agenda of family law reform.

The chapter presents more detailed case studies of Argentina, Brazil, and Chile, respectively. I argue that Argentina is the most successful case of reform due to the absence of the authoritarian legacy and the convergence among issue network proposals, executive commitment, and partisan interests. Brazil is the middle case. The authoritarian legacy did not help or hinder reform, but the drafting of a new constitution, weak executive commitment, and the inchoate party system made it harder to promote coherent policy. In Chile, a pronounced authoritarian legacy proved to be a major obstacle to reform. Institutional and opposition senators blocked the government's proposals, and the potential for division within the governing coalition compelled activists to treat gender issues with caution.

Issue Networks under Democratic Governance

As Chapter 3 described, civil law experts convened in special commissions by military governments in the 1960s and 1970s placed the question of equality in family rights and obligations on the policy agenda. The partial reforms eventually adopted by these governments formed part of projects of legal modernization that emulated legal practices in the Northern Hemisphere. By the time Latin American countries made transitions to democracy in the 1980s and 1990s, however, family equality had become an integral part of what was meant by a democratic society. If democracy were to mean more than elections and interparty competition, democratic regimes would need to grant citizens equal rights and foster conditions of equal opportunity. Those who were aware that the law continued to discriminate against women and sought to do something about it – feminist activists, lawyers, and government officials – were the key advocates of family equality, though their precise composition and tactics differed across countries.

Legal issue networks were inspired by principles of democracy and equality as well as by international agreements such as the United Nations Convention on the Elimination of All Forms of Discrimination Against Women (CEDAW), endorsed by the General Assembly in 1979, and legal reforms in Western countries. Since the early twentieth century, various international conferences and treaties had helped consolidate global norms on gender equality in the family, society, and politics.[4] The first article of the Bogotá Convention on Women's Civil and Political Rights, endorsed by American states in 1948, called for full legal equality between men and women. In the same year, the United Nations' Universal Declaration of Human Rights affirmed that men and women were entitled to equal rights in marriage. Finally, CEDAW obliged states to eliminate all legal restrictions on women's full and equal participation in economy and society (Convention on the Elimination of All Forms of Discrimination Against Women 1979).[5]

---

[4] For an overview of such norms, commitments, and documents in the world and in Latin America, see Binstock (1997); Corrêa (1994); Organization of American States/CIDH (1998); United Nations (1996).

[5] CEDAW "brings together, in a comprehensive, legally binding form, internationally accepted principles on the rights of women – and makes clear that they are applicable to women in all societies" (Boutros-Ghali 1996: 41). The convention obliges signatory states to combat discrimination, which it defines as "any distinction, exclusion or restriction made on the basis of sex which has the effect or purpose of impairing or nullifying the recognition, enjoyment or exercise by women irrespective of their marital status, on a basis of equality of men and women, of human rights and fundamental freedoms in the political, economic, social, cultural, civil or any other field" (Convention on the Elimination of All Forms of Discrimination Against Women 1979).

Since CEDAW carries the weight of law in signatory countries, citizens may file suits in national courts on the grounds that their rights have been violated under CEDAW, and judges may make decisions based on CEDAW in addition to (or instead of) local laws.[6] CEDAW was ratified by Brazil and Argentina in 1984 and Chile in 1989.[7]

"Demonstration effects" were another factor that inspired issue networks to advocate for policy change. A demonstration effect (also called contagion, diffusion, emulation, or snowballing) refers to the process by which political changes in some countries encourage change in other countries with similar problems or traditions (Huntington 1991: 100). Reforms of family law in Western Europe created demonstration effects for Latin America. In France, a 1965 reform expanded women's property rights and a 1970 reform furthered family equality by replacing the concept of "paternal power" with "parental authority," and substituting the notion of husband as household head with spousal cooperation. A German law approved in 1976 granted spouses complete equality in household decision making. In the same year, Italy introduced a law declaring that spouses should make household decisions through mutual agreement (Glendon 1989). Legal changes in Europe set a standard that Latin America hoped to emulate or, at least, to not be seen to lag too far behind.

Feminist activists played an important role in issue networks organized for family equality. During the transitions to democracy in the southern cone, feminists succeeded in convincing politicians and parties of the importance of gender equality, and secured pledges from them to advance gender equality after assuming power. In Brazil, hundreds of feminist groups had emerged by the early 1980s, consolidated a distinctive and autonomous identity, and forged links with popular women's organizations. Feminists convinced candidates from all political parties to endorse key elements of the feminist agenda and lobbied Congress to eliminate discrimination against women in the civil code (Alvarez 1990; Pitanguy 1996). In Chile, the National Coalition of Women for Democracy (Concertación Nacional de Mujeres por la Democracia) mobilized women for the 1989 elections and pressed demands on politicians about women's rights. The coalition sensitized mainstream politicians to gender issues, and most of its proposals were incorporated into

[6] However, CEDAW is rarely applied in practice. A feminist lawyer whom I interviewed in Buenos Aires said that the treaty had not been invoked in a single judicial opinion. She mentioned that other international treaties, such as the Inter-American Convention on Human Rights, had been invoked by local judges. Interview with Marcela Rodriguez, Buenos Aires, July 10, 1998. To apply CEDAW, the regional feminist lawyers' network CLADEM (Latin American Committee for the Defense of Women's Rights) has organized workshops for judges to educate them about the content of CEDAW and other international agreements.

[7] In fact, the Argentine constitutional reform of 1994 incorporated CEDAW into the country's magna carta: The treaty is annexed to the end of the text itself. By 1998, CEDAW had been ratified by nineteen Latin American countries, but not by the United States.

the platforms of political parties contesting the 1989 elections. The presidential campaign of Patricio Alywin, for example, promised legal reform, equal opportunities in the workplace, and the creation of a state agency on women (Chuchryk 1994; Valenzuela 1998). In Argentina, feminist mobilization was less visible than in the other two countries. Nonetheless, pressure from elite feminist groups convinced political parties to address gender discrimination in their election platforms, and parties made special efforts to appeal to the female electorate (Feijoó 1998; Feijoó and Nari 1994). The electoral platform of Radical Party president Raul Alfonsín called for the elimination of legal discrimination against women and specifically mentioned the need to grant women equal parental rights in the family.

Besides feminist activists, issue networks included lawyers and legal scholars, many of whom were men. These legal scholars played a particularly important role in civil code reform in Argentina, and were active in Chile as well. Lawyers believed that old laws granting fathers, but not mothers, the right to exercise *patria potestad* needed to be changed to reflect society and modern principles of law. As Chapter 2 explained, *patria potestad* refers to the rights and obligations of parents over the person and property of their minor children. Before the changes analyzed in this chapter, mothers could exercise *patria potestad* only when the father was incapacitated. Fathers held *patria potestad* even after a legal separation, and even when the mother had full custody over the children. Without the fathers' authorization, mothers could not inscribe their children in the civil registry, choose children's names, obtain a legal document such as a passport for their children, enroll them in school or university, or make decisions about major medical procedures (Soto 1982).

The final key actors in issue networks were state agencies on women's rights. Created in response to demands from women's movements, these federal government agencies existed to propose legislation, advise and/or coordinate government policy on women, and to advocate women's interests within the state (Htun 1998: 18). In Argentina, President Raul Alfonsín assumed power in 1983 and created the National Women's Directorate within the Ministry of Health and Social Action. In 1984, the directorate convened a group of scholars to propose reforms to the civil code. Later, in 1987, Alfonsín created a Women's Subsecretariat and appointed leading feminist Zita Montes de Oca as its president. In 1985, when Brazil's first civilian president in over twenty years took office, he created a National Council on Women's Rights within the Ministry of Justice and staffed it with feminists who had extensive connections to women's groups (Alvarez 1990; Pitanguy 1996). One of the first tasks undertaken by the council was the promotion of women's rights in the new constitution and in the ordinary law. In Chile, the creation of a state agency on women was a long-running demand of the women's movement. Following his assumption of power in 1990, President Patricio Alywin created the National Women's Service, endowed with a large budget, and assigned it the task of proposing legal reforms to advance women's status (Chuchryk 1994; Matear 1996; Valenzuela 1998).

In summary, transitions to democracy in the southern cone granted issue networks of feminist activists, lawyers and legal scholars, and officials in state women's agencies the freedom to organize around proposals for family equality reform. To understand the policy successes and failures of the three countries, however, we need to look at the factors that conditioned the influence and the effectiveness of issue networks. The country case studies that follow pay close attention to the convergence of interest among these networks, the executive, and parties in Congress (in the case of Argentina and Brazil) and the authoritarian legacy (in the case of Chile).

Argentina

Conditions in Argentina in the 1980s were particularly auspicious for legal reform on gender issues. Supreme Court Justice Gustavo Bossert recalled: "Everything changed with democracy. When the authoritarian government left the scene, censorship and self-censorship ended."[8] The clean slate produced by the terms of transition granted the Radical Party government, which assumed power in 1983, considerable political space to legislate its social agenda. The Radicals sought to eliminate authoritarian attitudes and institutions from state and society and to build a liberal democracy in Argentina by guaranteeing individual rights, protecting human rights and the rule of law, reducing the influence of the Roman Catholic Church on politics, and pushing the military back into the barracks. The government ratified CEDAW in 1984, which required it to "assume a commitment" to "granting equality between men and women" (Dirección Nacional de la Mujer 1984: 11).

The fact that Argentina is the most successful case in this chapter seems surprising. Much scholarship on gender issues around the Argentine transition has been directed at the Madres de la Plaza de Mayo, the mothers who marched in the plaza fronting the presidential palace to protest the disappearances of their children, raising international awareness of the abuses of the dictatorship and contributing to the return of civilian rule. But the Madres were not advocating for women's liberation: In fact, their success depended on the deployment of traditional women's roles (Navarro 1989). Feijoó and Nari argue that the prominence of the Madres retarded the achievement of a feminist agenda. The Madres' success promoted a "new *marianismo*" in Argentine politics, bringing back "the traditional worship of the Mary-mother characteristic of the most conservative sectors of Argentine society" (1994: 121). This chapter shows that, while the Madres dominated the public sphere with a traditional gender ideology, Argentine

[8] Interview, Buenos Aires, August 11, 1998.

liberal feminists, including men, worked behind the scenes to produce profound changes in women's legal rights.

In the early 1980s, the liberal agenda of the Radical Party government converged with proposals of issue networks seeking to legislate on family equality. What were the concerns of these issue networks? The central problem was that the law was out of sync with social reality and with democratic, egalitarian principles. Argentine law vested *patria potestad*, or parental power, in husbands. Mothers could exercise *patria potestad* only when the father was incapacitated. In other words, fathers held *patria potestad* even after a legal separation, and even when the mother had full custody over the children. The law also distinguished between children born to married parents and those born to nonmarried parents, granting "marital" children more rights than "nonmarital" children. Completing the family equality agenda in Argentina thus required that *patria potestad* be shared between mother and father and that all children be considered equal in terms of inheritance, support, health, social services, and the like.

By the time Argentina made the transition to democracy in the 1980s, women had gained a significant amount of independence and power, and many children were born out of wedlock. In the early 1980s women made up 35 percent of the economically active urban population (FLACSO 1993: 39). Between 1970 and 1990, moreover, the number of economically active women had grown by almost 50 percent (ibid.: 41). In 1980, some 19 percent of households were headed by women, compared with 5 percent in 1960 (in Buenos Aires city, 27 percent of households were headed by women in 1980) (ibid.: 35). Fifty percent of children were born to parents not legally married (an increase from 40 percent in 1960). In the city of Buenos Aires, the rate was around 40 percent (from 26 percent in 1960), and in some of the provinces, as high as 80 and 90 percent (ibid.: 28). The fact that Argentina had no divorce law contributed to the high rates of "illegitimacy" and also to pressure to grant children equal rights.

The first group of participants in what became the family equality issue network group was feminist organizations and legislators. Shared *patria potestad* had been on the feminist agenda for decades. In the 1940s, María Florentina Gomez Miranda had presented a proposal for shared *patria potestad* to the national Congress of the Radical Party.[9] In 1975, feminist legislators in Congress secured the sanction of a law creating *patria potestad indistinta* (the indistinct exercise of parental power), permitting either father or mother to exercise parental power without consulting the other parent. One month later, President Isabel Perón vetoed the law, arguing that indistinct parental power "is out of sync with our customs and in practice will translate into a dislocating element for the family, the fundamental cell of our

---

[9] Interview with María Florentina Gomez Miranda, Buenos Aires, July 29, 1998.

society."[10] In the 1980s, elite feminist organizations revived their efforts to expand women's rights in the family. The multiparty "Group of Women Politicians," founded in 1971, reorganized itself after having disbanded during the military government (1976–83) and began to lobby for laws on *patria potestad*, divorce, and removal of all distinctions among children.[11] The "Association of Women in Legal Careers" was founded in 1982, and immediately endorsed equal *patria potestad*.[12] The group held seminars, press conferences, and interviews; organized public demonstrations; and circulated petitions.[13]

The second group consisted of lawyers. After the return to civilian rule, new ideas in legal doctrine began to dominate legal journals and magazines, conferences and seminars of jurists, and legal professional organizations. Prominent civil jurists such as Gustavo Bossert, Augusto Belluscio, and Eduardo Zannoni spearheaded debates about family law reform, building upon a consensus in the legal community that updating family law was necessary in light of social changes and international trends. Male jurists wrote the family law bills presented in Congress, offered expert testimony, and gave statements to the popular media.[14] Many of the progressive male jurists collaborated with the feminists in the seminars and public events. As Diaz recalled, "there was coordinated work between the women's movement and liberal jurists toward the same objective."[15] Male "liberal feminists" argued that democratization in the country required democratization in the family. As Bossert recalled, "since the 1960s, we insisted on the need to grant men and women equal rights. But it crashed up against the authoritarian model. Equalizing men and women went against authority. It was perceived as an attack on the legitimate family."[16] The link between the authoritarian polity and the authoritarian household – famously captured by Chilean feminist theorist Julieta Kirkwood (1990) – was acted upon by Argentine male liberal feminists in the 1980s.

The final group consisted of officials of the Radical Party government, whose 1983 election platform called for women's equality in the exercise of *patria potestad* and the removal of any other discriminatory norms (Unión

---

[10] *Boletín Oficial*, September 30, 1975, p. 5088.

[11] *Buenos Aires Herald*, May 24, 1983.

[12] Ethel Diaz was invited by the International Federation of Women in Legal Careers to form the Argentine branch in 1975. However, the military coup of 1976 made the functioning of the organization impossible. Diaz waited until the political opening of 1982 to establish the organization. After its founding, the central goal of the group was to legislate shared *patria potestad*.

[13] Various fliers and newspaper reports from 1982–85, Archives of Ethel Diaz.

[14] Interviews with Eduardo Zannoni, Gustavo Bossert, Cecilia Grosman, Haydee Birgin; Buenos Aires, July and August 1998.

[15] Interview with Ethel Diaz, August 4, 1998.

[16] Interview with Gustavo Bossert.

Cívica Radical 1983).[17] The government established a National Women's Directorate in the Secretariat of Human Development and the Family and, as mentioned earlier, ratified CEDAW shortly after assuming office. The Women's Directorate, headed by feminist Zita Montes de Oca, convened a workshop in August 1984 to identify existing legal discrimination against women and formulate proposals for reform (Dirección Nacional de la Mujer 1984).[18] Participants in this workshop included feminist activists such as Haydee Birgin and Leonor Vain; civil judges Augusto Belluscio, Eduardo Zannoni, and Gustavo Bossert; and legal scholar Cecilia Grosman. The workshop took CEDAW as a starting point of discussion, particularly the article of the convention specifying that the spouses have equal rights and responsibilities during marriage. As a result of deliberations in the workshop, the Executive branch submitted a bill on family law reform to Congress.

These issue networks for family equality acquired allies across the political spectrum. The feminist groups "worked without political preferences. We didn't care who was a Radical, who was a Peronist. We worked with all the parties."[19] The same was true with the jurists. Although most liberal jurists had closer ties to the Radical Party, Eduardo Zannoni and Gustavo Bossert wrote the bills submitted by Peronist legislators. Even conservatives approved of the reforms. Conservative jurist Guillermo Borda (former Supreme Court Justice and minister of the interior during the government of General Onganía) had said as early as 1978 that "*patria potestad* should be shared by father and mother, because the law needs to reflect the reality of life, and in the reality of life *patria potestad* is shared."[20] Roman Catholic bishops were similarly supportive (Criterio 1985). Though sectors of all parties endorsed women's equal rights, party leaders left the vote to the conscience of each legislator.

A few groups expressed opposition to shared *patria potestad*. One feminist activist recalled: "It wasn't so obvious that the laws would be passed, because of resistance from conservatives who wanted only one boss in the family. They believed that having two bosses would make the family break up."[21] The Corporation of Catholic Lawyers issued a statement claiming that a system of shared or indistinct *patria potestad* would create domestic disputes and justify excessive state intervention in the family. In their view, equality between the spouses needs to recognize and conform to the "distinctive

---

[17] The platform's section on women, titled "Women's Location in the Modern World," called for the protection of pregnant women and single mothers, shared *patria potestad* and the end to legal discrimination, the extension of maternity leave, and the promotion of women's labor, cultural development, and social security benefits (Unión Cívica Radical 1983: 69).

[18] In 1987, the Women's Directorate was subsumed into the new Subsecretariat on Women in the Health and Social Action Ministry (Montes de Oca 1997: 25).

[19] Interview with Ethel Diaz.

[20] *La Opinión*, July 9, 1978.

[21] Interview with Ethel Diaz.

characteristics of both sexes."[22] Some legislators opposed the bill in Congress, claiming that shared parental power would destroy the unity of the family.[23] Yet the opposition to family equality reform had no partisan basis and was ultimately unable to block the bill. The law approved by Congress granted shared parental power to mothers and fathers and rendered "marital" and "extramarital" children equal under the law (Ley 23.264, sanctioned on September 25, 1985).

Brazil

The constitution-making process that followed the Brazilian transition to democracy generated significant civic mobilization. Feminist issue networks spearheaded by the state agency on women held workshops around the country to solicit popular proposals for constitutional reform. The result was a success: Brazil's 1988 Constitution contained a clause declaring men and women to be equal in family matters and had several other provisions resulting from feminist lobbying. The civil code, however, contradicted the Constitution, and by 2001, had still not been reformed. Under the ordinary family law upheld by the code, husbands were considered to be the head of the household. Thus, during the early period of democratic politics, family equality advanced in the Constitution but not in the civil code. Why? Unlike in Argentina, family law reform was not a salient issue in Brazil. Feminist lawyers and activists had lobbied to reform the code since the late 1970s but, after the transition, were more concerned about the Constitution than the code. After the Constitution had been approved, the women's agency in the state lost its power, and other actors in the executive demonstrated little interest in equal rights. Meanwhile, the Brazilian political system proved to be an unpropitious context for parties and legislators to champion issues such as family law.

Constitution Making in Brazil

New regimes usually give birth to new constitutions. Constitutions create institutions that regulate political competition, ideally rendering uncertain the outcome of competition while binding relevant parties to this outcome (Przeworski 1991). Constitutions also protect civil rights. In Latin America, some constitutions have assumed the additional function of guaranteeing that the state will provide to its citizens services such as housing, education, family planning, health care, and social security, as well as uphold workers' rights, including a minimum wage and a "thirteenth" salary; promote sportsmanship; and protect national cultural patrimony.

---

[22] *La Prensa*, November 5, 1981.
[23] This view was upheld by Deputy Tomas Gonzales Cabañas, member of the congressional commission debating the proposed reforms.

These regulative and representative functions of constitutions explain why new regimes want the chance to create their own. Not all regimes have this opportunity. Out of the three countries considered in this chapter, only Brazil had the opportunity to craft a new constitution immediately after their transition to democracy.[24] Constitution making provided an opportunity for feminists in the state women's agency and civil society to convince legislators to recognize women's equality, including in family matters.

Shortly after assuming office in 1985, Brazilian president José Sarney proposed a constitutional amendment that empowered Congress to act as a constituent assembly and draft a new constitution. President Sarney had originally appointed a fifty-member commission to prepare the first draft of the Constitution. Two women participated in the group, including São Paulo feminist lawyer Florisa Verucci, who proposed various articles on women's equal rights within the family and on the legal recognition of stable unions. The commission's draft, however, was too liberal for President Sarney, who refused to forward it for consideration by Congress (Rosenn 1990; Verucci 1991). In 1986, the 559-member Congress divided itself into eight committees (each with three subcommittees) and began to write the Constitution from scratch. Each subcommittee devoted several sessions to testimonies and proposals from civil society organizations. The degree of popular participation in the constitution-making process was unprecedented and the final document strongly emphasized social rights and social policy (Rosenn 1990: 776–7). As one jurist pointed out, Congress "had the task, unspoken but understood by all, of programming urgently needed social and economic reforms" (Ferreira Filho 1992: 14).

The National Council on Women's Rights (the Conselho Nacional dos Direitos da Mulher, or CNDM) spearheaded feminist mobilization around the constitution-making process. In response to demands by feminist movements, President Sarney created the CNDM in 1985 and staffed it with feminists with a long history of activism. For its "Women and the Constitution" (Mulher e Constituente) campaign, the CNDM organized seminars and public forums all over Brazil where lawyers, feminists, legislators, and the general public analyzed women's legal situation and formulated proposals for change (CNDM 1986).[25] Women's agencies in state and municipal governments, and coalitions of women's groups, cooperated with the CNDM in sponsoring the meetings and soliciting proposals. In some states, feminists

---

[24] Argentina's Constitution was reformed significantly only in 1994, after most family equality reforms had been approved.

[25] The CNDM worked in other areas as well. Between 1985 and 1989, the council launched public policies and educational campaigns on reproductive rights and women's health, domestic violence, rural women's rights and agrarian reform, day care, and labor market discrimination (Alvarez 1990; Linhares Barsted 1994; Pitanguy 1996; Schumaher and Vargas 1993).

placed suggestion boxes in the streets to gather proposals from women; in others, they held meetings in the state legislature and in universities (ibid.).

Women's proposals for constitutional change were summarized in a "Women's Letter to the National Constituent Assembly" that was released to the press and distributed to legislators. The letter called for explicit recognition of the equality of men and women, equal rights in marriage and the family, the recognition of families constituted by stable unions, equal pay for equal work, job protection for pregnant workers, a ban on workplace discrimination, more rights for domestic servants, social security for women workers in rural areas, the right to day care in the workplace, the right to family planning and reproductive health, the criminalization of domestic violence, and the decriminalization of adultery (Pimentel 1987).

The CNDM staged demonstrations around the country, held a sit-in at the Congress in Brasília, and organized the twenty-six female legislators into what came to be known as the "Lipstick Lobby" (*a bancada do batom*) to press feminist demands. Most of the CNDM's proposals were accepted with little controversy, although industrialists expressed resistance to the extension of maternity leave and Church groups opposed the guarantees of family planning (Alvarez 1990: 252–3). Proposals for the decriminalization of abortion submitted by delegates from the leftist Workers' Party (PT) provoked a massive controversy and prompted evangelical delegates to introduce a proposal to ban abortion under all circumstances. In the end, both feminists and conservative lobbies agreed to withdraw their proposals, and the new constitution was silent on the issue of abortion (ibid.: 254–5).

According to the CNDM's former president, 80 percent of the women's movement's proposals were included in the final constitutional text (Pitanguy 1996: 70). The 1988 Constitution included several provisions that expanded women's rights and reflected principles of gender equality. Article 5 of the Constitution states that "men and women have equal rights and obligations," and Article 226 on the family recognizes that "the rights and duties referring to conjugal society are equally held by husband and wife" (Constituição da República Federativa do Brasil 1996). Most legal scholars believe that constitutional guarantees of equality in the family tacitly revoke the inequalities contained in the civil code.[26] Studies of jurisprudence reveal that the new Constitution improved the treatment of women in family law cases. In the past, for example, decisions about parental custody were frequently conditioned on the mother's sex life: If she had other partners, even following a de facto separation, it was difficult for her to gain custody of her children. Women whom the court considered to be of bad moral conduct were also unlikely to be granted alimony payments (Pimentel, Giorgi, and Piovesan

---

[26] Interview with Silvia Pimentel, São Paulo, December 1, 1997; interview with Desembargador Silvio Capanema de Souza, Rio de Janeiro, December 11, 1997; interview with Denise Dora, Rio de Janeiro, July 1997.

1993). Following 1988, a woman's "moral conduct" decreasingly entered into legal arguments and judgments because of the widespread idea that spouses should be treated equally (ibid.). Still, so long as the old laws remain on the books, Brazilian law will be contradictory regarding family equality. Feminist jurists believe that civil code reform is urgent so that the Constitution can be made effective (Verucci 1991).

Much of Congress's activity after 1988 has been devoted to implementing and amending the Constitution. Extremely wide ranging, the Constitution contained numerous clauses that needed to be implemented by congressional action. One survey ranked it as the fifth longest in the world. The Constitution also upheld some of the more problematic aspects of the political system and included controversial clauses that Brazil's presidents have undertaken great efforts to eradicate. Lamounier notes that the Constitution

aggravated existing fiscal imbalances, maintained and in some cases expanded state economic interventionism and nationalism, and took no steps to attenuate the unparalled battery of incentives to party fragmentation generated by Brazil's electoral system and party legislation. In fact, it ratified the questionable combination of a presidential system with multipartyism and a highly permissive proportional electoral system, gave a lease on life to old-fashioned nationalist rhetoric and paternalistic welfare provisions, and, last but not least, confirmed in a democratic way, with strong support from labor unions, the corporatist system established by Vargas's dictatorship (1937–1945) – which had been branded as fascist throughout the preceding forty years. (1999: 176)

Many of this "wildly detailed" Constitution's articles establish goals and rights that require not only legislative action but also budgetary outlays and public programs in order to be effective. It has been estimated that the Constitution requires 285 statutes and forty-one complementary laws in order to be effective (Rosenn 1990: 778). A minority of progressive Brazilian jurists argues that programmatic norms do not require complementary legislation or administrative measures, but are automatically applicable. In their view, the judiciary's role is to apply constitutional rights directly, even in the absence of implementing legislation (Piovesan 1992: 70–1).[27] Several important new laws were passed to make the Constitution effective, including the Children and Adolescents' Statute of 1990, the Code of Consumer Protection of 1990, the stable union laws of 1994 and 1996, laws on racially motivated crimes of 1989 and 1990, and a 1994 law granting domestic workers the right to maternity leave with pay. At the same time, there

---

[27] The Constitution establishes two mechanisms for the judiciary to force legislators and administrative agencies to apply the Constitution. The judiciary can issue a declaration of unconstitutionality by omission to compel legislative or administrative action within thirty days. The judiciary can also issue a mandate of injunction if it finds that a lack of regulations render infeasible the exercise of constitutional rights and liberties.

have been several attempts to reform the Constitution, including a plebiscite on the establishment of a parliamentary system of government, held in 1993 (it lost), and a 1997 amendment permitting the president to run for reelection.

The Slow Pace of Civil Code Reform in Brazil

After the new Constitution was promulgated in 1988, the major obstacle to completing the family equality agenda lay in Brazil's Civil Code, which had hardly been reformed since its adoption in 1916. As mentioned in Chapter 3, the military government of General Geisel presented a bill overhauling the civil code to Congress in 1975. The bill was approved only in 2001.[28] Unlike in Argentina, civil code reform was not a salient policy issue in democratic Brazil. Neither the Executive nor parties in Congress were particularly concerned about expediting reforms to the code. After discussing how feminists mobilized under military rule to include family equality in the civil code reform, this section turns to explaining why the issue lacked prominence in the late 1980s and 1990, focusing first on the Executive branch and then on parties and legislators in Congress.

Issue networks headed by feminist activists were primarily responsible for putting family equality on the agenda of civil code reform in the 1970s. The original reform bill proposed by the Geisel government in 1975 was more egalitarian than the old 1916 Code, but still discriminated against women. The bill recognized the husband as the *chefe da sociedade conjugal*, or head of community property, and his will prevailed in the event of a spousal disagreement, though the wife had recourse to a judge (Pimentel and Verucci 1981). The prospect of civil code reform mobilized the newly formed Brazilian Women's Center (CMB) of Rio de Janeiro to national political action. CMB feminists proposed a list of changes to the civil code bill and traveled to Brasília to testify in the Chamber of Deputies about the need to ensure gender equality in the reforms.[29] The feminists claimed that the civil code violated principles of gender equality and failed to reflect women's roles in society. CMB feminists declared that "Brazilian women today face a dilemma: society asks for their participation everywhere – in the labor force, as homemakers, as mothers, as voters – yet the equality granted them in the Constitution is taken away by the civil code" (Centro da Mulher Brasileira 1975). The

---

[28] In general, Brazil has been notoriously slow to reform and redraft its civil code throughout its history as an independent country. The first Constitution of the Brazilian Empire, adopted in 1824, called for a new civil code to be drafted as soon as possible. After six attempts, a civil code of independent Brazil was finally promulgated on January 1, 1916, some 92 years later (Moreira Alves 1992). Four efforts were made to reform the 1916 Code during the twentieth century (the last of which was the Geisel bill).

[29] Documents in the archive of Comba Marques Porto, at the National Archives in Rio de Janeiro.

group collected signatures from the public to annex to their amendments to demonstrate public support for the reforms.[30]

The congressional commission ceased deliberations on the civil code bill when the government closed Congress temporarily in 1977. After Congress reopened later in the year, the debate about divorce dominated the agenda. In the meantime, the women's movement had grown throughout the country. Feminists mobilized nationwide to debate gender equality, and two lawyers from São Paulo, Silvia Pimentel and Florisa Verucci, formulated the "Outline of a New Women's Statute," based on consultations with women's organizations and prominent jurists in various parts of the country. In 1981, when Congress began to debate the civil code again, Verucci and Pimentel presented the "Outline" to Jarbas Passarinho, then president of the National Congress, accompanied by approximately fifty other feminist activists. The "Outline" was undersigned by forty-nine women's groups and 800 individuals from all over the country (Pimentel and Verucci 1981). The "Outline" proposed that the concept "head of household" be eliminated, that there be greater equality in the marital property regime and freedom to choose the family name, that the old term "paternal power" be replaced with the more egalitarian "parental authority," and that a woman's "deflowerment" be removed as a legitimate reason for the annulment of marriage (ibid.).

In 1982, a woman deputy and woman senator introduced civil code reform bills based on the "Outline" in their respective chambers. In the meantime, Pimentel and Verucci sent letters to women's groups around the country, asking them to organize public demonstrations, debates, and presentations and to send telegrams to legislators and letters to newspapers to inform the public about the need to reform the civil code (Pimentel and Verucci 1983a, b). Later in the year, the most important proposals contained in the "Outline" were incorporated in the consensus bill issued by the *relator*,[31] conservative deputy Ernani Sátiro from Paraíba. Sátiro stated to the press that although he was unsympathetic to "feminist radicalism," the proposals were in line with trends in modern civil law (Pimentel and Verucci 1983b).

At this point, feminist activists decided to abandon the attempt to secure the approval of the "Outline" on its own, that is, as a reform to the existing code, and to work instead for approval of the bill overhauling the civil code completely. This decision seemed justified because they could take advantage of the legislative momentum behind the larger bill. However, including the "Outline" as part of the big bill subjected it to the delays faced by such a large piece of legislation. The situation illustrates a potentially important trade-off in legislative strategy. On the one hand, harnessing a specific proposal to a larger package has the advantage of gaining the support of a

---

[30] *Tribuna da Imprensa*, February 28, 1976.

[31] In the Brazilian Congress, the *relator* is the committee member charged with reviewing and elaborating a formal opinion of each bill discussed.

more comprehensive coalition. On the other hand, the size of the package compounds the legislative delays prior to approval, as consensus is reached and details are ironed out. The larger the package, the greater the chance that a single "poison pill" will delay, or even thwart, the entire proposal. And the bill to overhaul Brazil's civil code faced numerous delays. In 1984, the Chamber of Deputies approved the bill, which included the changes proposed by the feminist lawyers, and sent it to the Senate. Yet not until November 1997 did the Senate approve the bill and send it back to the chamber. The bill contained over 2,000 articles, each of which had been considered in committee and some of which had been revised numerous times.[32]

Why couldn't the National Council on Women's Rights (CNDM) build on its success in promoting gender equality in constitution making to champion the cause of civil code reform? Not long after the new Constitution was promulgated, the CNDM entered into crisis. At the end of 1988, a new minister of justice reduced the CNDM budget by 72 percent, interfered in its plans and operations, and tried to fire some staff and hire others. In 1989, the president, staff, and consultative council of the CNDM all resigned in protest (Pitanguy 1996). Under the subsequent Collor (1990–2) and Franco (1992–4) administrations, the CNDM continued to exist, though at a very low level, in line with these governments' failure to prioritize gender equality issues.

Under the administration of Fernando Henrique Cardoso (1994–2002), however, the CNDM was partially revitalized. The CNDM's president, Rosiska Darcy D'Oliveira, a feminist and close personal friend of the Cardosos, assumed a public presence and succeeded in raising awareness of the Platform for Action endorsed at the 1995 World Conference on Women in Beijing. She forged agreements with different government ministries detailing actions to be taken to implement the platform, traveled around the country to raise awareness of women's rights, and encouraged the creation of women's agencies in dozens of municipalities.[33] The CNDM's president did not, however, champion the issue of civil code reform in the same way that the old CNDM had mobilized around constitution making. The agency gained a large consultative council, but continued to suffer from a skeletal staff and low institutional status. In spite of the fact that first lady Ruth Cardoso is a well-known feminist, the Cardoso administration in general was similar to its predecessors in the low priority it attached to gender equality issues. The president devoted his attention to macroeconomic stabilization, state reform, and projecting Brazil's presence in regional and international politics. During the Cardoso administration, moreover, the institutional status

---

[32] *Folha de São Paulo*, November 27, 1997. The Senate bill included all the original changes proposed by Pimentel and Verucci, and other sections dealing with tort law, the age of legal majority, inheritance law, and contracts (*Veja*, November 26, 1997).

[33] Interview with CNDM president Rosiska Darcy D'Oliveira, Rio de Janeiro, July 1997.

of the CNDM was reduced even further. In March 2000, the executive arm of the CNDM was demoted to an administrative unit within the Human Rights Department of the Human Rights Secretariat of the Justice Ministry, and its staff cut to a mere two employees (*Fêmea*, March 2000).[34]

The delays in approving the civil code must also be seen in light of some general institutional features of the Brazilian political system. In Brazilian politics, it is difficult to legislate on "public goods" issues such as the civil code unless the Executive takes a strong interest. Why? Political parties and legislators in Congress face few incentives to champion national policy issues; as a result, the Brazilian Congress "has seldom been able to legislate on issues of national concern" (Ames 1995a: 325). Ames writes:

Many if not most deputies spend the bulk of their time arranging job and pork barrel projects for their benefactors and constituents. Though electorally successful parties span a wide ideological range, some of the largest "center" parties are really just shells for deputies with no policy interests at all. Few parties organize around national-level questions; the Congress, as a result, seldom grapples with serious social and economic issues. (1995b: 407)

A mutually reinforcing combination of an "inchoate" party system, nonprogrammatic parties, and personalistic incentives faced by legislators explains this state of affairs. Let us explore each of these factors in turn.

Mainwaring and Scully argue that Brazil has an "inchoate," or weakly institutionalized, party system (1995). On their four criteria of party system institutionalization – low electoral volatility, parties with stable roots in society, a generalized perception of parties and elections as legitimate, and parties with clear internal rules and structures – Brazil ranks low (1995; see also Mainwaring 1999: 26–39). There is high volatility in popular support for parties: Between 1982 and 1986, volatility in voting for parties in the Chamber of Deputies was 49 percent, and between 1986 and 1990, 45 percent (Mainwaring 1999: 108). Parties lack stable roots in society. Brazil has a high rate of split-ticket voting and low party identification among voters, and parties have very short organizational histories. In 1994, for example, parties founded before 1950 received only 13 percent of the total lower-chamber vote (compared with 98 percent in the United States, 75 percent in Mexico, 70 percent in Argentina, and 42 percent in Chile) (ibid.: 32). The oldest of the six largest parties in Brazil was founded in 1966 (PMDB), though its bases of support have changed considerably. Two of the six largest parties were created in 1979, one in 1984, one in 1988, and one in 1995 (ibid.: 123). Surveys also show that voters lack confidence in parties and do not see them as central actors in determining the country's progress. In

[34] In May 2002, however, President Fernando Henrique Cardoso issued a decree law that turned the National Women's Council into a State Secretariat. The new agency is called the State Secretariat for Women's Rights (Secretaria de Estado dos Direitos da Mulher, SEDIM). Information at: http://www.mj.gov.br/sedh/cndm.

these respects, Brazilian parties fare among the worst in all of Latin America (Inter-American Development Bank 2000: 181–2; Mainwaring 1999: 126–7). Moreover, Brazil's party system is highly fragmented: In the 1990s, eighteen parties had representation in the Chamber of Deputies, including eight "effective" parties (Mainwaring 1997: 74; 1999: 96).

Second, the vast majority of Brazilian parties are "nonprogrammatic" parties, that is, they fail to maintain consistent, principled positions on national issues. With the exception of some parties on the left, the major parties in Brazil resemble the "catch-all" parties that emerged in Europe after World War II in that they aim to win elections by advocating uncontroversial positions that appeal to as many people as possible (Kirchheimer 1990). The nonprogrammatic nature of Brazilian parties is made more salient by internal party weakness. Even when parties do adopt positions, party leaders are rarely willing or able to compel party representatives to uphold them. As Mainwaring puts it, party "platforms have little significance because the representatives have no obligation to follow them. Although party legislation grants the parties the means of expelling recalcitrant representatives and of imposing discipline in congressional votes, such measures are rare. Party programs are seldom binding on politicians" (1999: 141).[35] The frequency of party switching in the Brazilian Congress is both cause and symptom of the parties' ideological incoherence. For example, between 1987 and 1990, 40 percent of deputies switched parties (Ames 1995a: 335). In many of these cases, politicians moved between one party and its archenemy (Mainwaring 1999: 143). In other countries, we might expect party ideology to help explain the voting behavior of deputies. In Brazil the opposite holds: "[R]ather than a determinant of issue positions and electoral tactics, party is a consequence" (Ames 1995: 335).

Brazil's electoral rules are a major, if not the primary, contributing factor to its inchoate party system and the weak, nonprogrammatic nature of most parties. Deputies for the national legislature are elected through open-list proportional representation from the states, each of which forms a large, multimember district (the number of seats per state ranges from eight to seventy, with lightly populated states overrepresented). Most voters cast votes for individual candidates, though seats are allocated among parties according to the d'Hondt method (Ames 1995b: 408). Importantly, Brazil's "birthright" candidate rule allows incumbents to seek reelection automatically; parties cannot deny the use of the party label to incumbents. This rule denies party leaders a major source of leverage with which to impose

---

[35] Some recent research has demonstrated, however, that during the Cardoso administration, Brazilian parties were disciplined in congressional voting, something attributable to the president's legislative powers as well as the internal organization of Congress (Figueiredo and Limongi 2000). Others disagree, maintaining that party unity is low and congressional voting explicable by other factors (Ames 2001; for a review, see Amorim Neto 2000i).

discipline on representatives and is arguably the major reason for party in-discipline. Brazil's electoral rules have other consequences. They generate in-centives for politicians to cultivate personal reputations among voters rather than the collective reputation of the party. This "undermines parties' ability to develop and maintain collective reputations for consistent public pol-icy" (Carey 1997: 79). Moreover, the electoral rules mean that politicians rely primarily on geographical bases of support in order to get reelected, and thus devote a considerable amount of energy to bringing pork to their constituencies. This distracts their attention from substantive questions of national policy. "If legislators are devoted mainly to serving a constituency, then they are less willing to bear the significant costs of acquiring expertise on complex policy questions. As a result, the quality of public policy – another collective good for which parties might claim credit – suffers" (ibid.: 79).

Yet congressional inaction on national "public goods" issues need not be an obstacle to civil code reform if the executive takes an interest. Brazilian presidents exercise considerable control over the scope and content of leg-islative behavior. Between 1964 and 1985 (the period of military rule), the military kept Congress running, but changed the constitution, party sys-tem, and legislative rules several times in order to maintain a tight rein over national politics. The president's extraordinary legislative powers contin-ued into the democratic period because of provisions of the Constitution of 1988. Presidents can implement provisional measures (*medidas provisórias*) that have the force of law for up to thirty days without legislative approval. Though these decrees are supposed to expire in thirty days unless Congress approves them, in practice, they are reissued on a regular basis and thus remain in force (Mainwaring 1997: 62–3). Presidents may also declare bills of their own initiative to be "urgent," a labeling that obliges both houses of Congress to vote on the bill within forty-five days. If they fail to do so, the bill immediately moves to the top of the legislative agenda, displacing other items (ibid.: 64–5). The vast majority of bills approved in Brazil's Congress originate in the executive: Between 1989 and 1997, the Executive wrote 86 percent of the bills enacted by Brazil's Congress (Figueiredo and Limongi 2000: 155). Presidential control over the legislature could potentially work in favor of civil code reform, given that the Executive submitted the bill to Congress in 1975. But the Geisel administration responsible for the original bill left power in 1979, and subsequent administrations demonstrated less interest in it. A lack of executive commitment to civil code reform, combined with Brazil's inchoate party system and unprogrammatic parties, contributed to the delays in civil code reform.

Chile

When Chile made the transition to democracy in 1990, its family laws were more restrictive and unequal than in Argentina and Brazil. Fathers had the right to exercise *patria potestad* and husbands controlled marital property. After twelve years of democratic governance, Chile's laws still lagged behind Argentina and Brazil. Divorce remained illegal, as the previous chapter showed, and men controlled marital property. Women did, however, acquire shared *patria potestad*, and marital and nonmarital children gained equal rights, though eight years after the transition and after considerable delay and controversy. This chapter seeks to explain the troubled fate of family equality reform in Chile. Why is the marital property regime still unequal? Why was there more controversy surrounding the achievement of equal *patria potestad* and children's equality than in Argentina or Brazil? The state women's agency had a solid institutional position and various powers, including the power to submit women's rights legislation for consideration by Congress. Yet the legacy left by the former authoritarian regime and continuing military power in politics limited the political space to legislate family equality. Part of the legacy was an electoral system that created incentives for parties of the left and the Christian Democrats to govern in a coalition. The need to preserve the unity of the coalition compelled political leaders to exercise caution on controversial issues.

Chile's Authoritarian Legacy
The terms of Chile's transition established a tutelary role for the military, making the achievement of democracy seem fragile and even uncertain. The armed forces retained substantial ideological and financial autonomy (Garretón 1995; Linz and Stepan 1996). Pinochet continued as commander in chief and enjoyed exclusive rights to nominate candidates for top army positions. Retired military chiefs were granted seats in the National Senate. The military retained significant autonomy over its budget (including 10 percent of the revenue from the state-owned copper company); an amnesty law was passed to protect military members from prosecution; Pinochet and his allies were represented on the National Security Council; and the military kept control over the National Intelligence Service (CNI) (Linz and Stepan 1996).

Moreover, in the transition negotiations, democratic leaders had agreed to abide by the Constitution crafted by the military. The 1980 Constitution created authoritarian enclaves in the political system, including the presence of nine "institutional" senators appointed by Pinochet and a Supreme Constitutional Court with the power to veto laws sanctioned by Congress (all of whose seven members had been appointed by Pinochet) (Garretón 1995; Linz and Stepan 1996). The presence of the nine institutional senators denied the governing coalition a majority in the Senate. To get legislation passed, the coalition had to not only exercise strict discipline within its own ranks but also forge deals with the opposition and the institutional senators. The government was able to forge some agreements with the right on a new tax law and redistributive social policies, but not on gender issues (Baldez 2001; Weyland 1997). As we see below, the presence of appointed senators enhanced the power of conservative views in the legislature, posing an obstacle to family equality. Four institutional senators sat on the Senate's constitution committee, which considered the family law bills submitted to Congress. All four of these senators held socially conservative views on family law issues and tended to oppose the government's proposals (Londregan 2000).

Coalitional Politics in Chile

Coalitional politics in Chile in the 1990s evolved in response to the period of military rule. The electoral system installed by outgoing military rulers created strong incentives for political parties to group into coalitions. Fear of the military and the need to consolidate the transition in spite of continued military power and prerogatives, moreover, increased the importance of maintaining unity within the coalition. Before leaving office the Pinochet government rewrote the electoral rules to encourage centripetal political competition and to enable the legislative overrepresentation of parties of the right that had supported the Pinochet government. Military rulers wanted to avoid the political polarization that had provoked the 1973 coup and believed that appropriate electoral incentives could moderate politics and compel politicians to appeal to voters with centrist messages (Rabkin 1996; Siavelis and Valenzuela 1996). To achieve these ends, the 1989 electoral law established sixty legislative districts (each with two representatives) and rules requiring that one party receive twice as many votes as the next party in order to capture both seats in the district. These rules, which allowed the runner-up party to gain the second seat by receiving 33.4 percent of the vote, benefited the second largest party list (Siavelis 1997). To have a realistic chance of gaining seats under the system, Chilean parties had to group into two large coalitions and dispute elections with a common slate.

The formation of the bigger coalition, which united the Christian Democrats (DC) and the left in the Concertacíon, represented the biggest difference in Chilean politics between the 1990s and the pre-1973 period. During the Allende government (1970–3), the DC had opposed the left. Military rule, however, produced a critical political realignment. Although the DC, as the largest and center party, could have theoretically aligned with either the left or the right, the common history of opposition to the military government made the alliance with the left much more obvious (Rabkin 1996; Scully 1995). As a result, virtually the entire spectrum of the former opposition to military rule became coalition partners. The Concertación won every election held in the 1990s, but the binomial system has resulted in a disproportionality between the popular vote received by the right and its seats in Congress.[36]

---

[36] In the 1989 elections, the right gained 34 percent of the vote and won 40 percent of the seats in the chamber; in the 1993 elections, for example, the right won 37 percent of the vote and got 41 percent of the seats in the chamber (Scully 1995).

The Concertación has proven to be an enduring political alliance, and discussions over fielding a common slate of candidates for congressional elections have not been nearly as fractious as discussions among parties of the right (Scully 1995). Politicians in the Concertación agree on the need to consolidate democracy, to defend human rights, and to follow free market economic policies. Yet there is a potentially explosive division between the Christian Democrats and the left parties on social and family issues, and even within the ranks of Christian Democracy itself. Several senior DC politicians tend to vote with the left on human rights questions but with the right on social and ethical issues (Londregan 2000). As we see below, these divisions proved consequential for family law reform. When bills to reform the marital property regime and *patria potestad* hit the Senate, some Christian Democratic senators ended up voting with senators from the right, and against their coalition partners from the Democratic and Socialist parties to force modification of the government's original bills.

SERNAM and the Family Equality Agenda
One arena where coalitional politics was at work was the government women's agency, SERNAM (the National Women's Service). SERNAM's internal dynamics illustrate how the need to preserve unity within the governing coalition had a muting effect on advocacy of "progressive" issues during the 1990s in Chile. In line with commitments made during the transition process, SERNAM was created by the new democratic government in 1991. SERNAM had offices in the thirteen administrative regions of the country, and was headed by a director of ministerial rank. SERNAM has run a nationwide network of information centers on women's rights, a violence prevention program, a support program for women heads of households, a program directed at women agricultural workers, and a microcredit program; trains police officers and other public servants on gender issues; and advises and coordinates public policies toward women executed by other ministries (SERNAM 1996). One of SERNAM's central objectives was to propose legal reforms aimed at eliminating discrimination against women (Alvear 1994). SERNAM's legal reform department drew up a series of proposed reforms to laws on women's rights in marriage, the equality of children, domestic violence, workplace discrimination, and constitutional equality. The Executive presented most of these proposals to Congress in the first few years following democratization.

From the beginning, however, conflicts plagued SERNAM. The first site of conflict was Congress, where politicians from the right disputed the very existence of the agency. In line with women's movement demands, the Alywin administration had agreed to create SERNAM by law so that the agency would be permanent (Baldez 2001: 13–14). During congressional debates over the bill to create SERNAM, however, politicians from the right objected to the gender equality discourse justifying the agency and to the idea that government should play a role in promoting gender equality in society.

The right charged that a women's bureaucracy was an unacceptable invasion of personal liberty, imposed in totalitarian fashion a monolithic understanding of women's roles, and discriminated against men.[37] Conflicts also appeared within SERNAM itself due to ideological and political differences between leftist feminist and Christian Democratic women working within the agency. The feminists (headed by subdirector Soledad Larraín, a leader of the Socialist Party) wanted SERNAM to take a protagonistic stand on divorce, reproductive rights, and women's quotas, and to collaborate on public policies with feminist NGOs.[38] The Christian Democrats, led by SERNAM's director, Minister Soledad Alvear, did not want SERNAM to raise these issues.[39]

The Christian Democrats were worried that a more "progressive" stand on social issues would risk antagonizing the right and putting the democratic transition in jeopardy. The socialists, led by Larraín, did not believe that engaging issues of divorce and reproductive rights, even though these alienated the right and conservative sectors of the DC, would endanger the transition. As a matter of principle, Larraín questioned the rule of consensus endorsed by other Concertación politicians: She maintained that issues dividing the Socialists and the Christian Democrats could be debated without threatening the unity of the Concertación. In 1992, however, Larraín was removed from the position of subdirector of SERNAM, and the agency was consolidated as a Christian Democratic space.[40] For most of the 1990s, SERNAM avoided addressing controversial issues such as divorce, therapeutic abortion, rape, and reproductive rights, both internally and in Chilean society at large. To preclude criticism from the Church, the opposition, and the media, SERNAM "effectively self-censored internal debate on vital issues which affect women" (Matear 1996).[41]

---

[37] See *El Mercurio* editorials: April 12 and 29, July 4, 1990; January 16, 1991; congressional debates on the law creating SERNAM.

[38] Interview with Soledad Larraín, Santiago, April 27, 1998.

[39] See, e.g., "Sernam no apoyará una ley de divorcio," *El Mercurio*, November 27, 1991.

[40] Interview with Soledad Larraín.

[41] SERNAM's careful approach on gender issues trickled down into civil society. Financial dependency on SERNAM made feminist nongovernmental organizations (NGOs) reluctant to serve as protagonists of divorce and reproductive rights. Because of Chile's high income level, foreign funding of domestic social movements and NGOs, particularly from European donors, was reduced after the return to democracy (Barrig 1997). To survive, most feminist NGOs had to retool themselves as research and consulting firms. Their biggest client was SERNAM, who contracted feminist NGOs to conduct research, policy analysis, and policy design (Alvarez 1998b; Barrig 1997). The existence of contractual relations between feminist organizations and SERNAM reduced the former's capacity for political intervention. Feminist NGOs self-censored their political claims because, as one of Barrig's sources pointed out, "the government is not going to consult with institutions or people who pressure it on issues outside of the official agenda or who exceed the threshold of its tolerance" (Barrig 1997).

Family Equality in Congress

Family equality was a prominent issue on the policy agenda in Chile, but aspects of the authoritarian legacy and coalition dynamics served as a brake on reform. Certain actors in the Executive branch, particularly in SERNAM, were strongly committed to reform; political parties held clear positions on the issue; and some legislators were willing to labor for change on family equality. But other, socially conservative politicians in Chile opposed the family equality agenda. These politicians included not only members of the political opposition on the right but also institutional senators and politicians from the Christian Democratic Party of the governing coalition. Because they desired to maintain unity within the governing coalition, the presidency, SERNAM, and even politicians from the left felt the need to tread carefully and not advocate potentially divisive issues too forcefully. It is worth repeating a quote from Democratic Party senator Sergio Bitar, cited in the previous chapter:

What you have to avoid at the beginning [of the transition] is the accumulation of factors provoking polarization.... For us, the first fundamental task was the struggle to strengthen democracy, to confront the dictatorship, to combat the archaic institutions of designated and lifelong senators, to launch a big effort in the area of human rights ... this generated a degree of national unity that was very important, including an important linkage to the Catholic Church.[42]

SERNAM also made some errors in legislative strategy that compounded the problems faced by family equality in Congress. Opposition by politicians on the right was directed less toward the marital property regime and *patria potestad* than toward other parts of the bills in which these two issues appeared. Discord over the more controversial issues of adultery and illegitimacy delayed changes to marital property and *patria potestad* more than would have been the case had these issues been the subject of separate bills. Furthermore, Chilean society was polarized over the divorce bill at the same time that family equality reforms were being considered by Congress. The absolutist position conservatives adopted against divorce almost certainly spilled over into family equality debates, particularly the proposal to eliminate distinctions between children born in and out of wedlock, which, conservatives maintained, posed a threat to the institution of marriage.

The first bill aimed to grant women equality in the administration of marital property and to decriminalize adultery. The default marriage regime in Chile is the *sociedad conyugal* (community property), of which the husband is the designated administrator. Under community property rules, women forsake the right to control the property they own prior to marriage and

---

[42] Interview with PPD Senator Sergio Bitar, Santiago, June 12, 1998.

the property they inherit or gain during the marriage.[43] In 1991, SERNAM presented a bill in Congress to change the default marriage regime to *participación en los gananciales* (participation in acquests). Under this system, husband and wife are each recognized as the legitimate executors of their personal property during marriage. Upon termination of the marriage, however, all property acquired by both spouses for the duration of the marriage is lumped together and split evenly between the two spouses. The system is broadly egalitarian: It avoids placing women in a subservient position to men, and by splitting property evenly at the end, recognizes the value of women's nonmonetary contributions to the household (Alvear 1991; Alywin 1991; Barros 1991). In 1993, the Chamber of Deputies voted unanimously to approve the bill.

Modifying the criminal code on adultery was a far more controversial enterprise. The Chilean criminal code had treated male and female adultery according to separate standards. Whereas a woman committed "adultery" by sleeping with a man who was not her husband, a man committed "adultery" only by maintaining a mistress for an extended period of time or conducting an extramarital affair in a scandalous manner (Programa de Asesoria Legislativa 1991). SERNAM proposed to remove sex discrimination in the law by making single acts of adultery a crime whether committed by a man *or* a woman. At the same time as they approved changes to the marital property regime, the Chamber of Deputies voted to decriminalize adultery altogether rather than adopt the government's proposal, which would "democratize" it by establishing equal standards for women and men.

Opposition by conservative senators forced a modification of the chamber's version of the bill on property and adultery. The Senate opted for modifications presented by the right-wing Renovación Nacional Party establishing *participación en los gananciales* as an alternative, but not the default, marital property regime, and in line with the government's original proposal, adultery continued to be a crime with equal standards for men and women. Senators from the right and conservative Christian Democratic senators believed that granting equal rights in the administration of marital property was against natural law and would undermine family unity. They also felt that decriminalizing adultery would weaken the family and communicate the wrong message about family values (Londregan 2000: chapter 7). Yet establishing "participation in acquests" as an alternative marital property regime produced few concrete effects. In 1995, a mere 2,000 of the 88,000 couples contracting marriage chose this regime; 1,800 out of 62,000 in 1996; and 820 out of 27,000 in the first six months of 1997 (Claro 1997). The vast majority of Chilean couples continued to marry under the old community property regime managed by the husband.

[43] The Married Women's Reserved Property Act of 1925 granted women exclusive control over the income earned from independent work, the only property women may dispose of without their husband's authorization.

A second bill was introduced into Congress by SERNAM in 1993. Called the *ley de filiación*, the bill had three key components. First, the bill granted women shared *patria potestad*. Second, it erased the distinction among legitimate, illegitimate, and natural children to establish the equality of all children before the law. Previously, illegitimate children had no inheritance rights and suffered from discrimination in the Catholic schools, armed forces, and police department. Third, the law permitted the free investigation of paternity and admitted biological evidence as proof. There had been many restrictions on the investigation of paternity, creating a situation on where the establishment of paternity was up to the will of the (undeclared) parent (Programa de Asesoria Legislativa 1994).

The Lower House approved the *ley de filiación* unanimously in 1994, but the bill encountered fierce opposition in the Senate. The proposal to grant women equal parental authority encountered little opposition, but had the unfortunate fate to be linked to the more contentious proposal about the equality of children. Because senators from the right and hard-line bishops thought it undermined the legitimate family, the *ley de filiación* generated tremendous controversy in Chile. Conservatives maintained that the new bill threatened to devalue the family in society at large and to reduce the importance of marriage in the eyes of children (Libertad y Desarollo 1997b). Others claimed the law was unconstitutional since, by weakening the family, it contradicted the constitutional principle establishing the family as the essential nucleus of society.[44] The Roman Catholic Church official in charge of family matters argued that a mere law could not change the reality of the unequal status of legitimate and illegitimate children; other bishops said that children's equality would change the concept of the family in Chilean culture and infringe upon the rights of legitimate children.[45]

Part of the conservative opposition stemmed from the consequences of the *ley de filiación* for inheritance rights. Chilean law grants little choice over how one may bequeath one's estate. Individuals may allocate only 25 percent of their estate at will; the rest is allocated in fixed quantities to children and the surviving spouse. The *ley de filiación* granted "illegitimate" children the same rights to their parents' estate as "legitimate" children. Since parents cannot write 75 percent of their own wills, it is impossible to deny or reduce further the inheritance rights of "illegitimate" children. As a result, some conservatives made libertarian-style arguments against the *ley de filiación*, claiming that it was an assault on freedom to force parents to support their illegitimate children. Although parents should feel morally obliged to care for their offspring, they argued, it is not the government's role to see that

---

[44] *El Mercurio*, May 23, 1998.
[45] See, e.g., the op-ed piece by Bishop Orozimbo Fuenzalida Fuenzalida, "Filiación, Verdad o Ideologías?" *El Mercurio*, June 11, 1998. On the other hand, several bishops, including the Archbishop of Santiago, expressed support for the law.

they do so.[46] In spite of this conservative opposition, the *ley de filiación* was eventually approved by the Senate in 1998.

Conclusion

By the 1980s and 1990s, the family equality reforms considered in this chapter were long past due. Since women made up around 35 percent of the labor force and female school enrollment equaled men's, it seems odd that patriarchal norms still dominated family life. Moreover, legal-related issue networks had expanded beyond their earlier core of middle-class male lawyers as second-wave feminist movements that mobilized in the 1970s and 1980s to advocate women's rights and bring about a return to democracy also focused their attention on the law. They were joined by the executive women's agencies created by new democratic governments to coordinate policy on gender issues. Empowered by international treaties such as CEDAW, this coalition of reformers worked in public and behind the scenes to mobilize awareness about equality in the family. Yet legal changes, though they may have seemed obvious in the context of evolving social practices, were not so easy. What should have been a matter of routine policy making – adjusting the civil code to conform to widely accepted standards of equality – was so only in Argentina. Reform proved a lengthy process in Brazil and a contentious one in Chile.

Does the uneven success of family equality reforms imply that Latin America's new democracies are hostile to women's gender interests? Even though outcomes might not match the rosy expectations held by feminist movements around the time of transitions to democracy, there are reasons not to be too pessimistic about democratic politics. In the first place, Argentina's experience in the 1980s shows that, given a harmony of interests among issue networks in civil society, parties in Congress able to coordinate their legislative behavior, and actors in the executive branch, new democracies can make reasonably good strides toward instituting gender equality in the law. Second, though Brazil's experience with delayed legal reform arouses cause for concern, legislative paralysis in Brazil is not unique to gender policy issues. Although in some respects presidents have been able to accomplish a great deal, numerous policy proposals, some of extreme national importance such as fiscal reform, administrative reform, and social security, have met a similar, or worse, fate in the Brazilian Congress. If Brazil succeeds in reforming its party and electoral system, the result may be more legislative coherence across issue areas. Finally, Chile's right-wing parties and public intellectuals hold conservative views on marriage, divorce, family planning, and abortion, and oppose legal reforms that threaten those beliefs. Yet the right's position, though disagreeable to feminists and

---

[46] Interview, Santiago, June 1998.

liberals, cannot be easily dismissed as hostile to women's gender interests, for it reflects an alternative vision of gender. Democracy creates conditions for proponents of different views to engage one another in public deliberation, but the outcomes of such deliberation are open-ended.

A final question concerns whether the presence of more women in power would have helped the cause of family equality reforms. There is evidence that women bring new proposals to the political agenda and work through various stages of the legislative process to defend women's rights (Jones 1997b; Swers 2002; Thomas 1994). Yet in Argentina in the 1980s, Brazil in the 1980s and 1990s, and Chile in the 1990s (the time when bills were under consideration), women held a small minority of seats in Congress and few exercised leadership in political parties. (In the 1990s, women's presence in Agrentine politics grew dramatically thanks to a quota law. For details, see Htun and Jones 2002). To the extent that women are more likely than men to sponsor and work for the passage of women's rights bills, women's greater numbers will make such bills more salient. Indeed, the growth in women's presence in power in Latin America in the 1990s (from 9 percent of the lower house of Congress in 1990 to 15 percent in 2002) has coincided with the formation of multiparty women's political alliances, greater debate, and more legislative output on women's issues (Htun 1998). In a pinch, however, party unity and the need for political survival have proven more decisive than gender identity in shaping women's legislative behavior (Alatorre 1999; Rodríguez 1998). Women are not above politics: Their activities will be shaped by the institutional configurations, coalition dynamics, and party politics studied in this chapter.

6

Why Hasn't Abortion Been Decriminalized in Latin America?

Abortion is one of the most thorny policy problems faced by modern democracies. Few other issues provoke comparable moral outrage and political polarization. Feminist and liberals see abortion as a question of individual liberty, privacy, and public health; social conservatives maintain that prohibitions on abortion are necessary to protect human life, defend human rights, and uphold moral and family values. Abortion thus involves a "clash of absolutes" (Tribe 1992) between which there is seemingly little ground for compromise. Beneath the rhetoric and the ideology, however, serious public health questions surround the problem of abortion. In countries where abortion is illegal, many women undergo the procedure in clandestine circumstances at great risk to their health. Complications from botched abortions are a leading cause of maternal mortality in many countries and produce a major drain on the public health system. The black market in illegal abortions contributes to corruption and a lack of respect for the rule of law. The problem of abortion demands urgent resolution, yet there is little political will to entertain serious debates about decriminalization.

In Latin America, with the exception of Cuba, the legal status of abortion has changed very little since the promulgation of modern criminal codes in the late nineteenth and early twentieth centuries. These codes criminalized abortion in general, but most did not punish people for performing abortions when the pregnancy threatened the mother's life ("therapeutic" reasons). A large number of countries exempted from punishment "compassionate" abortions (if the pregnancy resulted from rape), and some countries permitted abortions in the event of fetal abnormalities. Only one country, Uruguay, admitted abortion on "social" grounds (though the criminal code of the Mexican state of Yucatan also admits "social" abortions).

The continuing criminalization of abortion in Latin America is puzzling for several reasons. First, the vast majority of Western European and North American countries liberalized strict abortion laws between the late 1960s and the 1980s. In the midst of these global abortion policy changes, laws in

Latin America stayed the same and in some cases grew even more restrictive. Second, at around the same time, Latin American countries introduced legal reforms pertaining to the rights and responsibilities of spouses in marriage, divorce, domestic violence, political participation, and labor law, among others. Abortion was virtually the only gender issue area where major change did not occur. Finally, the restrictive nature of the region's abortion laws in the late twentieth century contrasts to the early twentieth century, when several Latin American countries were vanguards in the field of abortion law. In 1922, Argentina became one of the first countries in the world to declare that abortion would not be punished when performed after rape. Brazil, Mexico, Uruguay, and Cuba then copied the Argentine law during criminal code reforms of the 1930s (Jiménez de Asúa 1942). Most European Catholic countries, including France, Spain, Italy, and Portugal, did not authorize post-rape abortions until the 1970s and 1980s. Latin American countries, in summary, moved from world vanguards of abortion liberalization to world laggards.

Why hasn't abortion been decriminalized in Latin America? This chapter analyzes the experiences of Argentina, Brazil, and Chile in an attempt to answer this question. Even though feminist reproductive rights networks have grown and gained influence under democratic politics, the transition to democracy has coincided with great efforts by antiabortion movements and the Roman Catholic Church to preclude United Nations conferences from endorsing abortion rights and to oppose abortion reform in domestic politics. The strength of antiabortion movements combines with public ambivalence about abortion to increase the political costs associated with abortion advocacy and decrease the benefits. Fearing the wrath of antiabortion movements and the Church, and judging that little will be gained politically by supporting decriminalization, most parties and politicians attempt to steer clear of the abortion issue. Unlike policy changes on other gender issues, such as domestic violence, sex equality in the family, and divorce, there is less consensus about the need to reform restrictive abortion laws, and the coalition supporting change is therefore relatively small.

Beyond the general failure to decriminalize, there are differences in the legal framework of the three countries. Both Brazil and Argentina permit abortions for women who have been raped and when the pregnancy threatens the life of the pregnant woman ("therapeutic" abortions); Chile does not permit abortion under any circumstance. Chile had permitted therapeutic abortions until 1989, when the Pinochet government changed the Health Code to ban all abortions. The political climate and debates about abortion in the three countries also vary, with Brazil the most liberal, Chile the most conservative, and Argentina occupying a middle position. In Brazil, a "legal abortion" movement has set up services in seventeen hospitals to see that victims of rape have access to abortion, and several bills to liberalize abortion have been considered in Congress. Debates about abortion have occurred in the Brazilian press, and the National Human Rights program has officially declared abortion to be a public health problem. Argentina is the middle case. There is almost no discussion about liberalizing abortion, but conservative attempts to ban abortion under all circumstances have failed. Chile is completely closed to discussions about liberalizing abortion: Since the transition to democracy, only one bill to reinstate therapeutic abortion has been presented in Congress. Most parliamentary debate on abortion centers on conservative proposals to increase the penalties for abortion-related crimes.

A brief note on terminology is in order. To "decriminalize" abortion means to legalize the practice. To "liberalize" abortion means to make laws less restrictive. Liberalization *stretches* existing law by adding more grounds for legal abortion. For example, a country that allows abortion only for risks to the mother's life or in the event of rape would liberalize by permitting abortion if the child would be born handicapped, if the pregnancy threatened the pregnant woman's mental health, if the pregnant woman could prove financial hardship, and so on. The puzzle in Latin America concerns not just the uniform failure to decriminalize, but also the inability of every country except for Cuba to stretch the grounds for legal abortion.

The abortion policy stalemate in Argentina, Brazil, and Chile contrasts to the early twentieth century, when Argentina and Brazil pioneered innovations in abortion legislation. This chapter begins with a brief discussion of this early history of abortion politics. The second part of the chapter analyzes the global and regional context of contemporary abortion politics to identify reasons for Latin America's failure to decriminalize abortion. The next three parts describe abortion politics in the 1990s and early 2000s in Brazil, Argentina, and Chile and explores differences in activities of the feminist reproductive rights movement. The pro- or antiabortion position of the president and the presence or absence of allies in Congress shaped the movement's strategies. Brazil's progressive position on reproductive rights in international forums, the unwillingness of Brazilian presidents actively to oppose abortion, and the availability of allies in Congress from the Workers' Party generated more space for the movement to promote abortion rights than in Argentina and Chile. In these latter two countries, presidents were more explicit opponents of abortion, and virtually no legislators or parties in Congress were willing to raise debates about liberalizing abortion.

Early History of Abortion Politics

In the context of the early twenty-first century, Latin American abortion laws seem conservative. At the time of their crafting, the laws were bold. As mentioned earlier, Latin American countries were among the first in the world to permit abortions for women who had been raped. Why? In much the same way that international agreements and ideas influenced the experts who drafted civil law reforms during military governments of the 1960s and 1970s, cosmopolitan theories were brought to bear on the criminal codes promulgated by the Radical Party governments of 1920s Argentina and the dictatorship of Getulio Vargas in Brazil in the 1930s and 1940s. Policy changes were accomplished through reasoned deliberation among elites, primarily upper-class male criminologists, doctors, and politicians who were motivated by new ideas in medical science and criminology and concerns about judicial corruption and public health. The public was hardly involved. What's more, Roman Catholic bishops did not contest early, liberalizing reforms.

Latin American abortion debates were influenced by a growing international movement for "compassionate" abortion provoked by the widespread rapes of women by invading armies during World War I. At the time, various courts in France absolved women of the crime of abortion; some even forgave infanticide. The single most important influence on the development of legislation in Latin America, however, was the work of Spanish criminologist Luis Jiménez de Asúa. Jiménez de Asúa became a full professor of criminal law at the University of Madrid at age twenty-two, wrote scores of books, and held honorary doctorates and professorships from universities in almost every Latin American country. Through his publications and speeches at regional and international meetings, Jiménez de Asúa spread the news of contemporary developments in criminology. After General Francisco Franco assumed power at the conclusion of the Spanish Civil War, Jiménez de Asúa emigrated to Buenos Aires where he remained until his death in 1970. His prolific academic work helped diffuse knowledge about European legal systems throughout Latin America (Cury Urzua 1992: 138). Jiménez de Asúa's proposals about abortion were analyzed by the most respected criminologists in Argentina, Brazil, and Chile, and cited in virtually every criminal code reform in the region (Hungria 1942; Ministerio de Justicia 1929; Soler 1945). Even those who did not agree with his proposals felt the need to respond to them (Ribeiro 1942, 1973).

In Argentina, the new criminal code approved in 1922 permitted abortion for reasons of medical necessity and rape, including the presumed rape of mentally handicapped women. The Senate Commission charged with finalizing the 1922 Criminal Code cited Jiménez de Asúa's work and recognized that the new code's abortion provisions would amount to "a true innovation in criminal legislation." In approving "compassionate" abortion, the commission felt that it would shield women from the anguish of mothering the children of men who had sexually assaulted them. Eugenics was another motivation. Argentine senators wanted to avoid the birth of physically or mentally handicapped children. As the commission noted in its justification for the new legislation:

The issue is seductive and its elaboration in this report may carry us far, leading us into the domain of eugenics, whose study is held to be of transcendental importance for some members of this Commission and whose problems should be of profound and intense interest to the legislators, educators, sociologists, and jurists of our country. Even criminal science is concerned about the application of [eugenic] principles to more effectively combat the rise in delinquency....

But now is not the moment to make, in this report, extensive remarks about eugenics and its relationship to delinquency. It shall be enough to say, to finish with this point, that even if the sterilization of criminals is not accepted by science, by criminal law, and by social consensus ... *it is indisputable that the law must permit abortion when it is practiced, with medical intervention, with the objective of perfecting the race.* The problem was raised in Europe during the last war due to the rape of numerous Belgian women by drunken, uncontrollable, or criminal soldiers. (Senado de la Nación 1919: 84) (emphasis added)

In the first decades of the twentieth century, ideas about eugenics were pervasive in the southern cone of South America. Eugenicist notions inspired immigration quotas favoring Northern Europeans and helped give rise to national ideologies of racial mixture and whitening, particularly in Brazil (Stepan 1991).

Argentina's abortion law was copied verbatim from a draft bill submitted for consideration in Switzerland by several lawyers in 1916.[1] Though the bill was not enacted in Switzerland, it served as the model for Argentina and other Latin American countries. In fact, the ambiguity of the translation from French and German provoked decades of arguments among Argentine lawyers, some of whom argued that the law permitted abortions only for mentally ill women.[2] At issue was the phrasing of the last part of Article 86, which states that abortion is unpunishable "if the pregnancy results from a rape or an assault on the chastity [*un atentado al pudor*] committed against a mentally handicapped or mentally ill woman [*mujer idiota o demente*]." The question was, does the clause refer to one or two objects? That is, is abortion permitted for a "normal" woman who has been raped, or merely

---

[1] Between 1912 and 1916, members of a technical commission meeting in Lugano debated various proposals about abortion law, and finally issued a statement recommending that abortion be decriminalized "if the pregnancy results from a rape, from an assault on the chastity of a mentally disturbed, unconscious, or inhabilitated woman, or from incest." Due to pressure from the Catholic party, however, the federal government rejected these recommendations, and Switzerland ended up authorizing abortion only in the event of medical necessity (Jiménez de Asúa 1942: 344–7).

[2] Most experts, including Jiménez de Asúa and Argentine thinkers Juan Ramos and Sebastian Soler, believed that the clause authorized abortions in the event of a rape of a "normal" woman *and* the rape of a mentally handicapped woman. Other experts, including prominent criminologist José Peco, held that the article permitted only eugenic abortions performed on mentally handicapped or mentally ill women who had been raped. (Peco was not personally opposed to compassionate abortions; rather, he believed that the article, as phrased, did not authorize them. In fact, the draft criminal code revisions Peco submitted to the Argentine Congress in 1942 proposed that abortions after a rape or act of incest be decriminalized, as long as they were performed during the first three months of pregnancy (Peco 1942: 245).)

for a mentally handicapped or mentally ill woman who has been subject to rape or assault? If the former, why not make one simple reference to rape, which would by extension include cases of mentally handicapped women? If the latter, why does the law repeat itself, since surely a mentally handicapped woman cannot get pregnant from an "assault on chastity" [*atentado al pudor*] that does not involve vaginal penetration?

Apparently, the Argentine Senate worked with the French translation of the German text of a draft bill written by several Swiss criminologists in 1916. The original text followed German law by using the two German words for rape: violent rape (*Notzucht*) and the rape of a mentally handicapped or mentally ill woman (*Schändung*). The French version translated *Schändung* as "*attentat à la pudeur d'une femme idiote, alienée, inconciente ou incapable de résistence.*" The Argentine Senate translated the French translation as "*atentado al pudor cometido sobre una mujer idiota o demente.*" If *Schändung* had simply been translated as "rape," which would have been more accurate, since Spanish has only one word for rape, the second clause of the abortion article would have read as follows: "if the pregnancy results from a rape or rape committed against a mentally handicapped woman." Read in the revised manner, the law refers to two rapes of two women, not merely mentally handicapped or mentally ill women (Soler 1945: 130–1).

Various attempts were made in Argentina to clarify Article 86. Criminal code bills submitted in 1937 by Eduardo Coll and Euzebio Gomez and in 1942 by José Peco proposed to redraft the abortion articles to make it clear that they included any and all rapes (Peco 1942; Ribeiro 1942: 81). A definitive reform was not enacted, however, until the military government of General Juan Carlos Onganía assumed power in 1966. As discussed in Chapter 3, the Onganía administration spearheaded a massive overhaul of the country's laws. Justice Minister Conrado Etchebarne organized small commissions of the country's most prominent jurists to propose reforms, the contents of which were, for the most part, forwarded to and enacted by Onganía without political interference. The commission charged with proposing criminal law reforms consisted of Sebastian Soler, Carlos Fontan Balestra, and Eduardo Aguirre Obaro.

Among the various articles the commission singled out for revision was Article 86, dealing with the conditions of unpunishable abortion. To make the law absolutely clear, the new article read that abortion would not be punished "if the pregnancy results from a rape for which a criminal suit has been initiated. If the victim of the rape is a minor or a mentally handicapped or mentally ill woman [*mujer idiota o demente*] the consent of her legal representative is required" (Ley 17.567 of 1967). In describing the motives behind the revision, the committee declared: "This was one of the provisions of the Code that gave rise to the most disparate interpretations, above all for including the phrase '*o de un atentado al pudor cometido sobre una mujer idiota o demente.*' We leave it perfectly clear that abortion is unpunishable when the pregnancy results from rape and that it is performed under the conditions specified by the law" (Soler, Fontán Balestra, and Aguirre Obarrio 1967: 2881). In one sense, the Onganía reform made the law stricter by requiring that a criminal suit be initiated for the abortion to be legal. On the other hand, it is indisputable that the reform clarified, in the liberal direction, the circumstances under which abortion would go unpunished.

Over the next two decades, the fate of the abortion article was tied to the various changes of political regime suffered by Argentina. Ironically, while military governments promoted a more "liberal" version of the abortion law, democratic governments restored the law to its historic, more ambiguous version. In 1973, a democratically elected civilian government revoked General Onganía's liberalizing criminal code reform. After assuming power, the government of Héctor Cámpora (a stand-in for former President Juan Perón, who was making a political comeback) revoked all of the criminal law reforms that had been issued during the previous military administrations. Then, the military government of the Proceso de Reorganización Nacional promulgated a new criminal code reform after seizing power in 1976. The Proceso's reform sought to reinstate the "scientific and technical advances" introduced by the Onganía administration, including the more liberal version of the abortion article. On the darker side, the same reform reinstated the death penalty in Argentina and prescribed life prison sentences for those convicted of subversive activities (Ley 21.338, sanctioned on June 25, 1976).

After the transition to democracy in 1983, the Radical Party government of Raul Alfonsín promulgated the much-celebrated "Law of the Defense of Democracy" (Law 23.077, sanctioned on August 9, 1984). Alfonsín's law revoked all criminal laws enacted under prior military governments and established procedural norms for the investigation and trial of human rights violations committed by the Proceso. One consequence of the Alfonsín reform was that Article 86, dealing with unpunishable abortions, was restored to its original, ambiguous form. In the 1990s, the historic debate over the proper interpretation of Article 86 continued. An authoritative doctrinal text by Carlos Fontan Balestra (1991) alleges that the article authorizes abortions performed for all women who have been raped; another text by Carlos Creus (1995) holds that the article permits abortions for mentally handicapped or mentally ill women only.

Nelson Hungria, the criminologist who wrote large parts of the Brazilian Criminal Code of 1940, remarked that the Argentine code of 1922 was one of the first in the world to condone the principle of compassionate abortion, and "our code followed its example" (1942: 279). Criminal codes promulgated in Mexico in 1931, Uruguay in 1933, and Cuba in 1936 also followed the Argentine model (Jiménez de Asúa 1942: 341). In Chile, a 1929 bill proposed decriminalization of compassionate abortion. The proposal, commissioned by a decree issued by President Carlos Ibáñez in 1928, mentioned theories about "compassionate" abortion elaborated by Luis Jiménez de Asúa at the Third Panamerican Scientific Congress in 1924 (Ministerio de Justicia 1929). Yet the reform was never enacted, and to this day, Chile's 1875 Criminal Code is still in effect.

It is noteworthy that these reforms were enacted at all, given that any exception to prohibitions on abortion contradicts Church doctrine, and that governments responsible for the reforms had close ties to the Church. The government of Getulio Vargas enacted Brazil's abortion reforms of 1940, and Vargas's regime cooperated with the Church on many issues, even declaring marriage indissoluble in 1934, as noted in Chapter 4. The military government of General Juan Carlos Onganía in late 1960s Argentina, which upheld permission for compassionate abortion and clarified the law to eliminate ambiguities in its application, was, like the Vargas regime in Brazil, on good terms with the Church.[3] Perhaps because these governments in power upheld the idea that abortion was morally wrong and should be treated as a crime, Roman Catholic bishops did not speak out when governments stretched abortion laws. To be true to its principles, which oppose abortion under any circumstances, the Church should have contested early changes. Because abortion was framed as a technical issue, however, the Church may have felt that its general position was safe. As we see below, however, Church opposition to abortion grew more intense in reaction to the threat posed by the feminist reproductive rights movement and the liberalization of abortion in North America and Europe.

Why Hasn't Abortion Been Decriminalized?

The 1990s and early 2000s would seem to have been a propitious time to change old laws restricting abortion, as the 1980s and 1990s saw the growth of feminist reproductive rights movements at the global, regional, and national levels and the consolidation of international norms on reproductive rights. The reproductive rights movement, which links think tanks, activist groups, private foundations, and, increasingly, international population agencies, seeks to expand women's decision-making autonomy over issues of reproductive and sexual health, including abortion. The movement worked with national delegations and U.N. officials to see that reproductive rights were recognized in the agreements reached at the International Conference on Population and Development in Cairo in 1994 and the Fourth World Conference on Women, held in Beijing in 1995.[4] Both the Cairo and

---

[3] In fact, when revising the civil code provisions on marital separation, the Onganía government incorporated suggestions made by Church officials.

[4] Reproductive rights movements were also active in regional politics, particularly at the string of Latin American Feminist Encuentros, held biannually beginning in 1981, and the regional preparatory meetings organized for the United Nations' Cairo and Beijing conferences (Sternbach et al. 1992). At the fifth Latin American feminist Encuentro held in Argentina in

Beijing documents committed governments to address the public health consequences of unsafe abortion, to help prevented unwanted pregnancies, to see that abortion is safe in countries where it is legal, and to provide safe medical assistance to women with abortion-related complications. The Beijing document also included a phrase calling on governments to "consider reviewing laws containing punitive measures against women who have undergone illegal abortions" (paragraph 106k, Platform for Action).

U.N. plans of action are statements of principle that, though they represent political commitments, are not binding on signatory countries. Yet the programs are of tremendous normative importance. The Cairo and Beijing documents, for example, helped legitimize feminist arguments in domestic politics and served as instruments of consciousness raising and political mobilization. As one activist put it:

[t]he Cairo Conference legitimized reproductive rights as a human rights concept. . . . If someone asks: what are reproductive rights? you can tell them. And this is not just your opinion, but a definition that has been debated and agreed to by a wide variety of countries and cultures.[5]

Feminist achievements in the international sphere were not uncontested, however. Tremendous controversy surrounded discussions on reproductive and sexual health at Cairo and Beijing when a coalition of conservative forces (including the Vatican, some Muslim countries, and Argentina) attacked the use of the word "gender" and attempted to eradicate clauses about reproductive rights from the final documents (Franco 1998).[6] At the follow-up conferences – Cairo Plus Five and Beijing Plus Five – held in 1999 and 2000, respectively, feminists tried to incorporate more progressive statements on abortion into the final documents, while antiabortion groups sought to backtrack on the agreements reached in 1994 and 1995. To block inclusion of abortion-related clauses, conservative groups attempted to preclude the adoption of *any* final document (Corrêa 2000: 1).[7]

1990, participants organized the Latin American and Caribbean Health and Reproductive Rights Network and resolved to establish September 28 as the "Day for the Legalization of Abortion in Latin America and the Caribbean." Every year the day provides an opportunity for the movement to organize demonstrations and seminars to promote abortion rights.

[5] Interview with Sonia Corrêa, Rio de Janeiro, July 31, 1997.

[6] The Vatican, as a permanent nonmember state observer at the United Nations, cannot vote in the United Nations General Assembly but can vote on policy recommendations issued at U.N. Conferences (CRLP 1999).

[7] Brazil and some other Latin American countries played important roles in these debates. In the preparatory meetings for Beijing Plus Five, Latin American countries (with the exception of Honduras and Nicaragua) formed a negotiating block called SLAC (for "Similarly Minded Latin American Countries" or "Some Latin American Countries"). SLAC helped broker an agreement so that both documents recommended, in addition to calling on countries to reconsider punitive laws for abortion, that health practitioners be trained to perform those abortions permitted by law.

Antiabortion activism in U.N. conferences was the product of two important trends in global abortion politics, trends that also help explain Latin America's failure to decriminalize. The first had to do with reform within the Roman Catholic Church. Beginning with his election in 1978, Pope John Paul II promoted changes to enhance the Church's institutional control and coherence, making it a more committed and effective opponent of abortion. The pope placed a high priority on Latin America, where he sought to counter the influence of liberation theology and replace its popular and participatory approach with a "Polish model" emphasizing unity, hierarchy, and discipline (Levine 1990: 35–6). The pope centralized power in the Church, reorganized the Papal Commission for Latin America, appointed theologically conservative bishops to Latin American posts, and took measures to discredit outspoken proponents of liberation theology such as Gustavo Gutiérrez (Peru) and Leonardo Boff (Brazil) (Blofeld 2001; Ghio 1991). These institutional changes increased the Vatican's ability to ensure that increasingly strict official views were reflected at all levels of Church activity. Pope John Paul II took a hard line on divorce, abortion, and birth control at a time when some sectors of the Church were calling for greater openness. Some observers have speculated that John Paul II's rigorous defense of traditional sexual morality stems from his background in the Polish Church. For Polish bishops operating during Communist rule, when the state controlled virtually all of civil society, defense of the family amounted to a defense of one of the last realms of human freedom (Whale et al. 1980: 40–1). Sexual morality, moreover, was one of the main points of conflict between the Church and the communist state that counted on abortion as its main method of birth control. Thus, though never an easy matter, liberalizing abortion laws became considerably more contentious after Karol Wojtyla became Pope.

The second trend was the growth of antiabortion movements. When, in the 1960s and 1970s, tens of Western European and North American countries modified their laws on abortion, antiabortion groups were largely dormant. The 1973 United States Supreme Court decision in *Roe v. Wade*, however, prompted a massive conservative outcry and sowed the seeds of the global antiabortion movement. Few policy changes have incited a comparable degree of outrage. For conservatives, *Roe v. Wade* was a "bolt from the blue," for it took a belief they assumed to be a basic fact of life – that the embryo is a person – and "threw it into the realm of opinion" (Luker 1984: 140). Conservatives saw the legalization of elective abortion as an assault on motherhood, sex roles, and the origins of human life, and maintained that the denial of these values in one society would represent a defeat for all societies. Antiabortion activists organized to fight and defend their views in multiple arenas – in the courts, the legislature, outside clinics, and at U.N. conferences, and over Medicare funding, foreign aid, and federal research money. U.S. foes of abortion also helped organize similar movements in

Latin America. The antiabortion network Human Life International (HLI) has a regional office in Miami and affiliates in virtually every Latin American country.

Latin American antiabortion activists have attempted to manipulate principles of human rights to their advantage. Arguing that democratic states seeking to protect human rights must defend innocent fetal life and forbid abortion, opponents of abortion maintain that the right to life at conception is the logical fulfillment of international norms on human rights. Former Argentine Justice Minister Rodolfo Barra, for example, argues that constitutional protections for fetal life are necessary to implement the general principles established in the Declaration of Human Rights endorsed by the United Nations in 1948 (Barra 1997). In this way, antiabortion claims resonate with the human rights discourse deployed by new democratic governments to distinguish themselves from authoritarian predecessors. Antiabortion claims couched within a human rights discourse may have a stronger purchase in societies with bitter memories of authoritarian and totalitarian rule. To prevent a return to the past, when state power was used arbitrarily against human life, postauthoritarian societies have placed particular emphasis on laws to protect the weak and the innocent. In Germany in 1976, for example, the Constitutional Court struck down a liberal abortion law, explaining that constitutional protection of all forms of life was an explicit response to the experience of the Holocaust (Glendon 1987: 6).

The antiabortion movement has successfully resisted domestic proposals to liberalize abortion and helped create a climate in which few people are willing to advocate abortion rights. In Brazil in 1993, for example, Senator Eva Blay of São Paulo introduced a bill to Congress that would decriminalize abortions performed during the first trimester of pregnancy and guarantee women access to abortions in the public health system. Blay organized a seminar in Congress and invited prolife and prochoice speakers from all over Brazil to participate. To protest the seminar and the bill, an antiabortion group amassed in the corridors of the Senate, waved banners, and insulted the senator, who called congressional security to escort her out of the building. Some senators told Blay that her abortion bill was important for Brazil and that they were personally in favor of it, but would not endorse it for fear of losing votes.[8] After the return to democracy in Argentina, several bills to liberalize abortion were presented in Congress, but none were discussed in commission or within political parties. As Alberto Maglietti, Radical Party senator and author of one of the bills to decriminalize abortion, recalled: "No one has demonstrated interest in considering this bill. It is an impolitic issue for the political environment of our country. To speak publicly in favor of abortion is impolitic."[9]

---

[8] Interview with Eva Blay, Sao Paulo, September 5, 1997.
[9] Interview, Buenos Aires, July 21, 1998.

Nonetheless, Latin American countries have succeeded in enacting legislation on other "impolitic" and controversial gender issues. Divorce is a good example. As Chapter 4 showed, divorce was illegal in Brazil and Argentina until the 1970s and 1980s, largely due to Church opposition and legislators' fear of the Church. During military rule in Brazil and shortly after the democratic transition in Argentina, big coalitions of reformers organized in civil society and Congress to demand divorce. In response, the Church threatened politicians and created a climate of intimidation reminiscent of its behavior on abortion. Bishops and priests lobbied legislators, spoke against prodivorce politicians from the pulpit, and organized public demonstrations. In spite of this pressure, divorce was made legal in Brazil in 1977 and in Argentina in 1983. The eruption of conflict between the government and Church over human rights, economic policy, and/or education opened a window of opportunity for reformers to legalize divorce.

Why hasn't this occurred in the case of abortion? Put another way, why could reformers defeat the Church on divorce but not on abortion? The abortion issue generates a unique degree of political polarization and moral outrage. Opponents of abortion see their role as an absolutist defense of human life, a position that leaves little room for political compromise. Though opponents of divorce felt strongly about the need to defend the institution of indissoluble marriage, this view was not as firmly held nor as widely shared as the idea that abortion involves the taking of innocent life. Moreover, the movement backing legal divorce was bigger than the abortion rights movement. Divorce reformers included politicians from across the political spectrum, lawyers, judges, professional associations, feminists, and members of the media. Public opinion polls showed overwhelming public support for divorce. The coalition for abortion rights, by contrast, has rarely involved more than a few isolated politicians, some health practitioners, and the feminist reproductive rights movement, and public opinion is more ambivalent.

Several features of the sociology of abortion in Latin America make it difficult to mobilize a big coalition for abortion reform. Though abortion rates are high, antiabortion laws are rarely enforced and public opinion largely condemns abortion. Because abortion is illegal, it is difficult to gather data on the practice. Data in Table 6.1 are estimates based on hospital admittances for abortion complications, interviews with medical practitioners, and surveys of women about family planning.

Argentina was not included in the multicountry study. Still, estimates suggest that women undergo between 350,000 and 400,000 illegal abortions per year (Durand and Gutiérrez 1998: 33). Latin American abortion rates are higher than in other industrialized countries. Based on data from around 1995, the Alan Guttmacher Institute estimated the abortion rate in Latin America to be 37 per 1,000 women aged fifteen to forty-four. In the United States, the rate was 23 per 1,000 women; in Canada, 16; in Germany, 8; in England, 16; and in the Netherlands, 7 (Alan Guttmacher Institute 1999).

TABLE 6.1. *Incidence of Abortion in Latin America*

Country	Annual number of abortions	Rate per 1,000 women	Average number of abortions per woman	Percentage of pregnancies that end in abortion
Brazil	1,433,350	36.5	1.3	31
Chile	159,650	45.4	1.6	35
Colombia	288,400	33.7	1.2	26
Dominican Republic	82,500	43.7	1.5	28
Mexico	533,100	23.2	0.8	17
Peru	271,150	51.8	1.8	30
Total	2,768,150	33.9	1.2	

Source: Alan Guttmacher Institute (1994).

Punitive laws on abortion are hardly ever enforced. In Brazil, for example, women are rarely prosecuted for having an abortion, and even when the police are called upon to investigate an illegal abortion, most cases are rejected by the courts and archived. Some 53 percent of a sample of 765 abortion cases heard in a Sao Paulo court between 1970 to 1989 were archived. Only 4 percent of the cases led to a conviction (Ardaillon 1997: 111). Based on her laborious analysis of court records of abortion trials, Ardaillon concludes that society is not interested in punishing abortion: "It is as if there is an enormous social investment in [abortion's] prohibition and little interest in its de facto criminalization" (1997: 105). Even when cases are brought to trial, juries and judges are seldom willing to convict. In Chile, on the other hand, there is greater willingness on the part of doctors, nurses, prosecutors, and judges to enforce laws on abortion. Between 1980 and 1989, some 1,939 people were prosecuted for abortion in Santiago's courts (Casas 1996).

Lax enforcement means that the middle classes have access to safe abortions in private clinics. Consequently, many Latin American observers do not see a real "need" for the liberalization of abortion laws.[10] (By contrast, prohibitions on divorce cut directly at middle-class interests.) Latin America's poor, who endure abortions in clandestine and dangerous circumstances, are the primary victims of abortion's illegality. Poor women in urban and rural areas tend to depend on untrained providers or traditional methods known to induce abortions, and are susceptible to infection, hemorrhage,

---

[10] This statement is my personal observation based on extensive field research in several Latin American countries (Argentina, Brazil, Chile, Mexico, Peru), interviews with hundreds of people in the field and at international conferences, and shorter trips to other countries (Costa Rica, Nicaragua, Venezuela).

TABLE 6.2. *Percent of Respondents Who Approve of Abortion Under the Circumstances Specified, by Country, Early 1990s*

Country	Risk to mother's health	Child born handicapped	Mother unmarried	Couple do not want more children
Argentina	77	59	18	25
Brazil	84	51	13	15
Chile	75	41	7	14
France	92	83	24	40
Spain	82	72	29	31
United States	85	53	28	25
43-country total	82	68	31	36

Source: World Values Survey.

damage to uterus or cervix, and adverse reactions to drugs (Alan Guttmacher Institute 1994). Whereas just 13 percent of higher income urban women suffer from postabortion complications, 44 percent of poor urban women and 54 percent of poor rural women suffer from complications (ibid.). Only around half of these women are hospitalized for treatment of these problems. Thus, it is not surprising that the most vocal proponents of abortion reform are feminist activists with left-leaning tendencies and a concern for social justice.

Though abortion is widespread, surveys show that people tend to disapprove of abortion unless the mother's health is at risk or, more infrequently, in the event of fetal anomaly. Table 6.2 describes results from the World Values survey, a study taken in forty-three countries between 1991 and 1994. (Responses from France, Spain, and the United States are presented for the purposes of comparison.)

National polls conducted in Argentina, Brazil, and Chile lend additional support to these results, for they demonstrate public support for laws that permit abortion on narrow grounds but less support for elective abortion. (Due to the sensitive nature of the abortion issue, there are relatively few surveys on this question.) One survey of 500 Buenos Aires residents revealed that 54 percent favored permission for abortion on narrow grounds, while only 27 percent supported elective abortion (Dubkin 1994: 115). In Brazil, a Datafolha poll conducted in 1997 of São Paulo residents revealed that 56 percent felt abortion laws should stay the same (compared with 37 percent in 1994), while only 21 percent believed that the law should be more permissive (fully 43 percent of those surveyed in 1994 thought the law should be liberalized). Nineteen percent thought abortion should be decriminalized. (In 1994, 18 percent favored decriminalization) (*Folha de São Paulo*, August 28, 1997). In Chile, a poll conducted by a newspaper in 2000 revealed that 78 percent of respondents agreed that abortion should be permitted if the mother's life is in danger, 55 percent agreed in the case of rape, and 54 percent agreed if the fetus is deformed (Blofeld 2001: 19), suggesting that most people believe that Chile's outright prohibition on abortion should be relaxed.

With the exception of Chile, these public opinion surveys imply little public support for a substantial revision of abortion laws. Moreover, since the illegality of abortion poses little health risk to middle-class women, and abortion-related punishments are rarely enforced, most politicians see little to be gained by jumping onto an abortion rights bandwagon.[11] And there are many costs involved in advocating abortion rights in light of opposition from the Vatican, antiabortion movements, and national bishops' councils. In spite of the efforts of feminist reproductive rights movements and a growing international consensus that punitive abortion laws should be reconsidered, few parties or politicians in Latin America are willing to engage the issue. These common factors help explain the general failure to decriminalize abortion in Latin America. Yet as the following sections of this chapter show, there are important differences in the political climate surrounding abortion in Brazil, Argentina, and Chile. Reproductive rights movements have responded in distinct ways to the abortion stalemate and to the opportunity structures provided by the government in power and the presence of allies in Congress.

Brazil: The Emergence of a "Legal Abortion" Movement

Beginning in the mid-1980s, Brazilian reproductive rights activists organized a nationwide effort to encourage public hospitals to perform those abortions permitted by law (so-called legal abortions). Though the Brazilian Criminal Code of 1940 permits abortions on "compassionate" grounds (that is, for women who have been raped), no administrative procedures existed to allow women who relied on the public health system to have access to abortions under these circumstances. Fearing criminal prosecution, doctors were reluctant to perform abortions on women who had been raped. Without a judge's authorization, how could they be certain that the woman's claims about rape were true and that the abortion was therefore legal? Though the framers of Brazil's criminal code acknowledged the problem of doctors' legal liability when introducing permission for "compassionate" abortion, they neglected to stipulate professional standards for doctors confronted by

---

[11] Many Latin Americans practice a "double discourse" when it comes to abortion. According to Shepard, "This phrase is widely understood to signify the art of espousing traditional and repressive socio-cultural norms publicly, while ignoring – and often participating in – the widespread flouting of these norms in private. Thanks to the ubiquity of the double discourse, in most Latin American countries the reproductive and sexual choices open to citizens are much wider than the official policies would lead one to believe" (2000: 114).

women whose pregnancies resulted from rape.[12] As a result, most of the burden of verifying the rape fell on doctors, few of whom had the time or the resources for potentially lengthy investigations, and women were left unattended.

The legal abortion movement sought to institutionalize procedures for hospitals to establish the legality of an abortion. Linking feminist reproductive rights activists and NGOs, doctors, gynecologists, and other health practitioners,[13] members of the media, workers in the Ministry of Health, and some congressmen, the movement has been successful in building public awareness about legal abortion and securing some changes. In 1985, the Rio de Janeiro state legislature passed a law requiring public hospitals to attend to legal abortions. At the request of Rio's Archbishop, Dom Eugenio Salles, the state governor vetoed the law, though a Rio de Janeiro municipal ordinance was adopted later in the year with the same purpose (Linhares Barsted 1993). In 1989, the São Paulo city government under Workers' Party mayor Luiza Erundina created a service for legal abortions at the Jabaquara Hospital. (The service was later established in other hospitals around the city.) At Jabaquara, a commission of doctors and social workers was appointed to receive petitions from women seeking abortions and, on the basis of supporting documentation (a police report and medical exam verifying a rape, for example) and the period of gestation, to authorize or decline the abortion. Explicit police authorization was not required (Araújo 1993; Dacah 1993). Between 1989 and 1996, some 311 women requested abortions at the Jabaquara Hospital, and 109 abortions were performed. The primary rationale for denying the abortion was that the pregnancy had advanced beyond twelve weeks (*Fêmea*, August 1997). By the end of 1999, sixteen public hospitals in Brazil had introduced legal abortion services, several municipalities had approved laws authorizing such services, and approximately 400 legal abortions had been performed (Neto 1999; *Fêmea*, August 1999).

---

[12] The issue of doctor liability was amply considered by criminologists in the early twentieth century. Nelson Hungria, author of Brazil's criminal code, wrote that "to avoid abuses, a doctor should act only with conclusive proof of the alleged rape unless the event was widely known or the rapist had already been convicted" (1942: 274). He continued: "For his or her own safety, the doctor should obtain the consent of the woman or her legal representative in writing or in front of credible witnesses. If there is a suit against the rapist, it would be advisable to consult the judge and public prosecutor . . ." (ibid.). Spanish criminologist Jiménez de Asúa acknowledged that without administrative procedures, the best and most reputable physicians would be the most reluctant to risk their careers by performing abortions, unfairly leaving women to abort on their own (1942: 393–4).

[13] The Brazilian Federation of Gynecological and Obstetrical Societies created, in 1996, a National Commission on the Legal Interruption of Pregnancy (Comissão Nacional de Interrupção da Gestação Prevista por Lei) and organized an Interprofessional Forum on the Realization of Legal Abortion (Fórum Interprofissional sobre Atendimento ao Aborto Previsto por Lei) to orient medical professionals (Neto 1999: 1).

To generalize these experiences for Brazil as a whole, two legislators from the Workers' Party introduced a bill (called the "legal abortion" bill) to the national Congress in 1991. The bill would require *all* of the country's public hospitals to perform abortions on women who had been raped or whose lives were at risk. Following the example of the municipal regulations established in São Paulo, the bill establishes that women can petition for an abortion by presenting either a police report or a report of an official medical exam (attesting to the occurrence of a rape) to a local health board. Provided that the board grants its approval, the local public health service would have to perform the abortion within seven days of the presentation of the petition.[14] The bill received support from feminist groups, labor unions, medical associations, members of the judiciary, the National Health Council, National Council on Population and Development, and even some Protestant priests. Feminist groups also organized a nationwide campaign in support of the bill, part of which involved gathering signatures (in places as exotic as Ipanema Beach in the city of Rio de Janeiro) on thousands of postcards to send to Congress.

Not surprisingly, the legal abortion bill has provoked vehement opposition from the Roman Catholic Church and antiabortion groups, with the latter lobbying fiercely for its defeat, even sending members to hold prayer services in the halls of Congress. The Brazilian Bishops' Council (CNBB) made a passionate appeal to legislators to vote against the bill, declaring that abortion "is always a grave and unacceptable assault on the fundamental right to life." Citing Pope John Paul II's encyclical *Evangelium vitae*, the bishops declared that whatever reasons, "as grave and dramatic as they seem, can never justify the deliberate suppression of an innocent being" (CNBB 1997). Supporters framed the bill as a question of social justice, arguing that the bill sought merely to implement the fifty-seven-year-old criminal code to allow poor women access to legal abortions. The antiabortion movement, by contrast, attempted to turn debate on the bill into a referendum on the morality of abortion after rape. The CNBB stated: "In the case of rape, the human being conceived is totally innocent and defenseless. How can it be punished with death?"

In spite of this pressure, the bill was approved by the Chamber of Deputies' Committee on Social Security and the Family in 1995, and in 1997 was approved by one vote in the Chamber of Deputies' Constitutional Committee. Interestingly, even some those committee members affiliated with the Catholic Caucus (Grupo Parlamentar Católico, or GPC) voted in favor of legal abortion (Aldana Santin 2000: 2). As is the usual practice on controversial social issues, no major political party took an official position, leaving legislators to "vote their conscience." Nor did President Cardoso make any public statement about the bill. Nonetheless, abortion opponents have

[14] Projecto de Lei (bill) 20/91.

succeeded in preventing the bill from being considered by the entire chamber and then passed to the Senate. By 2002, the vote of the whole chamber had been delayed several times.

According to a survey conducted by the feminist lobby CFEMEA in 1999, the vast majority of Brazilian legislators support the idea of legal abortion. Fully 87 percent of those who responded to the survey (a total of 273 deputies and senators)[15] endorsed the idea that the public health system should perform those abortions permitted by law. Thirty-six percent of legislators were favorable to expanding the conditions of legal abortion, while 42 percent believed the law should stay as it is (that is, permitting abortions in the event of rape or a risk to the mother's life). Nine percent expressed support for a law that would permit abortion under any circumstance, and only 7 percent believed abortion should be banned absolutely (Rodrigues 2000: 2–3). Legislators' views resemble those of the general public: 73 percent of those surveyed in a 1997 poll of São Paulo residents approved of the legal abortion bill (*Folha de São Paulo*, August 28, 1997). As Rodrigues notes, the problem faced by advocates of abortion rights is not so much conquering legislative opinion but generating enough political will to put the abortion issue on the congressional agenda. Abortion is not among the priority of most legislators, even those who express sympathy for the goals of the reproductive rights movement (ibid.).

In late 1998, the legal abortion movement scored a major victory when the Ministry of Health issued a rule to standardize the treatment of victims of sexual violence in public hospitals. Elaborated by officials in the Women's Health Unit, the rule (*norma técnica*) directs public hospitals to perform abortions at the request of women who have been raped; to conduct complete physical exams, give psychological consultations, and perform laboratory tests for sexually transmitted diseases and HIV/AIDS; and to gather forensic evidence for the prosecution of the aggressor. The rule guarantees that legal abortions be attended in Brazil regardless of the situation in Congress, and reflects a willingness on the part of senior officials in the Cardoso administration to engage the abortion issue, though not to endorse its legalization. (The Health Minister at the time, José Serra, was the governing party's candidate for president in the 2002 elections.) Feminist reproductive rights advocates, however, believe that a national law is still necessary since the Health Ministry's rule can be revoked by the Executive at any time (*Fêmea*, August 1999).[16]

---

[15] A total of 313 deputies and senators (53 percent of Congress) responded to the survey.

[16] Already in 1998, antiabortion deputy Severino Cavalcanti introduced a bill to Congress to suspend the Health Ministry's decree. In 1999 and 2000, respectively, the Committee on Social Security and the Family and the Constitutional Committee of the Chamber of Deputies voted to reject Cavalcanti's proposal. Cavalcanti and other abortion opponents argued that the Health Ministry's rule represented the first step toward the legalization of abortion (*Fêmea*, August 1999).

Meanwhile, a routine process of criminal code reform created the possibility of stretching Brazil's abortion law. In 1998 and 1999, a commission of legal experts deliberated over reforms to the 1940 Criminal Code.[17] In 1999, this committee presented its proposal, which upheld the general criminalization of abortion, to the Minster of Justice. According to the commission's only female member, there was no discussion about decriminalization, since they felt that any mention of this possibility would generate so much controversy in Congress as to preclude approval of a new Code (Wiecko de Castilho 1999: 2). Nonetheless, the proposal contained several changes to abortion law. First, it enabled judges to waive criminal penalties against women who had committed the crime of abortion. Second, it expanded the categories of legally permissible abortion to include three cases: (1) to prevent a grave and irreversible damage to the health of the pregnant woman; (2) when the pregnancy results from a crime against sexual freedom, and (3) in the event of defects that render the fetus inviable (*Jornal da Rede Saúde*, no. 18, September 1999). If approved by Congress, the commission's proposals will represent a small, though significant, liberalization of abortion law in the country, particularly the article permitting abortion for a risk to the pregnant woman's *health*, not just her life. Yet the process of criminal code reform has been stalled by high turnover in the Ministry of Justice and the different ideas of each new minister. (Six different individuals held the post of minister of justice during the second term of President Fernando Henrique Cardoso alone, which ran from 1998 to 2002.) Reportedly, however, the president intervened in at least one instance to make sure that the proposed changes with respect to abortion would be preserved in spite of personnel changes (ibid.). By 2002, the new code had still not been sent to Congress.

Why has Brazil been able to entertain a debate about legal abortion, and even to contemplate, in the criminal code reform, the expansion of conditions for legal abortion? In the first place, no Brazilian president since the return to democracy has adopted a firm position against abortion nor allied with the antiabortion movement. The Brazilian government has not tried to cultivate the favor of the Vatican by repressing the reproductive rights movement or attempting to ban abortion outright. By contrast, the position of the Brazilian government in international conferences, evidenced by its leadership in the SLAC coalition at Beijing Plus Five, has been relatively progressive (see note 7). Moreover, some sectors of the government endorse the goals of the legal abortion movement. For example, the National Human Rights Program, released in May 2002 by the Ministry of Justice, proposes that "abortion be considered a public health issue, with guaranteed access

---

[17] Traditionally, criminal codes are divided into two parts: the general part, which deals with overall principles, and the special part, which defines crimes. The general part of the code was reformed in the early 1980s, but a committee to consider changes to the special part of the code was created only in 1997.

to legal abortions in the public health services" (Ministerio da Justiça 2002). Though no Brazilian president has actually advocated liberalizing abortion, their failure vehemently to oppose abortion generates political space for the legal abortion movement to operate. Most Brazilian political parties, while they will not support abortion, will also not defend restricting it. When, in 1995, a constitutional amendment proposal to include a clause protecting life at the moment of conception came up for a vote, the whips of all major political parties, in a departure from the normal practice, instructed their deputies to vote against the proposal; only one party left the vote open (*Fêmea*, April 1996). As noted earlier, party leaders rarely close the vote on controversial social issues.

The reproductive rights movement has allies in the leftist Workers' Party (PT). Though the party had only around 10 percent of the seats in Congress in the 1990s, PT deputies have been the most prominent sponsors of bills to liberalize abortion. Of course, not all of the PT supports abortion rights. Historically, the party has wavered on the issue of abortion because of close ties between some sectors of the PT and the Church. For example, in the 1994 elections, the PT party platform initially endorsed the decriminalization of abortion. Under pressure from the Church, however, the party later removed mention of abortion from its program (Haas 2001: 263). Nonetheless, the presence of the PT in Congress and the willingness of several PT deputies to serve as advocates of abortion reform keeps abortion on the congressional agenda. In Argentina and Chile, by contrast, most presidents have actively opposed abortion, and feminist reproductive rights movements have found few allies in Congress willing to raise the abortion issue (though in Argentina, feminists found allies willing to oppose conservative efforts to ban abortion altogether). As a result, the movements there have focused more on expanding the state's commitment to family planning and women's reproductive health and less on the legality of abortion.

Argentina: Policy Stalemate

In dramatic contrast to the situation in Brazil, the Argentine government, at least under President Carlos Menem in the 1990s, has actively opposed abortion. In 1994, Menem proposed that the presidents gathered for the Fourth Ibero-American Summit in Cartagena, Colombia, sign a declaration that explicitly condemned abortion. Although Menem was unable to convince the other presidents, he received a letter from Pope John Paul II thanking him for "his initiatives aimed at promoting family values and defending life."[18] Then, the Argentine government spearheaded opposition to abortion at the Cairo and Beijing conferences, developing, together with the Vatican and Iran, reservations to the consensus documents declaring that the concept of

---

[18] *Clarín*, July 1, 1994.

reproductive health not be interpreted to endorse abortion (Dinardi, Gogna, and Ramos: 11–12). In 1998, Menem issued a presidential decree declaring March 25 the "Day of the Unborn Child." (The date was selected to coincide with the Roman Catholic Feast of the Annuciation.) With copious references to international agreements such as the Universal Declaration of Human Rights, the Convention on Children's Rights, and even the Cairo and Beijing conferences, the decree declared that "the international community has identified the child as a dignified subject of special consideration [*un subjeto digno de especial consideración*]" (Decreto 1406/98). Though the text insisted that "the protection of life is not an ideological or religious question, but rather something that emanates from human nature," most Argentine observers believed that the decree was part of a governmental effort to charm the Vatican.

Menem attempted to use the process of constitutional reform to advance his antiabortion position. During the constitutional convention held in 1994, Menem and his justice minister, Rodolfo Barra, attempted to add a phrase to the Constitution granting the right to life "at conception in the maternal womb until natural death," in order to produce legal closure on the issues of abortion and euthanasia. At a dinner in the presidential palace hosted for delegates from the ruling Peronist party, Menem asked the delegates to work as hard as possible to guarantee inclusion of the phrase in the Constitution.[19] Church officials joined with antiabortion movements and with the conservative "Tradition, Family and Property" group to lobby delegates, organize demonstrations, and circulate petitions. Cardinal Antonio Quarracino, Archbishop of Buenos Aires, declared on television that "delegates who vote for abortion will pass into history as criminals, because abortion is, was, and will be simply and terribly a crime: the killing of an innocent being."[20] Two other proposals to ban abortion, one by veteran Peronist politician Antonio Cafiero and another by the leader of right-wing party MODIN, were also presented to the convention.

Opposition political parties, feminists, and the medical and legal communities mobilized to defeat these antiabortion proposals. As in Brazil, Argentine parties were unwilling to advocate for abortion rights but also unwilling to support outright bans on abortion. (Nonetheless, there was no Argentine equivalent to the Brazilian Workers' Party that gave the reproductive rights movement a toehold in Congress through the actions of sympathetic legislators.) Legislators from the opposition Radical and Frepaso parties claimed that delegates lacked a mandate to legislate on the abortion issue, since no political party had mentioned the issue in its electoral campaign for delegates to the convention. Moreover, the framework agreement signed by Alfonsín and Menem (called the "Pacto de Olivos") precluded

[19] *Clarín*, July 9, 1994.
[20] *Página 12*, July 12, 1994

the constitutional convention from introducing any modification to the first part of the Constitution elaborating "declarations, rights and guarantees."[21] These procedural issues allowed people to oppose the antiabortion proposal without having to express support for abortion.

Meanwhile, over a hundred women's groups formed an alliance (called MADEL) to defeat the "life at conception" proposal. MADEL lobbied delegates, organized street demonstrations, and disseminated their arguments through the news media. In the process, "the women's movement underwent a hitherto unheard-of political and organizational experience that marked a turning point in its history" (Dinardi et al.: 13). Several major newspapers and magazines at the time provided extensive coverage of the abortion debates and results of investigative reports into women's varying experiences with and attitudes toward abortion (ibid.). Feminist legislators and activists from the governing Peronist party confronted the president's position. The National Women's Council, in spite of being organizationally dependent on the presidency, made public their opposition to the "life at conception" clause at press conferences and open letters.[22] The position of Peronist women angered party leaders close to the president. After the convention, the president of the Women's Council, Virginia Franganillo, was asked to resign from her position. Following the 1995 elections, the council was completely reorganized and staffed with women known not to be feminists.[23] In the end, the convention delegates implicitly rejected the "life at conception" proposal by failing to consider it in the plenary.

The antiabortion movement and the support it has received from the Menem presidency limited the political space for the feminist reproductive rights movement and its medical and legal allies to advocate the liberalization of abortion laws. Instead, the movement focused on expanding the state's commitment to women's reproductive health through the provision of family planning services and sex education. The ties forged between feminist groups in the constitutional reform fight of 1994 created an organizational base for this activism. Feminist groups and women legislators introduced a family planning bill to Congress, which was approved by the Chamber of Deputies in 1995. In the Senate, however, various senators proposed to prohibit distribution of IUDs, which they considered abortifacients, and to require that minors receive parental authorization before receiving contraceptives. The acrimonious debate delayed voting on the bill for so long that it had to be thrown out. Then, in April 2001, the Chamber of Deputies

---

[21] *La Nación*, July 11, 1994.

[22] In contrast to the alliance of women's groups, composed largely of those sympathetic to the political opposition, the Peronist women distinguished between their opposition to Menem's abortion proposal and their overall support for him (see *Página 12*, July 17, 1994). The issue of opposition to, or alignment with, the government precluded the formation of an alliance between women from the Peronist party and women from the opposition.

[23] Interview with Virginia Franganillo, Buenos Aires, July 17, 1998.

approved a similar bill, called the "Law on Sexual Health and Responsible Procreation," which proposed to create a national family planning program that would provide contraceptives in public hospitals, work on breast and cervical cancer prevention, and offer information about sexual health and the prevention of STDs (*Clarín*, April 19, 2001).[24] Meanwhile, ten Argentine provinces, the city of Buenos Aires, and several municipalities introduced legislation on reproductive health (Ramos 2001; Schlueter 2000).

After Menem left office in 1999, the political climate changed. The next president, Radical Party leader Fernando de la Rúa, still opposed abortion, though not as vigorously. Argentina ceased to ally automatically with the Vatican in international forums, publicly recognized that women's reproductive and sexual rights constitute part of human rights, and acknowledged the connection between high abortion rates and women's lack of access to health services.[25] In his speech before the United Nations in June 2000, Argentine foreign minister Enrique Candioti departed from previous policy by declaring that sexual and reproductive rights are a part of women's human rights (Candioti 2000: 4). The government drafted a federal plan on maternal mortality that called for improvement of family planning services, sex education, the prevention of sexual violence, and the reduction of unwanted pregnancies (Consejo Nacional de la Mujer 2000).

The government's relatively more liberal position created space for a Supreme Court ruling in January 2001 that authorized the abortion of a fetus suffering from anencephaly in the seventh month of pregnancy. Two lower courts had denied permission for the abortion, and the Supreme Court, for the first time in fourteen years, called the justices in from a summer recess to discuss the issue and submit its decision. In their public statements, the justices were careful to differentiate their decision from a more general permission for abortion, though they made clear that the juridical good they aimed to protect was the mother's mental health (*Clarín*, January 12, 2001).

Chile: Abortion Illegal Under any Circumstance

The Chilean Criminal Code, which dates from 1875, does not admit any exceptions to the criminalization of abortion. Since 1875, there have been

---

[24] The law is ambiguous on several points. Though the bill requires that public hospitals distribute contraceptives for free, and that these contraceptives be "nonabortive, impermanent, and reversible," it does not include a list of contraceptives. Rather than directly address the question of contraceptive provision to minors, the bill merely states that the law would not contradict the principle of parental power, nor the rights of children. Finally, the bill establishes that health professionals who find the use of contraceptives morally unacceptable can exercise a "right to free conscience" and opt out of applying the law (*Clarín*, April 19, 2001).

[25] Interview with National Women's Council president Carmen Storani, Buenos Aires, August 2000.

four attempts to redraft the criminal code, at least one of which proposed to decriminalize "compassionate" abortion.[26] Yet the reform was never enacted, and abortion continued to be criminalized under all circumstances. Then, in 1931, President Carlos Ibáñez promulgated a series of reforms to the Health Code, which included the legalization of therapeutic abortion and sterilization. The new article read:

> Only with therapeutic objectives may one interrupt a pregnancy or perform an intervention to sterilize a woman. The documented opinion of three doctors is required. When it is not possible to proceed in the above said manner, due to the urgency of the situation or the lack of doctors in the area, the doctor and witnesses should document what has been done, with the doctor remaining in charge of the depositions. (Article 226 of decree law 226, published in the *Diario Oficial*, May 29, 1931)

The law thus authorized doctors to perform abortions and sterilizations with "therapeutic objectives." Though no precise definition was offered of "therapeutic," it is commonly understood to refer to medical procedures necessary to avert a serious risk to the life or health of the pregnant woman or the child.

Chilean abortion law stayed the same until 1989, when the military government, on the eve of its departure from power, removed the Health Code's article authorizing doctors to perform therapeutic abortions. The new code stated: "It is prohibited to carry out any action whose objective is to provoke an abortion" (Law 18,826, enacted on September 15, 1989). The reform originated in a motion by a navy admiral, head of the government's legislative commission, and followed consultations among the governing junta and several doctors, academics, and one member of the Pope's international commission on theology (two of these experts, both from the University of Chile, expressed support for therapeutic abortion) (Valenzuela Carrazola: 3–4). The admiral later explained that the reform reflected the military government's commitment to protect human life and human rights (Casas 1993: 38–9). The change was not made public. One researcher who studied the issue in the early 1990s noted that only a few of the employees she interviewed in hospitals were aware that permission for therapeutic abortion had been repealed (Valenzeula Carrazola: 4). The modification of the Health Code

---

[26] The reform was ordered in a decree issued by President Carlos Ibáñez in 1928. The authors of the proposal, appeals court judges Eduardo Erazo and Rafael Fontecilla, followed many other Latin American countries in importing the theories about "compassionate" abortion elaborated by Spanish criminologist Luis Jiménez de Asúa at the Third Panamerican Scientific Congress. The proposed Article 92 read: "The woman who becomes pregnant as the result of rape may obtain permission from a judge to interrupt her pregnancy when, in consideration of her dignity, the circumstances under which conception occurred led to turmoil or deep moral suffering" (Ministerio de Justicia 1929: 33). Erazo and Fontecilla believed that it was unnecessary explicitly to decriminalize therapeutic abortion since this was already justified by the concept of "state of necessity" (Ministerio de Justicia 1929: xviii).

effectively placed Chile, along with El Salvador, Andorra, and Malta, into the small group of countries where abortion is forbidden under all circumstances.

As of 2002, Chilean law continued to forbid abortion under any circumstance. Since the return to civilian rule in 1990, virtually no politician or government official has been willing to entertain debates about liberalizing abortion, and only one bill has been presented in Congress to reinstate therapeutic abortion. This bill was sponsored by a group of deputies from the Socialist and Democratic (PPD) parties and led by Adriana Muñoz, a feminist (Camara de Diputados, Session 41, September 17, 199, Boletín 499–07). The bill received support from various medical practitioners (e.g., Gayán 1993), but generated consternation among the women who had united in the Concertación de Mujeres por la Democracia (the multiparty women's alliance that helped usher in the democratic transition), since they had earlier agreed to avoid controversy by suppressing issues such as divorce and abortion during Chile's first democratic government (1990–4).[27] The bill was archived before reaching the floor of the Chamber, and Muñoz was vilified by abortion opponents, leading to her defeat in the parliamentary elections of 1993. Since then, few legislators have been willing to express any support for changes to abortion law, ceding much of the initiative on the abortion issue to parties of the right. Only the Socialist Party and the Communist Party have officially endorsed the reinstatement of therapeutic abortion.[28]

Chilean abortion opponents argue that permission for therapeutic abortion is medically and legally unnecessary, since advances in medical science have greatly reduced the number of circumstances in which the life of the mother and the fetus come into conflict. In these rare events, however, the law does not punish actions taken by doctors to defend the mother's life. Chile's conservative think tank Libertad y Desarollo (Liberty and Development) argues that Chile's Health Code "does not punish those actions that, being necessary to protect the life of the mother and executed with that intention, endanger the life of the child" (Libertad y Desarollo 1991). In other words, the law permits therapeutic abortion, as long as it is an indirect consequence of a medical procedure and not its principal aim:

If, for example, the life of a pregnant woman is threatened by an infection that requires major surgery, from which the death of the fetus could result, the performance of such an operation is permitted according to current legislation ... because the operation in the example is conducted with the intention of saving the mother's life and not with the intention of causing an abortion.... (Ibid.)

---

[27] Muñoz argued that she did not break the pact since her bill proposed not to legalize abortion, but rather to reinstate an old law permitting therapeutic abortion. Interview, Santiago, April 24, 1998.

[28] See, e.g., the statement of Socialist Party president Camilo Escalona to *La Tercera*, February 16, 1995.

These arguments resemble St. Thomas Aquinas's dictum that the moral status of an action lies in its intention and recall early Roman Catholic doctrine, which did not oppose therapeutic abortion.[29]

Most legislative activity on abortion in Chile has surrounded proposals from politicians on the right seeking to extend prison terms for those convicted of abortion crimes. One of the bills, sponsored by Unión Demócrata Independiente (UDI) Senator Hernan Larraín, introduces the concept of "effective repentance" to create incentives for women to help the police apprehend abortion practitioners by granting them a reduction in sentence. The bill also proposes to redefine abortion from a "crime against public morality" to "homicide" (Blofeld 2001: 20; Larraín 1994). The bill was approved by the Constitutional Commission and the Health Commission in 1998, but in 1999 was defeated by a narrow margin on the Senate floor, with thirteen senators voting in favor and fifteen against. (In line with Chilean political practice, eight senators who had "paired" their votes abstained from the final vote.)[30] Larraín reported in an interview that he won even though the bill lost because he managed to divert the terms of the Chilean abortion debate away from the issue of liberalization and toward the question of punitive strategies and whether abortion should be considered the legal equivalent of homicide (Blofeld 2001: 53).

This political climate precludes much activism on abortion, but Chilean feminist activists have still attempted to expand the state's commitment to reproductive health. Historically, the Chilean state has taken a relatively active role in family planning. Beginning in the 1960s, when the Christian Democratic government of the period sought to combat extremely high rates of maternal and infant mortality stemming from abortion complications, the government has provided family planning services through the public health system. Conservatives made some efforts to shut down family planning during the Pinochet dictatorship, but these were ultimately unsuccessful. In theory, contraceptives are available to all women of child-bearing age. In practice, there is considerable resistance to providing minors with contraceptives without parental authorization. Feminists and health officials also complain that sterilization is difficult to obtain. Regulations dating from 1975 permit the public health system to sterilize only women meeting all of the following criteria: over thirty years old, more than four children, a history of at least three caesarian sections, medical reasons justifying the operation, and the documented consent of their spouse.[31] In the 1990s, among the goals

---

[29] As Chapter 2 mentioned, many theologians have felt that if abortion is the indirect consequence of a medical procedure designed to save the mother, it may be morally valid, since the primary intention is to protect life, not abort the fetus. As a result, some Church thinkers voiced support for therapeutic abortion until 1930, when the encyclical *Casti connubii* harshly condemned abortion, including therapeutic abortion (Noonan 1970).

[30] Communication between Mireya Zuleta Reyes and Bonnie Shepard, November 2, 1999.

[31] Interview with Rene Castro, director of the Maternal and Infant Health Program, Ministry of Health, Santiago, April, 1998.

of the Ministry of Health's Maternal and Infant Health Programs was the reduction of unwanted pregnancies and the risks associated with abortion (Ministerio de Salud 1993: 5).

In the mid- to late 1990s, Chilean feminist politicians drafted a reproductive rights bill similar to that approved by the Chamber of Deputies in Argentina. In 2000, Socialist deputy Fanny Pollarolo and nine others introduced to Congress a bill that would guarantee citizens the right to sex education and contraception. One deputy who cosponsored the reproductive rights bill affirmed to the press the existence of an agreement not to discuss the issue of abortion.[32] The Open Forum on Health and Reproductive Rights (an NGO) has held meetings and demonstrations every year to commemorate the Latin American Day for the Decriminalization of Abortion, but when they circulated a draft bill to introduce permission for abortion on several grounds (risk to the mother, rape, and fetal anomaly), no politician was willing to touch it.[33]

Conclusion

The common failure of Latin American countries to liberalize abortion, in spite of their openness to gender-related policy changes in other areas, confirms that gender policy issues need to be disaggregated. We need to reconsider the impression left by the experiences of the United States and Western Europe, where policies on women's parental and property rights, liberal divorce, and elective abortion changed sequentially between the 1960s and 1980s. The simultaneity of these reforms suggested that they were part of a single package, that change on one issue would lead to change on the next. Latin American experiences show otherwise and imply that abortion is a unique policy issue. Few other policies generate a similar amount of moral controversy and political polarization. Abortion invokes deep questions: As Kristin Luker puts it, abortion is merely "the tip of the iceberg" beneath which are complex world views about motherhood and morality (1984). The fact that abortion-related penalties are rarely enforced, that middle-class women have access to safe abortions, and that the majority of respondents in public opinion surveys see little need to change the law makes politicians and parties more reluctant to endorse change on abortion than on other gender issues.

Latin American experiences with abortion also suggest that abortion policy may be getting harder to change over time. In the 1980s, the Vatican became a more committed and effective opponent of abortion, and began to use international conferences in the 1990s to advance its position. Meanwhile, the antiabortion movement mobilized on a global scale in reaction

---

[32] *El Mercurio*, April 17, 2001.
[33] Interview with Lidia Casas, Santiago, April 14, 1998.

to liberalizing changes in North America and Western Europe. By the time the abortion debate arrived in Latin America, reproductive rights advocates had to confront these highly organized foes, as well as a global climate in which antiabortion activists were scoring major victories. In the late 1980s and early 1990s, several Eastern European countries, including Poland, the Slovak Republic, and Hungary, restricted liberal communist-era abortion laws after democratic transitions (Githens 1996; Zielinska 2000).[34]

Two scenarios might change the outlook for abortion politics in the region: The growing participation of women in political decision making and the increase in religious competition. Women's presence in political leadership has grown steadily. From an average of 9 percent in 1990, by 2002, women's representation in the lower houses of Congress had increased to 15 percent. Women's share of the Senate grew from an average of 5 percent in 1990 to 12 percent in 2002. And whereas women occupied 9 percent of ministerial posts in 1990, by 2002 this had increased to an average of 13 percent and as high as 40 percent in some countries (Htun 2002; Inter-American Dialogue 2001). Will these women produce change on abortion? There is some reason to be skeptical. In the past, women seen as defenders of abortion rights have been politically handicapped. For example, Graciela Fernandez Meijide lost the election for governor of Buenos Aires province in Argentina in 1999 after she failed effectively to respond to charges from her opponent that she supported abortion.[35] After presenting a bill to Congress to reintroduce therapeutic abortion, Chilean deputy Adriana Muñoz was defeated at the polls after being pilloried by the right opposition and labeled an "abortionist." Biases against women in politics are made worse by suspicions that women seek radical changes to gender relations. Many women in power fail to advocate on behalf of women's rights. Data gathered in Argentina between 1993 and 1995, for example, showed that 58 percent of women legislators presented no bills related to women's rights issues (Htun and Jones 2002).

On the other hand, there are examples of women leaders spearheading significant changes to abortion policy. In 2000, Rosario Robles, then mayor of Mexico City for the left PRD party, introduced legislation to modify the

---

[34] In Poland in 1993, a 1956 law that permitted elective abortion during the first trimester of pregnancy was replaced by a law that criminalized abortion except for medical grounds or when the pregnancy resulted from rape. Bishops of the Roman Catholic Church, who gained credibility and stature with the democratic transition, were instrumental in securing the abortion restrictions. Popular support for changing the abortion law was enhanced by the fact that the old liberal law was associated with the communist past (Githens 1996; Zielinska 2000). This was not the general pattern in all of Eastern Europe, however. In countries such as the Czech Republic and Bulgaria, permissive abortion laws were hardly affected by the democratic transition. In Romania, antiabortion laws were abolished after the fall of Ceausescu (Githens 1996).

[35] *Clarín*, October 19, 1999.

city's criminal code on abortion matters. The proposal, approved through support by the PRD and PRI parties, added two additional grounds for legal abortion: if the mother's health (not just her life) is at risk and if the fetus has birth defects. Robles agreed with the feminist movement that abortion is a public health problem posing grave risks for women, but she also sought to exploit the abortion issue for political advantage. Earlier in the year, the PAN-dominated legislature of the northern state of Guanajuato had voted to rescind permission for abortion for women who had been raped, triggering nationwide protest and indignation. Robles sought to distinguish her party from the conservative tendencies of the PAN and to exploit public fears that the PAN (whose leader, Vicente Fox, had recently been elected to the presidency) would impose a strict moral order in the country.

Growing religious diversity in Latin America is another factor that might affect abortion politics. The growth of Protestant evangelical churches,[36] particularly in Brazil and Chile, has reduced Roman Catholic hegemony in the region. We might think that the weakening of the Church would undermine some of the organized opposition to abortion. Brazil's giant *Igreja Universal do Reino de Deus*, for example, supports women's right to abortion in the event of rape.[37] Yet there are some reasons to doubt that Protestant growth will contribute to abortion law liberalization. Many Protestant churches, particularly Pentecostal churches, are equally or even more conservative than the Roman Catholic Church when it comes to gender issues. Most endorse a strict sexual division of labor based on male authority and female submissiveness in family life (Steigenga and Smilde 1999: 173).[38] Moreover, the Roman Catholic Church has responded to the Protestant threat with renewed attempts at evangelization and institutional reform. Between the late 1970s and late 1990s, the Church increased the number of bishops and parishes and successfully recruited seminarians at higher rates than before (Gill 1999: 33–4). Religious competition has reinvigorated, rather than marginalized, the presence of the Roman Catholic Church in political life.

When and if Latin American countries relax restrictions on abortion, their eventual policies may be more likely to resemble some European laws than

---

[36] In Latin America, it is common to refer to all Protestant churches as "evangelicals." The term includes both mainstream churches (Baptists, Presbyterians, Lutherans, etc.) and Pentecostals. The latter are the most active evangelicals in Latin America. More than the mainstream churches, Pentecostals emphasize "born again" conversions, fighting against "worldly" things in order to be in communion with Christ, charismatic acts such as speaking in tongues and divine healing, and millennialism (Steigenga and Smilde 1999: 176).

[37] Interview with Federal Deputy Aldir Cabral, pastor of the *Universal*, Rio de Janeiro, June 2002.

[38] Nonetheless, some studies have shown that in practice, participation in Pentecostal sects has enabled women to transcend their traditional gender roles and given women greater confidence (Steigenga and Smilde 1999: 173–5).

the permissive policies of the United States.[39] European laws, particularly the French law, are notable for their attempt to steer a middle course between the different values invested in the abortion debate. The first article of the French law, for example, declares that the "law guarantees the respect of every human being from the commencement of life" (quoted in Glendon 1987: 16). Yet in fact, the French permit abortion under a fairly wide range of circumstances, for the law allows abortion through the tenth week of pregnancy for women who claim to be in "distress."[40] The significant point here is that the law simultaneously permits abortion while purporting to answer one of the major concerns of antiabortion activists – the negation of fetal life – by admitting rather bluntly that questions of human life are at stake. At least in part because of the compromise forged by the wording of the abortion law, France has escaped the public conflict and polarization plaguing abortion in the United States (Glendon 1987; Outshoorn 1996). If Latin America is to liberalize abortion, reformers may need to seek compromise rather than outright victory.

[39] My characterization of U.S. law as permissive refers to the letter of the law only, since one must distinguish between abortion's legal status and its availability. By the latter criteria, U.S. policy is restrictive for, in contrast to many European countries, the public health system (Medicare) does not fund abortions.

[40] The law requires that women undergo counseling prior to abortion and imposes a one-week waiting period. There are no sanctions against women who *pretend* to be in distress, and the state pays 70 percent of the cost of nontherapeutic abortions (and 100 percent of medically necessary abortions).

7

Conclusion

Policy makers in Argentina, Brazil, and Chile faced tough choices on abortion, divorce, and gender equality in the family. The results were often surprising. Conservative military rulers adopted liberalizing reforms on family equality, sometimes more easily than democratic governments. In spite of their moral authority and strength in civil society, Roman Catholic bishops could be defeated, paving the way for the legalization of divorce. In an era when the majority of Western countries introduced elective abortion, Argentina and Brazil kept abortion a crime and Chile banned abortion under all circumstances. Chile modernized its economy and consolidated its democracy, but held on to the most conservative and restrictive laws on gender in Latin America.

Propositions

What propositions can be gleaned from these puzzling experiences? In the first place, *transitions to democracy will not necessarily lead to the liberalization of laws on gender and may in fact lead to the opposite.* The democracies of North America and Western Europe have developed some of the most liberal laws on gender in the world. Abortion and divorce are permitted, and women enjoy equal rights. Western laws have long served as models for legal reform in the rest of the world, particularly Latin America. It thus seemed safe to assume that when Latin American countries made the transition from authoritarian military regimes to democracy in the 1980s, they would seek to emulate the West's gender regime. Yet laws in Western countries are a product not merely of democracy but a long tradition of constitutional liberalism and the sturdiness of the institutions that sustain that tradition. Liberal traditions uphold the separation of the state from religion and the effective juridical – not just political – equality of citizens. Liberal countries believe that the state should exercise self-restraint in order not to infringe on the individual rights of citizens. It is harder for countries to construct these institutions of constitutional liberalism than to adopt electoral procedures and permit competitive party politics.

The failure of countries passing through the "third wave" of democratic transitions to modify all laws to conform to principles of gender equality and individual freedom should thus come as no surprise. What is surprising, perhaps, is that democracies may be more conservative than authoritarian regimes. By enabling citizen groups and institutions to mobilize and express their views, democracy opens the door to both liberal and illiberal influences on gender policy. While liberal issue networks seeking legal conformity with global standards and egalitarian principles may pressure governments, so may conservative networks and churches. The political clout and influence of churches is greater, moreover, in countries that lack a history of strong civil society organization. When liberal reformers are able to change policy, their success is not the automatic triumph of democracy but a result of shifts in power configurations that overcome the status quo.

The weakness of feminist movements and scarcity of women in politics are signs of, but not the main reasons for, democracy's illiberal tendencies. To be sure, feminist movements that mobilized around the transition lost momentum during democratic consolidation as political parties gained center stage and old patterns of cooptation, corruption, and infighting reasserted themselves (Friedman 2000). But in many countries, democracy has coincided with significant gains in women's representation in elected office and women's presence in senior executive posts. The adoption by many countries of women's quota laws requiring that political parties nominate a certain percentage of women for legislative office suggests that this trend is likely to continue. Yet women's presence in decision making is no guarantee of liberal policy. Not all women are liberals. And even when women's voices do bring liberal and feminist perspectives to decision making, they must still contend with forces opposing change and with political institutions reluctant to prioritize gender policy issues.

Projects of state modernization launched under military authoritarian rule have surprising consequences, for they open a window of opportunity for gender and family reforms. Military rulers often seize power to avert threats posed by politically mobilized popular classes and leftist movements. They may also desire to promote the rationalization of state and society to encourage investment, promote economic growth, and modernize. Military governments around the world have overhauled national laws, constitutions, state bureaucracies, economic policy, and state-owned enterprises in line with international principles of technical efficiency and modernity. When they decided to modernize the law, military rulers often called on legal technocrats – lawyers, legal scholars, and judges who had published in professional journals and participated in national and international legal conferences – to draft reform proposals based on the newest ideas and approaches. By the mid-twentieth century, modern tenets of the legal profession had come to incorporate principles of gender equality in family law. By giving technocrats free rein to craft legal reforms, military governments, even patriarchal ones, can open the door to liberalizing gender policy. In these circumstances, modernity trumps patriarchy.

Conflict between governments and dominant religious institutions may create opportunities for gender policy reform; cooperation between state and Church creates obstacles to change. Governments may uphold laws conforming to Church doctrine, not always because they agree with it, but because they need the Church's political support. The Church helps the state maintain social control; it also deploys symbols that help to legitimize state rulers and their policies. In countries where the vast majority of the population is Catholic, the Roman Catholic Church wields considerable political clout. To be sure, the power of churches lessened considerably in the nineteenth and twentieth centuries as many countries secularized their educational systems and seized control over areas traditionally under the Church's purview, such as hospitals, cemeteries, and records of birth, marriage, and death. But the Church's role as guardian of common ethics remained important, and the Church cares about few ethical issues more than those governing family life and intimate relations. Restrictions on divorce and abortion must be understood in this context. More liberal policies run the risk of alienating an important political ally. Regardless of their beliefs, many state leaders have been unwilling to risk the Church's wrath by legalizing divorce and abortion. But if Church-state relations sour, the government has less to lose by endorsing policies opposed by the Church. Periods of Church-state conflict may therefore be an ideal time for networks of reformers to push for liberal gender policy.

The configuration of democratic institutions – "authoritarian enclaves," coalitional dynamics, political party systems, executive-legislative relations, and electoral systems – shape patterns of policy on gender issues. Institutions affect the policy goals that are achievable and the issues that gain salience on the policy agenda. The presence of an authoritarian legacy may steer democrats away from certain policy courses and enhance the power of conservative actors to veto policy change. When the Executive enjoys a dominant position over law making, executive commitment to gender policy is necessary for change. In the absence of executive interest, parties and legislators must bear the burden of bringing an issue to prominence. However, there are few incentives for legislators to champion "public goods" issues such as gender policy when Congress is weak, and parties lack unity, clear ideological agendas, and defined policy positions. State agencies created to promote women's rights may serve as advocates of policy change, but their institutional status and responsibilities vary dramatically. Often these agencies lack the power to propose legislation and are handicapped by low budgets and inadequate staffing. The presence of more women in power many increase the visibility of gender policy issues, but since women are not above politics, their legislative behavior also responds to institutional constraints and party dynamics.

Timing matters. In the late twentieth century, abortion policy became harder to change in those countries where laws remained strict. In a historical path or sequence, earlier events alter the conditions for later ones (Pierson 2000: 252). Past policies shape the political goals and organizational structure of interest groups in a way that affects later policies (Pierson 1994: 40). Reform to abortion policy in some countries produced contradictory effects for countries further along in the sequence. On the one hand, the experience of early liberalizers such as the United States and Europe made matters easier for later liberalizers such as Latin America. Changes in the West helped forge widely accepted norms for modern and democratic countries, and these norms in turn legitimized the demands of Latin American reformers. On the other hand, early liberalizers made the challenges for later liberalizers more intense on at least one issue: abortion.[1] Abortion reform in the United States and Europe granted women discretion over their reproductive capacity, but also spurred an unprecedented conservative countermobilization and energized the Roman Catholic Church's activities. Thus, Latin American countries seeking to change their abortion laws faced obstacles to change that their predecessors in the United States and Europe had not.

Beyond Argentina, Brazil, and Chile

These propositions may help to shed some light on patterns of gender policy change beyond Argentina, Brazil, and Chile. My arguments should be particularly relevant to countries that have experienced political transitions and preserved hegemonic religious institutions, but may pertain to other countries as well. In Uruguay, technocrats working under a 1930s authoritarian regime decriminalized abortion in ways resembling the liberalizing reforms introduced by the dictatorships analyzed in this book. The course of Church-state relations in Poland and its effects on abortion policy bear many similarities to Chile's experience with divorce. The history of gender policy in Spain shows that democratic transitions can generate momentum for liberalizing reforms, but also that illiberal forces can use democracy to prevent further changes. Finally, Ireland's struggle to legalize divorce and failure to legalize abortion demonstrate the continued influence of religious institutions over policy. The strength of illiberal tendencies and power of religious ideas is not unique to Latin American democracies.

---

[1] The idea that lateness does not bring unequivocally good things is well established. Gerschenkron argued that countries trying to industrialize later, when the world economy was more advanced, faced higher entry costs to succeed. Barrington Moore, for his part, linked the challenges of late industrialization to the emergence of fascism in Japan and Germany (Gourevitch 1978: 885–7).

Uruguay

Shortly after a coup disrupted Uruguayan democracy in 1933, the president promulgated a criminal code that completely decriminalized abortion, the first of its kind outside the Soviet Union. How could an authoritarian and conservative regime that seized power intending to reverse the social reforms of the 1910s produce the singularly most unprecedented liberalization of reproductive rights in Latin America? The answer lies in how decisions about criminal law reform were made. The previous government had commissioned José Irureta Goyena, an internationally renowned Uruguayan criminologist, to draft a new criminal code for the country. Irureta Goyena was well known in international criminology circles for his prolific scholarship and for his fierce defense of the decriminalization of abortion (Hungria 1942; Ribeiro 1942). Given that criminal law modernization was seen as technocratic, the conservative government of General Gabriel Terra rubberstamped Irureta Goyena's draft, including the abortion articles. The 1933 Code punished only abortions performed without a woman's consent. Due to an outcry from conservative doctors and politicians, however, the Uruguayan Criminal Code was reformed again in 1938 (Lavrín 1995: 176–86). Abortions performed with a woman's consent were made a crime, but the code identified wide grounds for legal abortion and made punishments relatively light. Abortions could be performed for medical reasons or after rape, but also if the pregnancy created "economic anguish" for the woman.[2] As in Argentina and Brazil in the 1920s and 1940s, respectively, the restriction of decision making to small groups made liberalizing changes possible, even within the context of otherwise conservative contexts. Once the decision-making circle widened, however, ideological conflict curtailed the scope of reform.

Poland

Abortion politics in Poland shows how Church-state relations affect gender policy. The communist regime repressed the Church, attempted to impose atheism on the Polish people, and upheld policies the Church opposed, including a very liberal abortion regime. In communist Poland, abortion was widely available and even encouraged as a means of birth control. After the transition, however, the scenario changed and Church power reasserted itself. As the most important autonomous civil society institution to survive communist rule, the Church, along with schools, universities, and the press, provided the means through which the Polish nation preserved and asserted its national identity (Casanova 1994: 99). The Church, moreover, contributed to the emergence of the Solidarity movement by defending development of an independent civil society and helping to protect other groups, including students, workers, peasants, and even leftist intellectuals (ibid.: 106).

---

[2] See Articles 325 to 328 of the *Codigo Penal de la República Oriental del Uruguay* (Montevideo: Fundación de Cultura Universitaria, 1986).

Under democracy, the Church has enjoyed legitimacy and political clout. In lobbying for policies conforming to its principles, such as the elimination of liberal communist-era abortion laws, the Church has found allies in the country's growing antiabortion movement. Politicians seeking the Church's political support have joined the antiabortion cause, a position that also allows them to distance the democratic present from the communist past. Several policy changes, including a health ministry decree and a change to the code of medical ethics, started to roll back abortion rights in the early 1990s, culminating in a 1993 law criminalizing abortions performed on "social" grounds and by doctors in private practice (Zielinska 2000: 28–31). After parliamentary elections installed a majority of communist and leftist parties, however, the Polish Parliament approved a more liberal abortion law. This law, passed in 1996, permitted abortions for social reasons (such as hardship) and allowed doctors to perform abortions in their private practices. Yet in May 1997, one day before the Pope was to visit the country, the Polish Constitutional Tribunal ruled most aspects of the law unconstitutional for violating the fetus's right to life (ibid.: 32–3).

Spain

During the reign of General Franco, gender-related laws in Spain were conservative and restrictive. Divorce was not permitted and abortion was considered a crime under all circumstances. The civil code upheld male authority in the family and called on wives to obey their husbands; the code also forbade married women to engage in financial and legal transactions without their husbands' permission (Valiente 1995). These laws conformed to the position of the Roman Catholic Church, which "constituted the main institutional and ideological pillar of the regime" (Casanova 1994: 80).[3] After the transition to democracy, however, Spain introduced radical changes to laws on gender. The Spanish Constitution, adopted in 1978, introduced the principle of gender equality, admitted that marriages could be dissolved, and erased the distinction between legitimate and illegitimate children. The government abolished restrictions on family planning and contraceptives in 1978. In 1981, Spain adopted a divorce law, introduced changes to the marital property regime, and granted spouses equal parental rights. In 1985, a new law was passed to permit abortion, though on narrow grounds (to protect the mother's life or health, in the event of rape, and when the fetus would be born disabled) (Fuente Noriega 1986; Threlfall 1996: 115–51). In practice, the law is applied loosely, but observers from both left and right find it unsatisfactory. The right sees the law as a slippery slope to elective abortion; the left maintains that a partial decriminalization offers no solution to the problem of abortion (Gonzáles 1994: 232).

[3] The Spanish Catholic Church underwent major changes, however, and by the 1960s and 1970s, important sectors of the Church stopped supporting the Franco regime and began to call for liberalization and democratization (Casanova 1994: 81–7).

Since the transition, Spain has been unable to introduce additional abortion reforms. The Socialist government presented a bill to Congress that would permit abortion for economic and social reasons. The Socialists lost parliamentary elections in 1996, however, and the bill was narrowly defeated during the first week of the new, conservative administration. Another liberal abortion bill (which would have permitted abortion for pregnancies creating "personal, social, or family conflicts" for the woman) was presented to Congress in 1998. The bill was voted on three times, and each time the vote ended in a tie. Later in the year, the bill was considered again, and defeated by only one vote (Fleishman 2000: 298). Both the ruling party (Partido Popular) and the opposition Socialists closed the vote on the abortion issue by instructing legislators to vote with the party line (smaller, nationalist parties allowed their representatives a free vote). Many observers believe that the Roman Catholic Church shifted the tide of the legislative standoff. The Church campaigned actively against the bill, and exploited its ties to the ruling party to promote its position.

Ireland

Irish law forbids abortion under any circumstance, and until 1995, divorce was not permitted. In 1983, Irish voters approved, in a referendum, a constitutional amendment protecting the life of the unborn child. In 1986, a campaign to amend the Constitution to permit legal divorce failed (as in Brazil, the Irish Constitution prohibited divorce), and in 1992, an amendment to the Constitution to permit abortion in cases where the mother's life was in danger also failed.[4] Ireland's Code of Medical Ethics forbids physicians to perform even therapeutic abortions (Gilheany 1998: 75). Divorce, however, was approved in a 1995 constitutional amendment referendum by a strikingly narrow margin: 50.3 to 49.7 percent. The divorce law is quite restrictive, requiring four years of separation and a court's judgment that no reasonable prospect of reconciliation exists (McKenna 1997). The amendment campaign pitted the country's political parties and leading politicians, including the president and prime minister, against Roman Catholic bishops and conservative interest groups. Though in the past, Irish politicians had been reluctant to oppose the Church, many confronted the bishops directly in order to discredit the Church's antidivorce campaign (Farrell 1995).

What explains Ireland's conservative laws? The strength of the Roman Catholic Church is a major factor. The Church has been the most powerful

---

[4] In 1992, the Irish Supreme Court ruled that abortion would be legal if the mother's life was in danger through the risk of suicide. The ruling obliged the Irish government to find some means to regulate these abortions, which it attempted to do through the ultimately defeated constitutional amendment proposal. However, Irish voters did approve amendments granting women the right to information about abortions abroad and the right to travel (Gilheany 1998: 66–7).

organization in Irish civil society, is the country's dominant interest group, and controls numerous educational, health, and social services (Gilheany 1998: 67; Mahon 1987). The Church's presence in education is surely one reason why Irish public opinion on morality and sexual ethics is considerably more conservative than in the countries of continental Europe and Great Britain, and why there is little space for more feminist and liberal discourses to resonate with the public. Conservative interest groups seeking to uphold restrictive laws, moreover, gained strength in the 1970s and 1980s. Conservative proposals to amend the Constitution to forbid all abortions were triggered by a 1973 Irish Supreme Court ruling that had thrown out anticontraceptive legislation. These groups "feared that, just as the [Irish] Supreme Court had read off from U.S. jurisprudence a right to privacy to justify the legalization of contraception, so it could find abortion on demand to be legal" (Gilheany 1998: 71). Influenced by antiabortion movements in the United States, the amendment campaign was also able to use the parish structure of the Roman Catholic Church in their campaign. In spite of mounting public awareness of the extent of illegal abortion and the flight of Irish women to Great Britain for abortions, Ireland's adherence to restrictive laws serves as additional evidence that laws on gender, including in European countries, are not converging around a uniform model. The Church remains a formidable force in democratic politics.

Gender, the State, and Democracy

This book offers one perspective on gender and the state, not a general account that can be applied to all questions of gender politics or all aspects of state power. Laws on abortion, divorce, and gender equality in the family are a major way the state contributes to the social construction of gender, but not the only way. Considerable work has been done on gender and the welfare state, birth control, equal rights legislation, education policy, sexual harassment law, affirmative action, equal pay, domestic violence, and numerous other policy areas (e.g., Gelb 1989; Gelb and Palley 1996; Gordon 1976; Mansbridge 1986; Mink 1998; O'Connor et al. 1999; Orloff 1993; Pedersen 1993; Petchesky 1990; Rhode 1989; Skocpol 1992). A general theory of gender and the state covering all of these issues may be unviable, however. The significance of "gender" depends on a subject's other social positions (class, race, ethnicity, religion, and so on), while the state, far from being a monolithic or unitary actor, exercises distinct forms of power, each of which "produces different effects, engenders different kinds of possible resistance, and requires a different analytical frame" (Brown 1995: 175). The objective of historical institutionalist social science, moreover, is less an encompassing theory valid for all times and places than sets of historically grounded propositions about probabilistic causal relationships (Katznelson 1997; Skocpol in Kohli et al. 1995). My arguments about state decision making on gender issues supplement normative theories (Benhabib 1992; Brown 1995; Cohen 2002; Fraser 1997; MacKinnon 1989; Okin 1989; Phillips 1991, 1995; Young 1997) and analyses of the effects of gender policy implementation on citizens' lives (Mink 1998; Weitzman 1985; William 2000). Research on gender and the state, as in other areas of scholarly inquiry, is ultimately a collective endeavor.

What is distinctive and important about the policies studied in this book? The decriminalization of abortion, legalization of divorce, and removal of impediments on the action of married women are policies that expand our negative liberties, particularly those that pertain to the private sphere. "Negative liberty" or "negative freedom," stemming from the ideas of Hobbes and Locke, refers to freedom *from* social or state interference in our actions. The idea is that "some portion of human existence must remain independent of the sphere of social control" (Berlin 1969: 123). Negative liberties protect citizens against state power and regulate relationships among citizens themselves; they also secure a sphere of private autonomy that helps us exercise rights of political citizenship, such as collective decision making and authorship of the laws governing our lives (Habermas 1996a).

Some may object that the expansion of negative freedoms means little if citizens do not enjoy basic capabilities and opportunities. Aren't legal permissions for abortion superfluous if the public health system fails to provide safe abortions at a low cost? What good is legal divorce if many people lack the means legally to formalize their marriages in the first place? Doesn't the enjoyment of negative liberties depend on certain material conditions? In Western democracies, the welfare state evolved precisely to guarantee the standard of living needed for citizens effectively to exercise the civil and political rights they had already been granted under the constitution and statutory laws. In many Latin American countries, by contrast, the sequence was reversed: States extended social protections, albeit partially, before negative liberties and political rights (O'Donnell 1999b). Though political rights were won when the third wave of democratization of the 1980s and 1990s instituted free and fair elections and competitive party politics, the universalization of civil rights remains incomplete. Very few Latin American countries are democratic legal orders. State agents perpetrate human rights abuses with impunity, pervasive discrimination continues, and large geographic areas are ruled by raw power rather than valid legal norms (Pinheiro 1999).

The extension of civil rights and the improvement of guarantees of private autonomy through reforms on abortion, divorce, and gender equality in the family are essential to a deeper democratization. The absence of social rights or the problem of arbitrary implementation does not detract from the importance of negative liberties. Those of us interested in the achievement of democracy must be concerned with all of these things. Indeed, issue networks that mobilized for change in Latin America were well aware that negative liberties and social rights needed to be developed together. Does this book offer any lessons for their future struggles?

I argued that disaggregating gender issues is a good analytical strategy. It may be that disaggregating gender issues is good political strategy as well. As an identity and principle of social differentiation, gender cross-cuts other identities and social categories. The content and significance of gender varies dramatically from context to context. This makes it enormously difficult to arrive at a comprehensive statement of women or men's gender interests. Moreover, the world's normative and ethical traditions uphold different ideas about gender and different prescriptions for gender policy. On certain issues, these traditions converge. Roman Catholicism, liberalism, socialism, and feminism, for example, shared a belief in equal parental and property rights. On other issues, such as divorce and abortion, ethical traditions diverged. This makes it difficult to formulate an agenda of gender *rights* that will appeal to diverse groups of people. Proposals seeking "progress" on "gender issues" may thus be poor strategy. The bigger and more comprehensive the target, the more likely it is that someone will find something to object to. In these cases of ethical and institutional conflict, change can still happen, but outside the procedures of routine decision making. Change requires shifts in power configurations that disable opponents and open windows of opportunity for reformers.

Gender-related policy proposals pass most easily when the agenda narrows. Proposals based on specific issues such as property rights reform or domestic violence, for example, have better prospects than omnibus "gender equality" proposals. Around the world, groups of women politicians have realized the greatest successes when they seek discrete goals such as quotas in political parties.[5] By agreeing to leave certain issues off the agenda – such as those that provoke division, like abortion – women from different parties and ideological tendencies have been able to unite on behalf of policy changes.[6] Aggregating gender issues, on the other hand, may be an effective strategy for the opponents of change. By linking issues, opponents can inflate the potential implications and consequences of change.

Future research might explore the ways that institutional rules and structures affect the possibility of disaggregating and aggregating gender issues. Work on agenda-setting powers has identified how, whether in the context of legislative committees or other institutional settings, certain procedures

---

[5] Greater presence in decision making is perhaps the one area where all women clearly have a common interest. "Although all women may not agree on the substance of specific policy outcomes, they do have a common interest in being present when policy is being made" (Friedman 2000: 291).

[6] In Mexico in the late 1990s, women leaders from the three major political parties were able to come together in support of a common agenda only by agreeing, in advance, to leave abortion off the agenda of national politics. Interview with Patricia Mercado, Mexico City, July 26, 2000.

structure the ways in which issues are disaggregated for consideration (e.g., Shepsle and Weingast 1995). The structure of volunteer-based social movements, by contrast, may create incentives for issue aggregation. Jane Mansbridge has shown that the interest groups supporting the U.S. Equal Rights Amendment (ERA) needed symbols and ideological incentives to motivate the volunteers who formed the base of the movement. In some cases, these volunteers – who were more radical than the segment of the U.S. population that supported the ERA – "preferred being right to winning." They exaggerated the probable effects of the amendment (such as the claim that it would require sending women into combat, which most of the U.S. public opposed), and thus inadvertently contributed to its defeat (1986).

The institutions of democracy permit both the aggregation and disaggregation of gender issues. These institutions are tools to promote interests: Some groups disaggregate issues to produce policy change, while others may endeavor to aggregate issues to preclude change.[7] Although studies such as this book identify the key factors shaping policy struggles over gender issues in particular countries at particular moments in history, the outcomes of such struggles in democratic regimes are never foreordained. Were it otherwise, democracy would not work. In a democracy, actors know what is possible, and they may even know what is likely, but they cannot be certain of what *will* happen. "Institutionalized uncertainty" is the sine qua non of democracy, for if outcomes were "either predetermined or completely indeterminate," few would have sufficient incentive to organize around their interests or to submit to the democratic process in the first place (Przeworski 1991: 12–13). Accepting democracy requires embracing procedures that ensure fair play but make no guarantee about outcomes. Democracy permits today's losers to mount a fresh challenge tomorrow and puts today's winners on notice that their victories are impermanent.

---

[7] Of course, institutions also affect the resources, organization, and strategies of different groups; see Skocpol (1992); Skocpol, Ganz, and Munson (2000).

References

Alan Guttmacher Institute. 1994. *Aborto clandestino: Uma realidade latinoamericana.* New York: Alan Guttmacher Institute.

Alan Guttmacher Institute. 1999. *Sharing Responsibility: Women, Society and Abortion Worldwide.* New York: Alan Guttmacher Institute.

Alatorre, Anna-Lizbeth. 1999. "Parties, Gender, and Democratization: The Causes and Consequences of Women's Participation in the Mexican Congress." B.A. Thesis, Harvard University.

Aldana Santin, Myriam. 2000. "Vozes da Igreja Católica na Câmara Federal." *Journal da RedeSaúde*, no. 21 (September).

Alessandri Rodríguez, Arturo. 1932. "Comentario a Sabioncello con Hausmann." *Revista de derecho y jurisprudencia* 29: 351–4.

Almond, Gabriel, and Sidney Verba. 1963. *The Civic Culture.* Princeton: Princeton University Press.

Alvarez, Sonia. E. 1990. *Engendering Democracy in Brazil: Women's Movements in Transition Politics.* Princeton: Princeton University Press.

Alvarez, Sonia A. 1998a. "...And Even Fidel Can't Change That!: Trans/national Feminist Advocacy Strategies and Cultural Politics in Latin America." Unpublished paper.

Alvarez, Sonia E. 1998b. "Latin American Feminisms 'Go Global': Trends of the 1990s and Challenges for the New Millenium." In Sonia E. Alvarez, Evelina Dagnino, and Arturo Escobar, eds., *Cultures of Politics: Politics of Cultures.* Boulder: Westview. Pp. 293–324.

Alvear, Soledad. 1991. "Régimen patrimonial del matrimonio." *El Mercurio.* September 8, 1991.

Alvear, Soledad. 1994. *Una mirada integral.* Santiago: Editorial Atena.

Alywin, Mariana. 1995. "Para su reflexión." *Ercilla*, no. 2981 (January 27): 23.

Alywin, Mariana, and Ignacio Walker. 1996. *Familia y divorcio: Razones de una posición.* Santiago: Editorial Los Andes.

Alywin, Patricio. 1991. "Modifica el código civil en materia de regimen patrimonial del matrimonio y otros cuerpos legales que indica. Mensaje de S.E. el presidente de la república." Cámara de Diputados. Session 26, August 6.

Ames, Barry. 1995a. "Electoral Rules, Constituency Pressures, and Pork Barrel: Bases of Voting in the Brazilian Congress." *Journal of Politics* 57, no. 2 (May): 324–43.

Ames, Barry. 1995b. "Electoral Strategy Under Open-List Proportional Representation." *American Journal of Political Science* 39, no. 2 (May): 406–33.

Ames, Barry. 2001. *The Deadlock of Democracy in Brazil.* Ann Arbor: University of Michigan Press.

Ames, Barry. 2002. "Party Discipline in the Chamber of Deputies." In Scott Morgenstern and Benito Nacif, eds., *Legislative Politics in Latin America.* New York: Cambridge University Press. Pp. 185–221.

Amorim Neto, Octavio. 2001. "The Puzzle of Party Discipline in Brazil." *Latin American Politics and Society* 44, no. 1: 127–44.

Antecedentes Parlamentarios. 1998. Ley 23.515. "Matrimonio civil-divorcio vincular." *Antecedentes Parlamentarios* 5, no. 7 (July). Buenos Aires: La Ley.

Aquinas, Saint Thomas. 1988. *The Summa of Theology.* In *St. Thomas Aquinas on Politics and Ethics,* trans. and ed. Paul Sigmund. New York: W. W. Norton. Pp. 30–83.

Araújo, Maria José de Oliveira. 1993. "Aborto legal no hospital do Jabaquara." *Estudos Feministas* 1, no. 2: 424–8.

Archibald, Katherine. 1988. "The Concept of Social Hierarchy in the Writings of St. Thomas Aquinas." In Paul Sigmund, ed., *St. Thomas Aquinas on Politics and Ethics.* New York: W. W. Norton. Pp. 136–42.

Ardaillon, Danielle. 1997. "Cidadania de corpo inteiro. Discursos sobre o aborto em número e gênero." Ph.D. dissertation, University of São Paulo.

Baer, Judith. 1999. *Our Lives Before the Law: Constructing a Feminist Jurisprudence.* Princeton: Princeton University Press.

Baldez, Lisa. 1998. "Democratic Institutions and Feminist Outcomes: Chilean Policy Toward Women in the 1990s." Working Paper no. 340, Department of Political Science, Washington University.

Baldez, Lisa. 2001. "Coalition Politics and the Limits of State Feminism in Chile." *Women and Politics* 22, no. 4: 1–36.

Baldez, Lisa. 2002. *Why Women Protest: Women's Movements in Chile.* New York: Cambridge University Press.

Baldez, Lisa, and John Carey. 2001. "Budget Procedure and Fiscal Restraint in Posttransition Chile." In Stephan Haggard and Mathew D. McCubbins, eds., *Presidents, Parliaments, and Policy.* New York: Cambridge University Press. Pp. 105–48.

Baltar da Rocha, Maria Isabel. 1993. "Política demográfica e parlamento: Debates de decisões sobre o controle da natalidade." Textos NEPO 25. Campinas: UNICAMP.

Baltar da Rocha, Maria Isabel. 1996. "O congresso nacional e a questão do aborto." Unpublished manuscript.

Barra, Roberto. 1997. *Los derechos del por nacer en el ordenamiento jurídico argentino.* Buenos Aires: Editorial Ábaco de Rodolfo Depalma.

Barrig, Maruja. 1997. "De cal y de arena. ONGs y movimiento de mujeres en Chile." Unpublished paper.

Barros, Enrique. 1991. "Por un nuevo régimen de bienes del matrimonio." *Estudios Públicos,* no. 43 (Winter): 139–66.

Barros, Enrique. 2002. "La ley civil ante las rupturas matrimoniales." *Estudios Públicos* 85 (Summer): 5–15.

Barros, Robert J. 1997. "By Reason and Force: Military Constitutionalism in Chile, 1973–1989." Ph.D. dissertation, University of Chicago.

Baumgartner, Frank R., and Bryan D. Jones. 1993. *Agendas and Instability in American Politics*. Chicago: University of Chicago Press.

Benhabib, Seyla. 1992. *Situating the Self: Gender, Community, and Postmodernism in Contemporary Ethics*. New York: Routledge.

Benhabib, Seyla. 1996. "Toward a Deliberative Model of Democratic Legitimacy." In Seyla Benhabib, ed., *Democracy and Difference: Contesting the Boundaries of the Political*. Princeton: Princeton University Press. Pp. 67–94.

Berlin, Isaiah. 1969. *Four Essays on Liberty*. London: Oxford University Press.

Berry, Jeffrey M. 1989. "Subgovernments, Issues Networks, and Political Conflict." In Richard Harris and Sidney Milkis, eds., *Remaking American Politics*. Boulder: Westview Press. Pp. 239–60.

Betto, Frei. 1992. "A questão do aborto por uma legislação em defesa da vida." In Thais Corral, ed., *Interrupção de gravidez*. Rio de Janeiro: REDEH. Pp. 11–18.

Bidart Campos, German. 1987. "La Corte suprema y el divorcio vincular." *El Derecho* 121 (1987): 522–34.

Bidau, José F., Abel M. Fleitas, and Roberto Martínez Ruiz. 1968. "Nota de la Comisión Redactora al Secretario de Estado de Justicia." *Anales de la legislación argentina*. Tomo 28-B. Buenos Aires: La Ley. Pp. 1811–12.

Binstock, Hannah. 1997. "Hacia la igualdad de la mujer: Avances legales desde la aprobación de la convención sobre la eliminación de todas las formas de discriminación contra la mujer." Paper prepared for CEPAL, Seventh Regional Conference on Women's Integration into Economic and Social Development in Latin America and the Caribbean, Santiago, November 19 to 21.

Blofeld, Merike. 1998. "The Politics of Abortion in Chile and Argentina: Public Opinion, Social Actors and Discourse, and Political Agendas." Paper prepared for the 1998 meeting of the Latin American Studies Association, Chicago, September 24–26.

Blofeld, Merike. 2001. "The Politics of 'Moral Sin': A Study of Abortion and Divorce in Catholic Chile Since 1990." *Nueva Serie FLACSO*. Santiago: FLACSO.

Borda, Guillermo, and Conrado Etchebarne. 1968. "Nota al poder ejecutivo acompañado el proyecto de ley 17.711." *Anales de la legislación argentina*. Tomo 28-B. Buenos Aires: La Ley. Pp. 1810–11.

Boutros-Ghali, Boutros. 1996. "Introduction." In *The United Nations and the Advancement of Women*. New York: United Nations. Pp. 3–74.

Brito, Eugenia. 1997. Roles sexuales: Diversas escenas. In Olga Grau, Riet Diesling, Eugenia Brito, and Alejandra Farías. *Discurso, género y poder. Discursos públicos: Chile 1978–1993*. Santiago: LOM Ediciones. Pp. 65–91.

Brown, Wendy. 1995. *States of Injury: Power and Freedom in Late Modernity*. Princeton: Princeton University Press.

Burdick, Michael A. 1995. *For God and the Fatherland: Religion and Politics in Argentina*. Albany: SUNY Press.

Butler Flora, Cornelia. 1984. "Socialist Feminism in Latin America." *Women and Politics* 4, no. 1 (Spring): 69–93.

Candioti, Enrique. 2000. "Igualdad entre los géneros, desarrollo y paz para el siglo XXI: Beijing +5." Intervención del Jefe de la Delegación Argentina, Embajador Enrique Candioti, Secretario de Estado de Relaciones Exteriores.

23a sesión especial de la asamblea general de las Naciones Unidas, June 8, 2000.

Cardoso, Fernando Henrique. 1979. "On the Characterization of Authoritarian Regimes in Latin America." In David Collier, ed., *The New Authoritarianism in Latin America*. Princeton: Princeton University Press. Pp. 33–57.

Carey, John. 1997. "Institutional Design and Party Systems." In Larry Diamond et al., eds., *Consolidating the Third World Democracies*. Baltimore: Johns Hopkins University Press. Pp. 67–92.

Carey, John. 2002. "Parties, Coalitions, and the Chilean Congress in the 1990s." In Scott Morgenstern and Benito Nacif, eds., *Legislative Politics in Latin America*. New York: Cambridge University Press. Pp. 222–53.

Carmines, Edward G., and James A. Stimson. 1980. "The Two Faces of Issue Voting." *American Political Science Review* 74, no. 1 (March): 78–91.

Carneiro, Nelson. 1973. "E a luta continua...." In *A Luta pelo divorcio*. Rio de Janeiro. Pp. 13–21.

Carneiro, Nelson. 1976. "Proposta de emenda à constituição no. 4, de 1975." In *Palavras. Leva-as ao vento* V. Brasília: Senado Federal. Pp. 153–61.

Carneiro, Nelson. 1985a. "Direitos civis da mulher casada." In *Palavras: Leva-as ao vento*, vol. 10. Brasília: Senado Federal. Pp. 43–54.

Carneiro, Nelson. 1985b. "...E a gota d'àgua venceu!" In *Palavras: Leva-as ao vento*, vol. 10. Brasília: Senado Federal. Pp. 123–33.

Carneiro, Nelson. 1991. "Ainda o código civil." In *Palavras: Leva-as ao vento*, vol. 12. Brasília: Senado Federal. Pp. 115–26.

Casanova, José. 1994. *Public Religions in the Modern World*. Chicago: University of Chicago Press.

Casas, Lidia. 1993. "La Despenalización del aborto." *Revista de la Academia de Derecho* 2 (October): 35–62.

Casas, Lidia. 1996. *Mujeres procesadas por aborto*. Santiago: Foro Abierto de Salud y Derechos Reproductivos.

Cascudo Rodrigues, João Batista. 1962. *A mulher brasileira: Direitos políticos e civis*. Rio de Janeiro: Renes.

Centro da Mulher Brasileira. 1975. "Texto do centro da mulher brasileira fazendo considerações sobre a situação da mulher e a constitucionalidade do novo Código Civil brasileiro." Rio de Janeiro, September 8.

Centro de Estudios Públicos (CEP). 1987. *Estudio social y de opinión pública en la población de Santiago*. Documento de Trabajo no. 83 (May).

Centro de Estudios Públicos (CEP). 1991a. *Estudio sobre opinión pública*. Documento de Trabajo no. 170 (December).

Centro de Estudios Públicos (CEP). 1991b. *Estudio social y de opinión pública, diciembre de 1990*. Documento de Trabajo no. 151 (February).

Centro de Estudios Públicos (CEP). 1991c. *Estudio social y de opinión pública, septiembre a octubre de 1991*. Documento de Trabajo no. 170 (December).

Centro de Estudios Públicos (CEP). 1995. *Tema especial. La Mujer chilena hoy: Trabajo, familia, y valores*. Documento de Trabajo no. 237 (August).

Centro Legal para Derechos Reproductivos y Políticas Públicas y Grupo de Información en Reproducción Elegida (CRLP/GIRE). 1997. *Derechos reproductivos de la mujer en México: Un reporte sombra*.

Cerda Varas, Fernando. 1943. "Regimen de participación en los gananciales establecido como regimen matrimonial ordinario o sin pacto expreso." In Federação Interamericana de Advogados, *Anais da Segunda Conferência*, vol. 5. Rio de Janeiro, August 7–12. Pp. 31–49.

CFEMEA. 1997. Dossiê. Aborto Legal.

Charlton, Sue Ellen M., Jana Everett, and Kathleen Staudt, eds. 1989. *Women, the State, and Development*. Albany: SUNY Press.

Charrad, Mounira. 2001. *States and Women's Rights: The Making of Postcolonial Tunisia, Algeria, and Morocco*. Berkeley: University of California Press.

Chuchryk, Patricia. 1989. "Subversive Mothers: The Women's Opposition to the Military Regime in Chile." In Sue Ellen Charlton, Jana Everett, and Kathleen Staudt, eds., *Women, the State, and Development*. Albany: SUNY Press. Pp. 130–51.

Chuchryk, Patricia. 1994. "From Dictatorship to Democracy: The Women's Movement in Chile." In Jane Jaquette, ed., *The Women's Movement in Latin America*. Boulder: Westview. Pp. 65–107.

Claro, Gloria. 1997. "La Mujer: Igualdad ante la legislación en el plano patrimonial." Unpublished manuscript.

CNBB. 1997. "Declaração da CNBB em favor da vida e contra o aborto."

CNDM. 1986. "Campanha 'Mulher e Constituinte.' Programa Geral de Campanha Aprovado pelo CNDM em 1985." Archive of Comba Marques Porto, National Archives, Rio de Janeiro.

Código Criminal do Imperio do Brasil. 1861. Ed. Carlos Antonio Cordeiro. Rio de Janeiro: Quirino e Irmão.

Código Penal de la República Argentina. 1887. Ed. Julian L. Aguirre. Buenos Aires: Félix LaJouane.

Código Penal de la República de Chile. 1889. Edición Oficial. Santiago: Imprenta Nacional.

Código Penal de la República Oriental de Uruguay. 1933. 2nd ed., Montevideo: Fundación de Cultura Universitaria, 1986.

Código Penal do Brazil [sic]. 1913. Ed. Antonio Bento de Faria. Rio de Janeiro: J. Ribeiro dos Santos.

Código Penal. 37th ed. São Paulo: Saraiva.

Cohen, Jean. 2002. *Regulating Intimacy: A New Legal Paradigm*. Princeton: Princeton University Press.

Cohen, Jean, and Andrew Arato. 1992. *Civil Society and Political Theory*. Cambridge: MIT Press.

Comisión Intersectorial para la Prevención de Embarazo Adolescente. n.d. "Jornadas comunitarias de conversación sobre afectividad y sexualidad. Guia de trabajo."

Comisión Nacional de la Familia. 1993. *Informe*. Santiago: SERNAM.

Conferencia Episcopal Argentina. 1984a. "Construyamos juntos la nación." *Criterio*, no. 1935 (November 22): 667–70.

Conferencia Episcopal Argentina. 1984b. "Democracia, responsabilidad y esperanza." *Criterio*, no. 1921 (April 26): 162–5.

Conferencia Episcopal Argentina. 1984c. "Mensaje de los obispos argentinos sobre el matrimonio indisoluble." *Criterio*, no. 1921 (April 26): 166–8.

Constitución Política de la República de Chile. 1980. 5th ed., Santiago: Editorial Jurídica de Chile, 1996.

Constituição da República Federativa do Brasil. 1996. 13th ed. Ed. Juarez de Oliveira. São Paulo: Editora Saraiva.

Convention on the Elimination of All Forms of Discrimination Against Women (CEDAW). 1979. Text in *The United Nations and the Advancement of Women.* New York: United Nations. Pp. 244–50.

Corral, Hernan. 1994. "Mujer y igualdad jurídica: El Derecho a los mismos derechos?" *Temas de Derecho* 9, no. 2 (July–December): 77–88.

Corral, Hernan. 1997. "Iniciativas legales sobre familia y divorcio: La perspectiva del derecho civil." In *Controversia sobre familia y divorcio.* Santiago: Ediciones Universidad Católica de Chile. Pp. 130–205.

Corrêa, Sonia. 1994. *Population and Reproductive Rights: Feminist Perspectives from the South.* London: Zed Books.

Corrêa, Sonia. 2000. "Pequim +5 e a discriminalização do aborto na América Latina." *Journal da RedeSaúde,* no. 21 (September).

Cousiño Valdés, Carlos. 1997. "Divorcio y opinión pública." In *Controversia sobre familia y divorcio.* Santiago: Ediciones Universidad Católica de Chile. Pp. 67–92.

Craske, Nikki. 1999. *Women and Politics in Latin America.* New Brunswick: Rutgers University Press.

Creus, Carlos. 1995. *Derecho penal. Parte especial.* Tomo 1. Buenos Aires: Astrea.

Criterio. 1985. "Cuestiones de familia" (Editorial). *Criterio* 58, no. 1941 (April 11): 113–14.

CRLP. 1999. *Reproductive Freedom News.*

Crossette, Barbara. 1998. "A Global Divide on Abortion Splits Poor from Rich." *New York Times,* June 7, 1998, sec. 4, p. 16.

Crummett, María de los Angeles. 1977. "El Poder Feminino: The Mobilization of Women against Socialism in Chile." *Latin American Perspectives* 4, no. 4 (Fall): 103–13.

Cury Urzua, Enrique. 1992. *Derecho penal. Parte general,* tomo 1. 2nd ed. Santiago: Editorial Jurídica de Chile.

Dacah, Solange. 1993. "As tentativas de legislar a interrupção de gravidez." In Thais Corral, ed., *Interrupção de Gravidez.* Rio de Janeiro: REDEH. Pp. 23–5.

Deus Simões, Solange. 1985. *Deus, pátria e família: As mulheres no golpe de 1964.* Petrópolis: Vozes.

Deutsch, Karl. 1971. "Social Mobilization and Political Development." In Jason Finkle and Richard Gable, eds., *Political Development and Social Change,* 2nd. ed. New York: Wiley. Pp. 384–405.

Díaz Vergara, Carlos. 1997. "Consecuencias económicas y sociales de la aceptación de una ley de divorcio vincular." In *Controversia sobre familia y divorcio.* Santiago: Ediciones Universidad Católica de Chile. Pp. 33–65.

Diamond, Larry. 1999. *Developing Democracy: Toward Consolidation.* Baltimore: Johns Hopkins University Press.

Dinardi, Graciela, Mónica Gogna, and Silvina Ramos. N.d. "The Politics of Abortion in Argentina: Reflections on the National Constitution Reform." Unpublished paper.

Dirección Nacional de la Mujer. 1984. "Taller 1: La Discriminación de la mujer en el derecho de la familia. Propuestas y recomendaciones ante la ratificación de la N.U. para la Eliminación de Todas las Formas de Discriminación contra la Mujer." Buenos Aires: Secretaría de Desarollo Humano y Familia.

Dolinger, Jacob. 1966. *A capacidade civil da mulher casada*. Rio de Janeiro: Biblos.

Domínguez, Jorge I. 1978. *Cuba: Order and Revolution*. Cambridge: Harvard University Press.

Domínguez, Jorge I. 1998. "Free Politics and Free Markets in Latin America." *Journal of Democracy* 9, no. 4 (October): 70–84.

Dore, Elizabeth. 2000. "One Step Forward, Two Steps Back: Gender and the State in the Long Nineteenth Century." In Elizabeth Dore and Maxine Molyneux, eds., *Hidden Histories of Gender and the State in Latin America*. Durham: Duke University Press. Pp. 3–22.

Dore, Elizabeth, and Maxine Molyneux, eds. 2000. *Hidden Histories of Gender and the State in Latin America*. Durham: Duke University Press.

Drogus, Carol Ann. 1997. *Women, Religion, and Social Change in Brazil's Popular Church*. Notre Dame: University of Notre Dame Press.

Dryzek, John. 1990. *Discursive Democracy: Politics, Policy and Political Science*. New York: Cambridge University Press.

Dubkin, Claudia. 1994. "Aborto." *Para Ti*, no. 3760 (August).

Durand, Teresa, and María Alicia Gutiérrez. 1998. "Cuerpo de mujer: Consideraciones sobre los derechos sociales, sexuales y reproductivos en la Argentina." In *Mujeres sanas: Ciudadanas libres (o el poder para decidir)*. Buenos Aires: Foro por los Derechos Reproductivos/CLADEM/FEIM. Pp. 3–44.

Dworkin, Ronald. 1984. "Liberalism." In Michael Sandel, ed., *Liberalism and Its Critics*. New York: New York University Press. Pp. 60–79.

Eckstein, Susan. 1989. "Power and Popular Protest in Latin America." In *Power and Popular Protest: Latin American Social Movements*. Berkeley: University of California Press. Pp. 1–60.

Engels, Friedrich. 1884. "The Origin of the Family, Private Property, and the State." In Robert C. Tucker, ed., *The Marx-Engels Reader*. New York: W. W. Norton, 1978.

Ergas, Yasmine. 1982. "1968–1979 – Feminism and the Italian Party System: Women's Politics in a Decade of Turmoil." *Comparative Politics* 14, no. 3 (April): 253–79.

Etchebarne, Conrado. 1967. "Disertación del secretario de estado de justicia Dr. Conrado J. Etchebarne: Pronunciada en el colegio de abogados de la ciudad de Buenos Aires, con motivo de la XVI conferencia interamericana de abogados." Buenos Aires: Secretaría de Estado de Justicia.

Familias por la Familia. n.d. "Treinta y tres razones para defender la familia y evitar el divorcio." Pamphlet.

Farrell, Michael J. 1995. "Irish Vote for Divorce Ends Era of Church's Social Dominance." *National Catholic Reporter* (December 8): 19.

Feijoó, María del Carmen. 1998. "Democratic Participation and Women in Argentina." In Jane S. Jaquette and Sharon L. Wolchik, eds., *Women and Democracy: Latin America and Central and Eastern Europe*. Baltimore: Johns Hopkins University Press. Pp. 29–46.

Feijoó, María del Carmen, and Marcela María Alejandra Nari. 1994. "Women and Democracy in Argentina." In Jane S. Jaquette, ed., *The Women's Movement in Latin America*. Boulder: Westview. Pp. 109–29.

Feijoó, María del Carmen, and Marcela M. A. Nari. 1996. "Women in Argentina During the 1960s." *Latin American Perspectives* 23, no. 1 (Winter): 7–26.

Ferreira Filho, Manoel Gonçalves. 1992. "Fundamental Aspects of the 1988 Constitution." In Jacob Dolinger and Keith S. Rosenn, eds., *A Panorama of Brazilian Law.* Miami: North South Center Press. Pp. 11–25.

Figueiredo, Argelina, and Fernando Limongi. 1999. *Executivo e legislativo na nova ordem constitucional.* Rio de Janeiro: Editora FGV.

Figueiredo, Argelina, and Fernando Limongi. 2000. "Presidential Power, Legislative Organization, and Party Behavior in Brazil." *Comparative Politics* 32, no. 2 (January): 151–70.

Filc, Judith. 1997. *Entre el parentesco y la política: Familia y dictadura, 1976–1983.* Buenos Aires: Editorial Biblos.

Finnis, John. 1998. *Aquinas: Moral, Political, and Legal Theory.* New York: Oxford University Press.

FLACSO. 1992a. *Mujeres latinoamericanas en cifras. Brasil.* Santiago: FLACSO.

FLACSO. 1992b. *Mujeres latinoamericanas en cifras. Chile.* Santiago: FLACSO.

FLACSO. 1993. *Mujeres latinoamericanas en cifras. Argentina.* Santiago: FLACSO.

FLACSO. 1995. *Latin American Women. Compared Figures.* Santiago: FLACSO.

Fleet, Michael, and Brian Smith. 1997. *The Catholic Church and Democracy in Chile and Peru.* Notre Dame: University of Notre Dame Press.

Fleischer, David. 1995. *Las Consecuencias políticas del sistema electoral brasileño: Partidos políticos, poder legislativo y gobernabilidad.* San José: IIDH/CAPEL.

Fleishman, Rishona. 2000. "The Battle Against Reproductive Rights: The Impact of the Catholic Church on Abortion Law in Both International and Domestic Arenas." *Emory International Law Review* 14 (Spring): 277–314.

Foley, Nadine. 1977. "Woman in Vatican Documents. 1960 to the Present." In James A. Coriden, ed., *Sexism and Church Law: Equal Rights and Affirmative Action.* New York: Paulist Press. Pp. 82–108.

Fonseca, Gelson. 1958. *Divórcio para os não-católicos.* Rio de Janeiro: José Konfino.

Fontan Balestra, Carlos. 1983. *Tratado de Derecho Penal*, tomo 4. Buenos Aires: Abeledo-Perrot.

Fontan Balestra, Carlos. 1991. *Derecho penal. Parte especial.* 13th ed. Buenos Aires: Abeledo-Perrot.

Fragoso, Heleno Cláudio. 1987a. *Lições de direito penal: A nova parte geral.* 11th ed. Rio de Janeiro: Forense.

Fragoso, Heleno Cláudio. 1987b. *Lições de direito penal: Parte especial*, vol. I. 9th ed. Rio de Janeiro: Forense.

Franco, Jean. 1998. "Defrocking the Vatican: Feminism's Secular Project." In Sonia E. Alvarez, Evelina Dagnino, and Arturo Escobar, eds., *Cultures of Politics: Politics of Cultures.* Boulder: Westview. Pp. 278–89.

Fraser, Nancy. 1997. *Justice Interruptus: Critical Reflections on the "Postsocialist" Condition.* New York: Routledge.

Fraser, Nancy, and Linda Nicholson. 1990. "Social Criticism without Philosophy: An Encounter between Feminism and Postmodernism." In Linda Nicholson, ed., *Feminism/Postmodernism.* New York: Routledge. Pp. 19–38.

Friedman, Elisabeth. 2000. *Unfinished Transitions: Women and the Gendered Development of Democracy in Venezuela, 1936–1996.* University Park: Pennsylvania State University Press.

Frohmann, Alicia, and Teresa Valdez. 1993. "Democracy in the Country and in the Home: the Women's Movement in Chile." FLACSO Series Estudios Sociales no. 55. Santiago: FLACSO.

Frug, Mary Joe. 1992. "A Postmodern Feminist Legal Manifesto (An Unfinished Draft)." *Harvard Law Review* 105, no. 5 (March): 1045–75.

Fuente Noriega, Margarita. 1986. *La patria potestad compartida en el código civil español*. Madrid: Editorial Montecorro.

Fukuyama, Francis. 1995. *Trust: The Social Virtues and the Creation of Prosperity*. New York: Free Press.

Furtado, Cid. 1975. Parecer No. 43 da Comissão Mista, sobre PECs 4 e 5 de 1975. Brasília: Congresso Nacional.

Gacitúa, Andrés. 1991. "Algunos aspectos de la realidad en las estadísticas demográficas y judiciales." In *Nos habíamos amado tanto: Un aporte al debate sobre divorcio en Chile*. Santiago: CORSAPS. Pp. 31–9.

Garretón, Manuel Antonio. 1995. "Redemocratization in Chile." *Journal of Democracy* 6, no. 1 (January): 146–58.

Gaudiem et spes. 1965. In *The Sixteen Documents of Vatican II*, ed. Marianne Lorraine Trouvé. Boston: Pauline Books and Media, 1999. Pp. 615–719.

Gauri, Varun. 1998. *School Choice in Chile: Two Decades of Educational Reform*. Pittsburgh: University of Pittsburgh Press.

Gayán, Patricio. 1993. "El Aborto terapéutico desde el punto de vista gineco-obstétrico." In *Simposio nacional: Leyes para la salud y vida de las mujeres. Hablemos de aborto terapéutico*. Santiago: Foro Abierto de Salud y Derechos Reproductivos.

Geddes, Barbara. 1995. "The Politics of Economic Liberalization." *Latin American Research Review* 30, no. 2: 195–214.

Geertz, Clifford. 1973. "Thick Description: Toward an Interpretive Theory of Culture." In *The Interpretation of Cultures*. New York: Basic Books. Pp. 3–30.

Gelb, Joyce. 1989. *Feminism and Politics: A Comparative Perspective*. Berkeley: University of California Press.

Gelb, Joyce. 1996. "Abortion and Reproductive Choice: Policy and Politics in Japan." In Marianne Githens and Dorothy McBride Stetson, eds., *Abortion Politics: Public Policy in Cross-Cultural Perspective*. New York: Routledge. Pp. 119–37.

Gelb, Joyce, and Marian Lief Palley. 1996. *Women and Public Policies*. New ed. Charlottesville: University Press of Virginia.

Germani, Gino. 1955. *Estructura social de la Argentina: Análisis estadístico*. Buenos Aires: Editorial Raigal.

Ghio, José María. 1991. "The Latin American Church in the Wojtyla's Era: New Evangelization or 'Neo-Integralism'?" Working Paper no. 159. University of Torcuato di Tella.

Ghio, José María. 1996. "The Catholic Church and Politics in Argentina." Ph.D. dissertation, Columbia University.

Gilfeather, Katherine. 1979. "Women Religious, the Poor, and the Institutional Church in Chile." *Journal of Interamerican Studies and World Affairs* 21, no. 1 (February): 129–55.

Gilheany, Barry. 1998. "The State and the Discursive Construction of Abortion." In Vicky Randall and Georgina Waylen, eds., *Gender, Politics and the State*. London: Routledge. Pp. 58–79.

Gill, Anthony. 1998. *Rendering unto Caesar: The Catholic Church and the State in Latin America*. Chicago: University of Chicago Press.

Gill, Anthony. 1999. "The Struggle to Be a Soul Provider." In Christian Smith and Joshua Prokopy, eds., *Latin American Religion in Motion*. New York: Routledge. Pp. 17–42.

Githens, Marianne. 1996. "Reproductive Rights and the Struggle with Change in Eastern Europe." In Marianne Githens and Dorothy McBride Stetson, eds., *Abortion Politics: Public Policy in Cross-Cultural Perspective*. New York: Routledge. Pp. 54–68.

Glendon, Mary Ann. 1987. *Abortion and Divorce in Western Law*. Cambridge: Harvard University Press.

Glendon, Mary Ann. 1989. *The Transformation of Family Law: State, Law and the Family in the United States and Western Europe*. Chicago: University of Chicago Press.

Glendon, Mary Ann, Michael Wallace Gordon, and Christopher Osakwe. 1982. *Comparative Legal Traditions in a Nutshell*. St. Paul: West Publishing.

Goldman, Wendy. 1991. "Women, Abortion, and the State, 1917–36." In Barbara Evans Clements, Barbara Alpern Engel, and Christine D. Worobec, eds., *Russia's Women*. Berkeley: University of California Press. Pp. 243–66.

Gomes, Orlando. 1984. *O novo direito de família*. Porto Alegre: Sergio Antonio Fabris Editor.

Gonzales, Encarna Bodelon. 1994. "Spain." In Bill Rolston and Anna Eggert, eds., *Abortion in the New Europe: A Comparative Handbook*. Westport: Greenwood Press. Pp. 229–36.

Gonzales, Victoria, and Karen Kampwirth, eds. 2001. *Radical Women in Latin America: Left and Right*. University Park: Pennsylvania State University Press.

Gonzales Moya, Carlos A. 1992. *Nueva ley de la mujer*. Santiago: Editora Jurídica Manuel Montt S.A.

Goode, William J. 1993. *World Changes in Divorce Patterns*. New Haven: Yale University Press.

Gordon, Linda. 1976. *Woman's Body, Woman's Right: A Social History of Birth Control in America*. New York: Grossman.

Gourevitch, Peter. 1978. "The Second Image Reversed: The International Sources of Domestic Politics." *International Organization* 32, no. 4 (Autumn): 881–912.

Grau, Olga, Raquel Olea, and Francisa Pérez. 1998. "El Género en apuros." Draft. Santiago: Corporación de Desarollo de la Mujer La Morada, Grupo Iniciativa Chile.

Grondona, Mariano. 1999. *Las Condiciones culturales del desarollo económico*. Buenos Aires: Ariel-Planeta.

Grosman, Cecilia. 1976. "Situación de la mujer en la familia argentina." *Universitas*, no. 51 (December): 319–41.

Grosman, Cecilia P. 1998. "El Derecho de familia en la Argentina en los umbrales del siglo XXI." Unpublished manuscript.

Grupo Iniciativa. 1999. "Encuesta nacional: Opinión y actitudes de las mujeres chilenas sobre la condición de género."

Gutiérrez, María Alicia. 1998. " 'Parirás con Dolor': Aborto, derechos sexuales y reproductivos en la cosmovisión eclesiástica." In *Nuestros cuerpos, nuestras vidas: Propuestas para la promoción de los derechos sexuales y reproductivos*. Buenos Aires: Foro por los Derechos Reproductivos. Pp. 75–93.

Gutmann, Amy, and Dennis Thompson. 1996. *Democracy and Disagreement*. Cambridge: Harvard University Press.

Guy, Donna. 2000. "Parents Before the Tribunals: The Legal Construction of Patriarchy in Argentina." In Elizabeth Dore and Maxine Molyneux, eds., *Hidden*

Histories of Gender and the State in Latin America. Durham: Duke University Press. Pp. 172–93.

Guzmán, Jaime. 1997. "Reflexiones acerca del divorcio." *Fundación Jaime Guzmán E.* (September).

Haas, Liesl. 2000. "Legislating Equality: Institutional Politics and the Expansion of Women's Rights in Chile." Ph.D. dissertation, University of North Carolina at Chapel Hill.

Haas, Liesl. 2001. "Changing the System from Within? Feminist Participation in the Brazilian Workers' Party." In Victoria Gonzáles and Karen Kampwirth, eds., *Radical Women in Latin America: Left and Right*. University Park: Pennsylvania State University Press. Pp. 249–71.

Habermas, Jürgen. 1990. "Discourse Ethics: Notes on a Program of Philosophical Justification." In *Moral Consciousness and Communicative Action*. Cambridge: MIT Press.

Habermas, Jürgen. 1996a. *Between Facts and Norms: Contributions to a Discourse Theory of Law and Democracy*. Cambridge: MIT Press.

Habermas, Jürgen. 1996b. "Three Normative Models of Democracy." In Seyla Benhabib, ed., *Democracy and Difference: Contesting the Boundaries of the Political*. Princeton: Princeton University Press. Pp. 21–30.

Hagopian, Frances. 1990. " 'Democracy by Undemocratic Means?' Elites, Political Pacts, and Regime Transition in Brazil." *Comparative Political Studies* 23, no. 2 (July): 147–66.

Hall, Peter. 1992. "The Movement from Keynesianism to Monetarism: Institutional Analysis and British Economic Policy in the 1970s." In Sven Steinmo, Kathleen Thelen, and Frank Longstreth, eds., *Structuring Politics: Historical Institutionalism in Comparative Analysis*. Cambridge: Cambridge University Press. Pp. 90–113.

Hall, Peter. 1993. "Policy Paradigms, Social Learning, and the State: The Case of Economic Policymaking in Britain." *Comparative Politics* 25, no. 3 (April): 275–96.

Hall, Peter, and Rosemary Taylor. 1996. "Political Science and the Three New Institutionalisms." *Political Studies* 44: 936–57.

Harrison, Lawrence, and Samuel P. Huntington, eds. 2000. *Culture Matters: Values and Human Progress*. New York: Basic Books.

Hart, H. L. A. 1994. *The Concept of Law*. 2nd ed. Oxford: Clarendon Press.

Hebblethwaite, Peter. 1990. "The Vatican's Latin America Policy." In Dermot Keogh, ed., *Church and Politics in Latin America*. New York: St. Martin's Press. Pp. 49–64.

Heclo, Hugh. 1978. "Issue Networks and the Executive Establishment." In Anthony King, ed., *The New American Political System*. Washington: American Enterprise Institute. Pp. 87–124.

Hegel, G. W. F. 1991. *Elements of the Philosophy of Right*. Ed. Allen W. Wood. Cambridge: Cambridge University Press.

Hortal, Jesus. 1991. *O que deus uniu: Lições de direito matrimonial canônico*. São Paulo: Edições Loyola.

Htun, Mala N. 1998. "Women's Political Participation, Representation, and Leadership in Latin America." Women's Leadership Conference of the Americas Issue Brief. Washington, D.C.: Inter-American Dialogue/International Center for Research on Women.

Htun, Mala. 2001a. "Advancing Women's Rights in the Americas: Achievements and Challenges." Working Paper. Leadership Council for Inter-American Summitry, North-South Center, University of Miami.

Htun, Mala. 2001b. "Women's Leadership in Latin America: Trends and Challenges." In *Politics Matters: A Dialogue of Women Political Leaders.* Washington, D.C.: Inter-American Dialogue. Pp. 13–26.

Htun, Mala. 2002. "Mujeres y poder político en Latinoamérica." In *Mujeres en el Parlamento. Más allá de los números.* Stockholm: International IDEA.

Htun, Mala N., and Mark P. Jones. 2002. "Engendering the Right to Participate in Decisionmaking: Electoral Quotas and Women's Leadership in Latin America." In Nikki Craske and Maxine Molyneux, eds., *Gender and the Politics of Rights and Democracy in Latin America.* London: Palgrave. Pp. 32–56.

Hungria, Nelson. 1942. *Comentários ao código penal,* vol. 5. Rio de Janeiro: Forense.

Hunter, Wendy. 1995. "Politicians against Soldiers: Contesting the Military in Postauthoritarian Brazil." *Comparative Politics* 27 (July): 425–43.

Huntington, Samuel P. 1991. *The Third Wave: Democratization in the Late Twentieth Century.* Norman: University of Oklahoma Press.

Inglehart, Ronald. 1997. *Modernization and Postmodernization: Cultural, Economic, and Political Change in 43 Societies.* Princeton: Princeton University Press.

Instituto de Docencia y Investigación Jurídica. 1973. *Informe sobre futura ley de divorcio vincular.* Valparaíso: Edeval.

Instituto Interamericano de Derechos Humanos (IIDH). 1997. *Protección internacional de los derechos humanos de las mujeres.* San José: IIDH/CLADEM.

Inter-American Bar Association (IABA). 1943. *Anais da segunda conferencia,* vol. 5. Rio de Janeiro, August 7–12.

Inter-American Bar Association (IABA). 1945. *Themes and Resolutions of the Fourth Conference of the Inter-American Bar Association.*

Inter-American Bar Association (IABA). 1969. *Resolutions, Recommendations, and Declarations approved by XVI Conference.* Caracas, Venezuela, November 1–8.

Inter-American Development Bank. 2000. *Development Beyond Economics. Economic and Social Progress in Latin America.* Baltimore: Johns Hopkins University Press.

Inter-American Dialogue. 2001. *Women and Power in the Americas. A Report Card.* Washington, D.C.: Inter-American Dialogue.

Jackman, Robert W., and Ross A. Miller. 1996. "A Renaissance of Political Culture?" *American Journal of Political Science* 40, no. 3 (August): 632–59.

Jacob, Herbert. 1988. *Silent Revolution: The Transformation of Divorce Law in the United States.* Chicago: University of Chicago Press.

Jaquette, Jane S. 1994. "Introduction: From Transition to Participation – Women's Movements and Democratic Politics." In Jane S. Jaquette, ed., *The Women's Movement in Latin America.* Boulder: Westview. Pp. 1–11.

Jaquette, Jane S., and Sharon L. Wolchik. 1998. "Women and Democratization in Latin America and Central and Eastern Europe: A Comparative Introduction." In Jaquette and Wolchik, eds., *Women and Democracy: Latin America and Central and Eastern Europe.* Baltimore: Johns Hopkins University Press. Pp. 1–28.

Jiménez de Asúa, Luis. 1942. *Libertad de amar y derecho a morir: Ensayos de un criminalista sobre eugenesia y euthanasia.* Rev. ed. Buenos Aires: Losada.

Jiménez de Asúa, Luis. 1943. *Cuestiones penales de eugenesia, filosofia y política*. Sucre: Facultad de Derecho, Ciencias Políticas y Sociales.

Jones, Mark P. 1997a. "Evaluating Argentina's Presidential Democracy: 1983–1995." In Scott Mainwaring and Matthew Soberg Shugart, eds., *Presidentialism and Democracy in Latin America*. New York: Cambridge University Press. Pp. 259–99.

Jones, Mark P. 1997b. "Gender and Legislator Policy Priorities in the Argentine Chamber of Deputies and the United States House of Representatives," *Policy Studies Journal* 25, no. 4 (Winter): 613–29.

Jones, Mark P., Sebastian Saiegh, Pablo T. Spiller, and Mariano Tommasi. 2002. "Amateur Legislators – Professional Politicians: The Consequences of Party-Centered Electoral Rules in a Federal System." *American Journal of Political Science* 46, no. 3 (July): 656–69.

Jones, Mark P. 2002. "Explaining the High Level of Party Discipline in the Argentine Congress." In Scott Morgenstern and Benito Nacif, eds., *Legislative Politics in Latin America*. New York: Cambridge University Press. Pp. 147–84.

Katzenstein, Mary. 1987. "Comparing the Feminist Movements of the United States and Western Europe: An Overview." In Mary Katzenstein and Carol Mueller, eds., *The Women's Movements of the United States and Western Europe*. Philadelphia: Temple University Press. Pp. 3–20.

Katznelson, Ira. 1997. "Structure and Configuration in Comparative Politics." In Mark Irving Lichbach and Alan S. Zuckerman, eds., *Comparative Politics: Rationality, Culture, Structure*. New York: Cambridge University Press. Pp. 81–112.

Kaufman, Robert, and Barbara Stallings. 1989. "Debt and Democracy in the 1980s: The Latin American Experience." In Barbara Stallings and Robert Kaufman, eds., *Debt and Democracy in Latin America*. Boulder: Westview Press. Pp. 201–23.

Keck, Margaret, and Kathryn Sikkink. 1998. *Activists Beyond Borders: Advocacy Networks in Transnational Politics*. Ithaca: Cornell University Press.

Kerber, Linda K. 1998. *No Constitutional Right to Be Ladies: Women and the Obligations of Citizenship*. New York: Hill and Wang.

Ketting, Evert, and Philip van Praag. 1986. "The Marginal Relevance of Legislation Relating to Induced Abortion." In Joni Lovenduski and Joyce Outshoorn, eds., *The New Politics of Abortion*. London: Sage Publications. Pp. 154–69.

King, Gary, Robert O. Keohane, and Sidney Verba. 1994. *Designing Social Inquiry: Scientific Inference in Qualitative Research*. Princeton: Princeton University Press.

Kirchheimer, Otto. 1990. "The Catch-All Party." In Peter Mair, ed., *The West European Party System*. Oxford: Oxford University Press. Pp. 50–60.

Kirkwood, Julieta. 1990. *Ser política en Chile: Los Nudos de la sabiduria feminista*. Santiago: Editorial Cuarto Propio.

Kissling, Frances. 1989. "Epilogo." In Ana María Portugal, ed., *Mujeres e iglesia: Sexualidad e aborto en América Latina*. Mexico: Distribuciones Fontamara. Pp. 113–18.

Klaiber, Jeffrey, S. J. 1998. *The Church, Dictatorships, and Democracy in Latin America*. Maryknoll: Orbis Books.

Klimpel, Felícitas. 1962. *La Mujer chilena (El Aporte femenino al progreso de Chile) 1910–1960*. Santiago: Editorial Andres Bello.

Kogut, Edy Luiz. 1976. *Análise econômica do fenômeno demográfico no Brasil*. Rio de Janeiro: Fundação Getulio Vargas.

Kohli, Atul, et al. 1995. "The Role of Theory in Comparative Politics: A Symposium." *World Politics* 48, no. 1 (October): 1–49.

Krotsch, Carlos Pedro. 1988. "Iglesia, educación y Congreso Pedagógico Nacional." In Ana María Ezcurra, ed., *Iglesia y transición democrática*. Buenos Aires: Pantosur. Pp. 205–50.

Lagomarsino, Carlos, and Jorge Uriarte. 1991. *Separación personal y divorcio*. Buenos Aires: Editorial Universidad.

Lamounier, Bolívar. 1999. "Brazil: Inequality against Democracy." In Larry Diamond, Jonathan Hartlyn, and Juan J. Linz, eds., *Democracy in Developing Countries: Latin America*, 2nd ed. Boulder: Lynne Rienner. Pp. 131–89.

Larraín, Hernan. 1994. "Moción: Aumenta penalización del aborto." República de Chile, Senado. Boletín 1302–07.

Lavrín, Asunción. 1995. *Women, Feminism, and Social Change in Argentina, Chile, and Uruguay, 1890–1940*. Lincoln: University of Nebraska Press.

Leonard, Virginia. 1989. *Politicians, Pupils, and Priests: Argentine Education since 1943*. New York: Peter Lang.

Levine, Daniel. 1973. *Conflict and Political Change in Venezuela*. Princeton: Princeton University Press.

Levine, Daniel H. 1990. "The Catholic Church and Politics in Latin America: Basic Trends and Likely Futures." In Dermot Keogh, ed., *Church and Politics in Latin America*. New York: St. Martin's Press. Pp. 25–48.

Levine, Daniel, and Scott Mainwaring. 1989. "Religion and Popular Protest in Latin America: Contrasting Experiences." In Susan Eckstein, ed., *Power and Popular Protest: Latin American Social Movements*. Berkeley: University of California Press. Pp. 203–40.

Lewis, Jane. 1992. "Gender and the Development of Welfare Regimes." *Journal of European Social Policy* 2, no. 3: 159–73.

Libertad y Desarrollo. 1991. "Comentários al proyecto que legaliza el aborto terapéutico." Serie Opinión. S11 (November).

Libertad y Desarrollo. 1997a. "Agenda de libertades culturales: Una evaluación política." *Temas Públicos*, no. 333 (April 25): 1–6.

Libertad y Desarrollo. 1997b. Boletín 1090–07. *Reseña Legislativa* 326 (March 15–28).

Libertad y Desarrollo. 1997c. "El Gobierno, la moral y la libertad de expresión." *Temas Públicos*, no. 332 (April 17): 1–3.

Linhares Barsted, Leila. 1993. "Ten Years of Struggle to Legalize Abortion in Brazil." In *Women: Watched and Punished*. Lima: CLADEM. Pp. 223–47.

Linhares Barsted, Leila. 1994. "Em busca do tempo perdido: Mulher e políticas públicas no Brasil: 1983–1993." *Estudos Feministas* 2, special issue (October): 38–54.

Linz, Juan J. 1973. "The Future of an Authoritarian Situation or the Institutionalization of an Authoritarian Regime: The Case of Brazil." In Alfred Stepan, ed., *Authoritarian Brazil*. New Haven: Yale University Press. Pp. 232–54.

Linz, Juan J., and Alfred Stepan. 1996. *Problems of Democratic Transition and Consolidation*. Baltimore: Johns Hopkins University Press.

Lipset, Seymour Martin, and Stein Rokkan. 1967. "Cleavage Structures, Party Systems, and Voter Alignments: An Introduction." In Seymour Martin Lipset and

Stein Rokkan, eds., *Party Systems and Voter Alignments: Cross-National Perspectives.* New York: Free Press. Pp. 1–64.

Locke, John. 1689. *A Letter Concerning Toleration,* ed. James H. Tully. Indianapolis: Hackett Publishing, 1983.

Londregan, John. 2000. *Legislative Institutions and Ideology in Chile.* New York: Cambridge University Press.

Lowi, Theodore J. 1964. "American Business, Public Policy, Case-Studies, and Political Theory." *World Politics* 16, no. 4 (July): 677–715.

Luciak, Ilja. 2002. *After the Revolution: Gender and Democracy in El Salvador, Nicaragua, and Guatemala.* Baltimore: Johns Hopkins University Press.

Luker, Kristin. 1984. *Abortion and the Politics of Motherhood.* Berkeley: University of California Press.

Lynch, Edward A. 1993. *Latin America's Christian Democratic Parties: A Political Economy.* Westport: Praeger.

MacKinnon, Catharine. 1989. *Toward a Feminist Theory of the State.* Cambridge: Harvard University Press.

Mahon, Evelyn. 1987. "Women's Rights and Catholicism in Ireland." *New Left Review* 166 (November-December): 53–77.

Mainwaring, Scott. 1986. *The Catholic Church and Politics in Brazil, 1916–1985.* Stanford: Stanford University Press.

Mainwaring, Scott. 1997. "Multipartism, Robust Federalism, and Presidentialism in Brazil." In Scott Mainwaring and Matthew Soberg Shugart, eds., *Presidentialism and Democracy in Latin America.* New York: Cambridge University Press. Pp. 55–109.

Mainwaring, Scott. 1999. *Rethinking Party Systems in the Third Wave of Democratization: The Case of Brazil.* Stanford: Stanford University Press.

Mainwaring, Scott, and Timothy Scully. 1995. "Introduction: Party Systems in Latin America." In Mainwaring and Scully, eds., *Building Democratic Institutions: Party Systems in Latin America.* Stanford: Stanford University Press. Pp. 1–34.

Mainwaring, Scott, and Matthew Soberg Shugart. 1997. "Conclusion: Presidentialism and the Party System." In Scott Mainwaring and Matthew Soberg Shugart, eds., *Presidentialism and Democracy in Latin America.* New York: Cambridge University Press. Pp. 394–439.

Mainwaring, Scott, and Alexander Wilde. 1989. "The Progressive Church in Latin America: An Interpretation." In Mainwaring and Wilde, eds., *The Progressive Church in Latin America.* Notre Dame: University of Notre Dame Press. Pp. 1–37.

Mansbridge, Jane J. 1986. *Why We Lost the ERA.* Chicago: University of Chicago Press.

Matear, Ann. 1996. "*Desde la Protesta a la Propuesta*: Gender Politics in Transition in Chile." *Democratization* 3, no. 3 (Autumn 1996): 246–63.

McBride Stetson, Dorothy, and Amy G. Mazur. 1995. *Comparative State Feminism.* Thousand Oaks: Sage.

McGee Deutsch, Sandra. 1991. "Gender and Sociopolitical Change in Twentieth-Century Latin America." *Hispanic American Historical Review* 71, no. 2 (May): 259–306.

McKenna, Megan. 1997. "Women's Rights and Divorce in Ireland." http://www.columbia.edu/cu/sipa/PUBS/SLANT/SPRING97/mckenna.html.

Meacham, Carl E. 1994. "The Role of the Chilean Catholic Church in the New Chilean Democracy." *Journal of Church and State* 36, no. 2 (Spring): 277–99.

Mecham, J. Lloyd. 1966. *Church and State in Latin America*. Chapel Hill: University of North Carolina Press.

Merryman, John Henry. 1985. *The Civil Law Tradition*. Stanford: Stanford University Press.

Mignone, Emilio. 1988. *Witness to the Truth: The Complicity of Church and Dictatorship in Argentina*. Maryknoll: Orbis Books.

Miller, Francesca. 1991. *Latin American Women and the Search for Social Justice*. Hanover: University Press of New England.

Ministerio da Justiça. 2002. *Programa Nacional de Direitos Humanos. PNDH II*. Brasília: Secretaria de Estado dos Direitos Humanos, Ministerio da Justiça.

Ministerio de Justicia. 1929. *Proyecto de Código Penal*. Santiago: Imprenta Nacional.

Ministerio de Salud. 1993. *Normas de Paternidad Responsable*. Santiago: Programa de Salud Materna y Perinatal, Ministerio de Salud.

Mink, Gwendolyn. 1998. *Welfare's End*. Ithaca: Cornell University Press.

Molyneux, Maxine. 1985. "Family Reform in Socialist States: The Hidden Agenda." *Feminist Review* 21 (Winter 1985): 47–62.

Molyneux, Maxine. 1988. "The Politics of Abortion in Nicaragua: Revolutionary Pragmatism or Feminism in the Realm of Necessity?" *Feminist Review* no. 29 (Spring 1988): 114–32.

Molyneux, Maxine. 2000. "Twentieth-Century State Formations in Latin America." In Elizabeth Dore and Maxine Molyneux, eds., *Hidden Histories of Gender and the State in Latin America*. Durham: Duke University Press. Pp. 33–81.

Montes de Oca, Zita. 1997. "Las Mujeres y el estado, el estado para las mujeres." In Marcela Rodriguez, Diana L. Staubli, and Patricia Laura Gómez, eds., *Mujeres en los '90: Legislación y políticas públicas*. Vicente Lopez, Argentina: Centro Municipal de la Mujer de Vicente Lopez. Pp. 25–46.

Moreira Alves, José Carlos. 1992. "A Panorama of Brazilian Civil Law from Its Origins to the Present." In Jacob Dolinger and Keith S. Rosenn, eds., *A Panorama of Brazilian Law*. Miami: North-South Center. Pp. 87–111.

Moreira Alves, Marcio. 1979. *A igreja e a política no Brasil*. São Paulo: Editora Brasilense.

Moreira Alves, Maria Helena. 1984. "Grassroots Organizations, Trade Unions, and the Church: A Challenge to the Controlled *Abertura* in Brazil." *Latin American Perspectives* 11, no. 1 (Winter): 73–102.

Morgenstern, Scott and Benito Nacif, eds. 2002. *Legislative Politics in Latin America*. New York: Cambridge University Press.

Morgenstern, Scott. 2002. "Explaining Legislative Politics in Latin America." In Scott Morgenstern and Benito Nacif, eds., *Legislative Politics in Latin America*. New York: Cambridge University Press. Pp. 413–45.

Morrisey, Francis. 1977. "The Juridical Status of Women in Contemporary Ecclesiastical Law." In James A. Coriden, ed., *Sexism and Church Law: Equal Rights and Affirmative Action*. New York: Paulist Press. Pp. 1–20.

Mouffe, Chantal. 1992. "Feminism, Citizenship, and Radical Democratic Politics." In Judith Butler and Joan W. Scott, eds., *Feminists Theorize the Political*. New York: Routledge. Pp. 367–84.

Munizaga, Giselle, and Lilian Letelier. 1988. "La Mujer y la acción hegemonizadora del regimen militar." In *Mundo de mujer: Continuidad y cambio*. Santiago: Centro de Estudios de la Mujer. Pp. 525–62.

Muraro, Rose Marie. 1989. "El Aborto y la fé religiosa en América Latina." In Ana María Portugal, ed., *Mujeres e iglesia: Sexualidad e aborto en América Latina*. Mexico: Distribuciones Fontamara. Pp. 81–94.

Navarro, Marysa. 1989. "The Personal Is Political: *Las Madres de la Plaza de Mayo*." In Susan Eckstein, ed., *Power and Popular Protest*. Berkeley: University of California Press. Pp. 241–58.

Navarro, Marysa, and Susan C. Bourque. 1998. "Fault Lines of Democratic Governance: A Gender Perspective." In Felipe Agüero and Jeffrey Stark, eds., *Fault Lines of Democracy in Post-Transition Latin America*. Miami: North-South Center Press. Pp. 175–202.

Nazzari, Muriel. 1995. "Widows as Obstacles to Business: British Objections to Brazilian Marriage and Inheritance Laws." *Comparative Studies in Society and History* 37, no. 4 (October): 781–802.

Neto, Jorge Andalaft. 1999. "Dez anos de serviços de aborto legal." *Journal da RedeSaúde*, no. 18 (September 1999).

Noonan, John T. 1970. "An Almost Absolute Value in History." In Noonan, ed., *The Morality of Abortion: Legal and Historical Perspectives*. Cambridge: Harvard University Press. Pp. 1–59.

O'Connor, Julia, Ann Shola Orloff, and Sheila Shaver. 1999. *States, Markets, Families: Gender, Liberalism, and Social Policy in Australia, Canada, Great Britain and the United States*. Cambridge: Cambridge University Press.

O'Donnell, Guillermo. 1979. *Modernization and Bureaucratic Authoritarianism: Studies in South American Politics*. Berkeley: Institute of International Studies, University of California.

O'Donnell, Guillermo. 1994. "Delegative Democracy." *Journal of Democracy* 5 (January): 55–69.

O'Donnell, Guillermo. 1999a. "On the State, Democratization, and Some Conceptual Problems: A Latin American View with Glances at Some Postcommunist Countries." In *Counterpoints: Selected Essays on Authoritarianism and Democratization*. Notre Dame: University of Notre Dame Press. Pp. 133–57.

O'Donnell, Guillermo. 1999b. "Polyarchies and the (Un)Rule of Law in Latin America: A Partial Conclusion." In Juan E. Méndez, Guillermo O'Donnell, and Paulo Sergio Pinheiro, eds., *The (Un)Rule of Law and the Underprivileged in Latin America*. Notre Dame: University of Notre Dame Press. Pp. 303–37.

Okin, Susan Moller. 1979. *Women in Western Political Thought*. Princeton: Princeton University Press.

Okin, Susan Moller. 1989. *Justice, Gender, and the Family*. New York: Basic Books.

Okin, Susan Moller. 1991. "Gender, the Public and the Private." In David Held, ed., *Political Theory Today*. Stanford: Stanford University Press. Pp. 67–90.

Okin, Susan Moller. 1999. "Is Multiculturalism Bad for Women?" In Joshua Cohen, Matthew Howard, and Martha Nussbaum, eds., *Is Multiculturalism Bad for Women?* Princeton: Princeton University Press. Pp. 7–24.

Olsen, Frances. 1993. "The Myth of State Intervention in the Family." In Martha Minow, ed., *Family Matters: Readings on Family Lives and the Law*. New York: New Press. Pp. 277–82.

Organization of American States/Inter-American Commission on Human Rights (OAS/CIDH). 1998. "Informe de la comisión interamericana de derechos humanos sobre la condición de la mujer en las américas." Washington, D.C.: Organization of American States.

Orloff, Ann Shola. 1993. "Gender and the Social Rights of Citizenship: The Comparative Analysis of Gender Relations and Welfare States." *American Sociological Review* 58, no. 3 (June 1993): 303–328.

Osnajanski, Norma, and Adriana Llano. 1985. "Informe especial: Divorcio." *Vivir*, no. 106 (March 1985). Pp. 19–27.

Outshoorn, Joyce. 1996. "The Stability of Compromise: Abortion Politics in Western Europe." In Marianne Githens and Dorothy McBride Stetson, eds., *Abortion Politics: Public Policy in Cross-Cultural Perspective*. New York: Routledge. Pp. 145–64.

Parekh, Bhikhu. 1999. "A Varied Moral World." In Joshua Cohen, Matthew Howard, and Martha Nussbaum, eds., *Is Multiculturalism Bad for Women?* Princeton: Princeton University Press. Pp. 69–75.

Pateman, Carole. 1989. *The Disorder of Women: Democracy, Feminism, and Political Theory*. Stanford: Stanford University Press.

PDC. 1994. "Democracia Cristiana, familia y rupturas matrimoniales. Once tesis de consenso." Santiago, July 14, 1994.

Peco, José. 1942. "Proyecto de Código Penal. Exposición de motivos presentado a la Camara de Diputados de la Nación Argentina." La Plata: Instituto de Criminologia.

Pedersen, Susan. 1993. *Family, Dependence, and the Origins of the Welfare State: Britian and France, 1914–1945*. Cambridge: Cambridge University Press.

Petchesky, Rosalind Pollack. 1990. *Abortion and Woman's Choice: The State, Sexuality, and Reproductive Freedom*. Boston: Northeastern University Press.

Petrocelli, José Luis. 1994. "Nupcialidade." In Sílvio Manoug Kaloustian, ed., *Família brasileira: A base de tudo*. São Paulo: Cortez.

Philippi, Julio. 1979. "Breve explicación de las principales modificaciones que contiene el proyecto sobre capacidad de la mujer casada, sobre sociedad conyugal y otras materias del derecho de familia." In Leslie Tomasello Hart and Alvaro Quintanilla Pérez, *Reformas al regimen matrimonial y de filiación*. Valparaíso: Edeval, 1981.

Phillips, Anne. 1991. *Engendering Democracy*. Cambridge: Polity Press.

Phillips, Anne. 1995. *The Politics of Presence*. New York: Oxford University Press.

Phillips, Roderick. 1988. *Putting Asunder: A History of Divorce in Western Society*. Cambridge: Cambridge University Press.

Pierson, Paul. 1994. *Dismantling the Welfare State? Reagan, Thatcher, and the Politics of Retrenchment*. Cambridge: Cambridge University Press.

Pierson, Paul. 2000. "Increasing Returns, Path Dependence, and the Study of Politics." *American Political Science Review* 94, no. 2 (June): 251–67.

Pimentel, Silvia. 1987. *A Mulher e a Constituinte: Uma contribuição ao debate*. São Paulo: Cortez Editora.

Pimentel, Silvia, and Florisa Verucci. 1981. "Esboço de um Novo Estatuto Civil da Mulher." Photocopy.

Pimentel, Silvia, and Florisa Verucci. 1983a. Letter to Brazilian women's movements, dated March 8.

Pimentel, Silvia, and Florisa Verucci. 1983b. Letter to Brazilian women's movements, dated November 3.

Pimentel, Silvia, Beatriz di Giorgi, and Flávia Piovesan. 1993. *A Figura/Personagem mulher em processos de família.* Porto Alegre: Sergio Antonio Fabris Editor.

Pinheiro, Paulo Sérgio. 1999. "The Rule of Law and the Underprivileged in Latin America: Introduction." In Juan E. Méndez, Guillermo O'Donnell, and Paulo Sérgio Pinheiro, eds., *The (Un)Rule of Law and the Underprivileged in Latin America.* Notre Dame: University of Notre Dame Press. Pp. 1–15.

Piovesan, Flávia. 1992. "Constituição e transformação social: A eficácia das normas constitucionais programáticas e a concretização dos direitos e garantias fundamentais." *Revista PGE/SP*, no. 37 (June): 65–74.

Pitanguy, Jacqueline. 1996. "Movimento de mujeres y políticas públicas en Brasil" In Geertje Lycklama, Virginia Vargas, and Saskia Wieringa, eds., *Triángulo de Poder.* Bogotá: Tercer Mundo Editores. Pp. 55–80.

Pollard, Miranda. 1998. *Reign of Virtue: Mobilizing Gender in Vichy France.* Chicago: University of Chicago Press.

Pope John XXIII. 1963. *Pacem in terris.* In Claudia Carlen Ihm, ed., *The Papal Encyclicals,* vol. 5. Wilmington, N.C.: McGrath, 1981. Pp. 107–29.

Pope John Paul II. 1988. *The Dignity of Women. Apostolic Letter Mulieris Dignitatem.* Dublin: Veritas Publications.

Pope Leo XIII. 1891. *Rerum novarum.* In Claudia Carlen Ihm, ed., *The Papal Encyclicals,* vol. 2. Wilmington, N.C.: McGrath, 1981. Pp. 241–61.

Pope Paul VI. 1968. *Humane vitae.* In Claudia Carlen Ihm, ed., *The Papal Encyclicals,* vol. 5. Wilmington, N.C.: McGrath, 1981. Pp. 223–36.

Portugal, Ana María. 1989. "Introducción." In Portugal, ed., *Mujeres e iglesia: Sexualidad e aborto en América Latina.* Mexico: Distribuciones Fontamara. Pp. 1–8.

Posner, Richard. 1992. *Sex and Reason.* Cambridge: Harvard University Press.

Potash, Robert A. 1996. *The Army and Politics in Argentina, 1962–1973.* Stanford: Stanford University Press.

Primero Concilio Plenario Chileno. 1946. *In urbe s. iacobi en Chile anno domini M.CM.XL VI celebratum Iosepho Maria S.R.E. Card. Caro Rodriguez S. iacobi en Chile Archiepiscopo Summi Pontificis PII PP. XII legato a latere praeside.* Chile, 1955.

Programa de Asesoria Legislativa (PAL). 1991. Regimen patrimonial del matrimonio: Proyecto que modifica el código civil y otros cuerpos legales. *Analisis Legislativo* 15, Año I.

Programa de Asesoria Legislativa (PAL). 1994. Proyecto de ley que modifica el Código Civil y otros cuerpos legales en materia de filiación. *Analisis Legislativo* 45, Año III.

Przeworski, Adam. 1991. *Democracy and the Market: Political and Economic Reforms in Eastern Europe and Latin America.* Cambridge: Cambridge University Press.

Przeworski, Adam, and Fernando Limongi. 1997. "Modernization: Theories and Facts." *World Politics* 49, no. 2: 155–183.

Rabkin, Rhoda. 1996. "Redemocratization, Electoral Engineering, and Party Strategies in Chile, 1989–1995." *Comparative Political Studies* 29, no. 3 (June 1996): 335–56.

Ramos, Silvina. 2001. "Mujeres, un paso adelante." *Clarín*, April 30, 2001.

Rawls, John. 1971. *A Theory of Justice.* Cambridge: Harvard University Press.

Rawls, John. 1993. *Political Liberalism.* New York: Columbia University Press.

Remmer, Karen. 1990. "Democracy and Economic Crisis: The Latin American Experience." *World Politics* 42, no. 3 (April): 315–35.

República Argentina. 1986. *Fallos de la Corte Suprema de la Nación*. Sept.-Dec. Tomo 308, vol. 2. Buenos Aires.

República de Chile. 1976. *Actas Oficiales de la Comisión Constituyente*. Sesión 191, celebrada en jueves 18 de marzo de 1976.

Reyes, Carmen. 1992. "La Familia chilena hoy: Fundamentos para políticas públicas orientadas al grupo familiar." In *La Familia en Chile*. Santiago: Centro de Estudios de la Realidad Contemporánea/Instituto Chileno de Estudios Humanisticos. Pp. 43–77.

Rheinstein, Max. 1972. *Marriage Stability, Divorce, and the Law*. Chicago: University of Chicago Press.

Rhode, Deborah. 1989. *Justice and Gender*. Cambridge: Harvard University Press.

Ribeiro, Leonídio. 1942. *O novo código penal e a medicina legal*. Rio de Janeiro: Jacinto.

Ribeiro, Leonídio. 1973. *Reforma do código penal*. Rio de Janeiro: São José.

Risse, Thomas, and Kathryn Sikkink. 1999. "The Socialization of International Human Rights Norms into Domestic Practices: An Introduction." In Thomas Risse, Stephen C. Ropp, and Kathryn Sikkink, eds., *The Power of Human Rights: International Norms and Domestic Change*. Cambridge: Cambridge University Press. Pp. 1–38.

Rodrigues, Almira. 2000. "Legislativo federal e os direitos das mulheres: Não falta sensibilidade e sim vontade política." *Jornal da RedeSaúde*, no. 21 (September).

Rodriguez, Marcela V. 1997. "La situación legal de los derechos reproductivos y sexuales en Argentina." In *Nuestros cuerpos, nuestras vidas: Propuestas para la promoción de los derechos sexuales y reproductivos*. Buenos Aires: Foro por los Derechos Reproductivos. Pp. 29–42.

Rodríguez, Victoria. 1998. "The Emerging Role of Women in Mexican Political Life." In Victoria Rodríguez, ed., *Women's Participation in Mexican Political Life*. Boulder: Westview. Pp. 1–20.

Rodríguez, Victoria, ed. 1998. *Women's Participation in Mexican Political Life*. Boulder: Westview.

Rosenn, Keith S. 1990. "Brazil's New Constitution: An Exercise in Transient Constitutionalism for a Transitional Society." *American Journal of Comparative Law* 38: 773–802.

Rouquié, Alain. 1984. *Poder militar e sociedad política en la Argentina*. Buenos Aires: Emece.

Sales Brasil, Francisco. 1953. *As Fontes do divórcio: Com um estudo completivo sobre o Projeto Nelson Carneiro*. Salvador: Editora Era Nova.

Samuels, David. 2003. *Ambition, Federalism, and Legislative Politics in Brazil*. New York: Cambridge University Press.

Santa Cruz, Lucía. 1996. "Sexo y Estado." *Libertad y Desarollo*, no. 58 (October): 18–21.

Schlueter, Vanessa. 2000. "The Politics of Sex: Democracy and Feminist Policy Change in Argentina." B.A. thesis, Department of Government, Harvard University.

Schmitter, Phillipe. 1979. "Still a Century of Corporatism?" In Phillipe Schmitter and Gerhard Lehmbruch, eds., *Trends toward Corporatist Intermediation*. Beverly Hills: Sage Publications. Pp. 7–52.

Schumaher, Maria Aparecida, and Elisabeth Vargas. 1993. Lugar no Governo: Álibi ou conquista? *Estudos Feministas* 1, no. 2. Pp. 348–65.

Scott, Joan Wallach. 1988. "Gender: A Useful Category of Historical Analysis." In *Gender and the Politics of History*. New York: Columbia University Press. Pp. 28–50.

Scott, Rosemary. 1949. "Capacity of Married Women to Contract." In Inter-American Bar Association, *Proceedings of the Sixth Conference held at Detroit, Michigan, May 22-June 1, 1949*. Washington, D.C. Pp. 194–5.

Scott, Samuel Parsons, ed. 1931. *Las Siete partidas*. Chicago: Commerce Clearing House.

Scully, Timothy R. 1992. *Rethinking the Center: Party Politics in Nineteenth- and Twentieth-Century Chile*. Stanford: Stanford University Press.

Scully, Timothy R. 1995. "Reconstituting Party Politics in Chile." In Scott Mainwaring and Timothy R. Scully, eds., *Building Democratic Institutions: Party Systems in Latin America*. Stanford: Stanford University Press. Pp. 100–37.

Senado de la Nación. 1919. *La Reforma penal en el Senado*. Informe y despacho de la Comisión de Códigos de la Cámara de Senadores de la Nación Argentina sobre el proyecto de Código Penal. Buenos Aires.

Serbin, Kenneth. 1996. "Church-State Reciprocity in Contemporary Brazil: The Convening of the International Eucharistic Congress of 1955 in Rio de Janeiro." *Hispanic American Historical Review* 76, no. 4 (1996): 721–51.

SERNAM. 1996. *Memoria: 1994–1996*. Santiago: SERNAM.

Shepard, Bonnie. 2000. "The 'Double Discourse' on Sexual and Reproductive Rights in Latin America: The Chasm between Public Policy and Private Action." *Health and Human Rights* 4, no. 2: 121–43.

Shepsle, Kenneth, and Barry Weingast, eds. 1995. *Positive Theories of Congressional Institutions*. Ann Arbor: University of Michigan Press.

Siavelis, Peter. 1997. "Executive-Legislative Relations in Post-Pinochet Chile: A Preliminary Assessment." In Scott Mainwaring and Matthew Soberg Shugart, eds., *Presidentialism and Democracy in Latin America*. Cambridge: Cambridge University Press. Pp. 321–62.

Siavelis, Peter. 2002. "Exaggerated Presidentialism and Moderate Presidents: Executive-Legislative Relations in Chile." In Scott Morgenstern and Benito Nacif, eds., *Legislative Politics in Latin America*. New York: Cambridge University Press. Pp. 79–113.

Siavelis, Peter, and Arturo Valenzuela. 1996. "Electoral Engineering and Democratic Stability: The Legacy of Authoritarian Rule in Chile." In Arend Lijphart and Carlos Waisman, eds., *Institutional Design in New Democracies: Eastern Europe and Latin America*. Boulder: Westview. Pp. 77–99.

Siero, Isabel. 1949. "Contractual Capacity of Married Women." In Inter-American Bar Association, *Proceedings of the Sixth Conference held at Detroit, Michigan, May 22-June 1, 1949*. Washington, D.C. P. 196.

Sigmund, Paul. 1988. "Thomistic Natural Law and Social Theory." In Paul Sigmund, ed., *St. Thomas Aquinas on Politics and Ethics*. New York: W. W. Norton. Pp. 180–8.

Sikkink, Kathryn. 1991. *Ideas and Institutions: Developmentalism in Brazil and Argentina*. Ithaca: Cornell University Press.

Simões, Solange de Deus. 1985. *Deus, patria e familia: As mulheres no golpe de 1964*. Petropolis: Vozes.

Skidmore, Thomas E. 1988. *The Politics of Military Rule in Brazil, 1964–1985*. New York: Oxford University Press.

Skinner, Quentin. 1986. "The Paradoxes of Political Liberty." *The Tanner Lectures on Human Values*. Salt Lake City: University of Utah Press.

Skocpol, Theda. 1992. *Protecting Soldiers and Mothers: The Political Origins of Social Policy in the United States*. Cambridge: Harvard University Press.

Skocpol, Theda, and Margaret Somers. 1980. "The Uses of Comparative History in Macro-Social Inquiry." *Comparative Studies in Society and History* 22 (April): 174–97.

Skocpol, Theda, Marshall Ganz, and Ziad Munson. 2000. "A Nation of Organizers: The Institutional Origins of Civic Voluntarism in the United States." *American Political Science Review* 94, no. 3 (September): 527–46.

Smith, Brian. 1982. *The Church and Politics in Chile: Challenges to Modern Catholicism*. Princeton: Princeton University Press.

Soler, Sebastián. 1945. *Derecho penal argentino*. Buenos Aires: La Ley.

Soler, Sebastián, Carlos Fontán Balestra, and Eduardo Aguirre Obarrio. 1967. "Exposición de motivos" for Law 17.567. In *Anales de la legislación argentina 1967*. Tomo 27-C. Buenos Aires: La Ley. Pp. 2873–4.

Soto, Moira. 1982. "La Patria potestad debe ser compartida." *Vosotras*, año 47, no. 2426 (November 3): 1–2.

Staudt, Kathleen. 1997. "Gender Politics in Bureaucracy: Theoretical Issues in Comparative Perspective." In *Women, International Development, and Politics: The Bureaucratic Mire*. Philadelphia: Temple University Press.

Steigenga, Timothy J., and David A. Smilde. 1999. "Wrapped in a Holy Shawl: The Strange Case of Conservative Christians and Gender Equality in Latin America." In Christian Smith and Joshua Prokopy, eds., *Latin American Religion in Motion*. New York: Routledge. Pp. 173–86.

Stepan, Alfred. 1978. *The State and Society: Peru in Comparative Perspective*. Princeton: Princeton University Press.

Stepan, Alfred. 1988. *Rethinking Military Politics: Brazil and the Southern Cone*. Princeton: Princeton University Press.

Stepan, Nancy. 1991. *"The Hour of Eugenics": Race, Gender, and Nation in Latin America*. Ithaca: Cornell University Press.

Sternbach, Nancy Saporta, et al. 1992. "Feminisms in Latin America: From Bogotá to San Bernardo." *Signs* 27, no. 2 (Winter): 393–434.

Stevenson, Linda. 1999. "Gender Politics in the Mexican Democratization Process." In Jorge Domínguez and Alejandro Poiré, eds., *Towards Mexico's Democratization*. New York: Routledge. Pp. 57–87.

Swers, Michele L. 2002. *The Difference Women Make: The Policy Impact of Women in Congress*. Chicago: University of Chicago Press.

Tabak, Fanny. 1983. *Autoritarismo e participação política da mulher*. Rio de Janeiro: Graal.

Tabak, Fanny. 1989. *A mulher brasileira no congresso nacional*. Brasília: Camara de Deputados.

Tarrow, Sidney. 1998. *Power in Movement: Social Movements and Contentious Politics*, 2nd ed. Cambridge: Cambridge University Press.

Thelen, Kathleen, and Sven Steinmo. 1992. "Historical Institutionalism in Comparative Politics." In Sven Steinmo, Kathleen Thelen, and Frank Longstreth, eds., *Structuring Politics: Historical Institutionalism in Comparative Analysis*. Cambridge: Cambridge University Press. Pp. 1–32.

Thomas, Sue. 1994. *How Women Legislate*. Oxford: Oxford University Press.

Thompson, Augusto F. G. 1982. *Escorço histórico do direito criminal luso-brasileiro*. Rio de Janeiro: Editora Liber Juris Ltda.

Threlfall, Monica. 1996. "Feminist Politics and Social Change in Spain." In Monica Threlfall, ed., *Mapping the Women's Movement*. London: Verso. Pp. 115–51.

Todaro Williams, Margaret. 1976. "Church and State in Vargas's Brazil: The Politics of Cooperation." *Journal of Church and State* 18, no. 3 (Autumn): 443–62.

Tomasello Hart, Leslie. 1989. *Situación jurídica de la mujer casada*. Valparaíso: Edeval.

Tomasello Hart, Leslie, and Alvaro Quintanilla Pérez. *Reformas al regimen matrimonial y de filiación*. Valparaíso: Edeval, 1981.

Tribe, Laurence. 1992. *Abortion: The Clash of Absolutes*. New York: W. W. Norton.

Tribunal Eclesiástico de Santiago. N.d. Instrucciones para las personas que solicitan los servicios del Tribunal Eclesiástico de Santiago en las causas matrimoniales.

Unión Cívica Radical. 1983. *Plataforma de gobierno*. Buenos Aires: El Cid Editor.

United Nations. 1996. *The United Nations and the Advancement of Women, 1945–1996*. New York: United Nations.

United Nations Development Program (UNDP). 1998. *Human Development Report*. New York: United Nations.

Valdés, Teresa, and Marisa Weinstein. 1997. "Corriendo y descorriendo tupidos velos." In *Chile 96. Análisis y Opiniones*. Santiago: FLACSO-Chile.

Valenzuela, María Elena. 1987. *La mujer en el Chile militar*. Santiago: CESOC.

Valenzuela, María Elena. 1998. "Women and the Democratization Process in Chile." In Jaquette and Wolchik, eds., *Women and Democracy: Latin America and Central and Eastern Europe*. Baltimore: Johns Hopkins University Press. Pp. 47–74.

Valenzeula Carrazola, Andrea. N.d. "Algunos antecedentes en torno al estado actual del aborto terapéutico en Chile." Unpublished paper.

Valiente, Celia. 1995. "Family Obligations in Spain." In Jane Millar and Andrea Warman, eds., *Defining Family Obligations in Europe*. Bath Social Policy Papers no. 23, University of Bath. Pp. 325–58.

Vallier, Ivan. 1970. *Catholicism, Social Control, and Modernization in Latin America*. Englewood Cliffs: Prentice Hall.

Vasallo, Marta. 1997. "Derechos reproductivos: Un desafío a la dinámica partidaria." In *Nuestros cuerpos, nuestras vidas: Propuestas para la promoción de los derechos sexuales y reproductivos*. Buenos Aires: Foro por los Derechos Reproductivos. Pp. 67–74.

Verucci, Florisa. 1987. *A mulher e o direito*. São Paulo: Nobel.

Verucci. Florisa. 1991. "Women and the New Brazilian Constitution." *Feminist Studies* 17, 3 (Fall): 551–68.

Vial Correa, Gonzalo. 1996. "Un estado corruptor?" *El Mercurio*, September 10.

Viotti da Costa, Emilia. 1985a. "The Fall of the Monarchy." In *The Brazilian Empire: Myth and Histories*. Chicago: University of Chicago Press. Pp. 202–33.

Viotti da Costa, Emilia. 1985b. "Liberalism: Theory and Pratice." In *The Brazilian Empire: Myth and Histories*. Chicago: University of Chicago Press. Pp. 53–77.

Vogel, Ursula. 1998. "The State and the Making of Gender: Some Historical Legacies." In Vicky Randall and Georgina Waylen, eds., *Gender, Politics and the State*. London: Routledge. Pp. 29–44.

Wainerman, Catalina H., and Rosa N. Geldstein. 1994. "Vivendo en Familia: Ayer y Hoy." In Wainerman, ed., *Vivir en familia*. Buenos Aires: Editorial Losada. Pp. 183–230.

Watson, Peggy. 1996. "The Rise of Masculinism in Eastern Europe." In Monica Threlfall, ed., *Mapping the Women's Movement*. London: Verso. Pp. 216–31.

Waylen, Georgina. 1994. "Women and Democratization: Conceptualizing Gender Relations in Transition Politics." *World Politics* 46, no. 3: 327–54.

Waylen, Georgina. 1998. "Gender, Feminism, and the State: An Overview." In Vicky Randall and Georgina Waylen, eds. *Gender, Politics, and the State*. New York: Routledge. Pp. 1–17.

Weir, Margaret. 1992. "Ideas and the Politics of Bounded Innovation." In Sven Steinmo, Kathleen Thelen, and Frank Longstreth, eds., *Structuring Politics: Historical Institutionalism in Comparative Analysis*. Cambridge: Cambridge University Press. Pp. 188–216.

Weir, Margaret, and Theda Skocpol. 1985. "State Structures and the Possibilities for 'Keynesian' Reponses to the Great Depression." In Peter B. Evans, Dietrich Rueschemeyer, and Theda Skocpol, eds., *Bringing the State Back In*. Cambridge: Cambridge University Press. Pp. 107–63.

Weitzman, Lenore J. 1985. *The Divorce Revolution: The Unexpected Social and Economic Consequences for Women and Children in America*. New York: Free Press.

Weyland, Kurt. 1997. "Growth with Equity in Chile's New Democracy?" *Latin American Research Review* 32, no. 1: 37–67.

Whale, John, et al. 1980. *The Man Who Leads the Church: An Assessment of Pope John Paul II*. San Francisco: Harper and Row.

Wiarda, Howard. 1973. "Toward a Framework for the Study of Political Change in the Iberic-Latin Tradition: The Corporative Model." *World Politics* 25 (January): 206–35.

Wiecko de Castilho, Ela. 1999. "Uma mulher na comissão revisora: Entrevista com Ela Wiecko de Castilho." *Journal da RedeSaúde*, no. 18 (September 1999).

Williams, Edward J. 1967. *Latin American Christian Democratic Parties*. Knoxville: University of Tennessee Press.

Williams, Joan. 2000. *Unbending Gender: Why Family and Work Conflict and What to Do About It*. New York: Oxford University Press.

World Bank. 2002. *Genderstats. Database of Gender Statistics*. http://genderstats.worldbank.org.

Yishai, Yael. 1993. "Public Ideas and Public Policy: Abortion Politics in Four Democracies." *Comparative Politics* 25, no. 2 (January): 207–28.

Young, Iris Marion. 1994. "Gender as Seriality: Thinking About Women as a Social Collective." *Signs* 19, no. 3: 713–38.

Young, Iris Marion. 1997. *Intersecting Voices: Dilemmas of Gender, Political Philosophy, and Policy*. Princeton: Princeton University Press.

Zakaria, Fareed. 1997. "The Rise of Illiberal Democracy." *Foreign Affairs* 76, no. 6 (November/December): 22–43.

Zannoni, Eduardo. 1998a. *Derecho de Familia*, tomo 1, 3rd ed. Buenos Aires: Astrea.
Zannoni, Eduardo. 1998b. *Derecho de Familia*, tomo 2. 3rd ed. Buenos Aires: Astrea.
Zielinska, Eleonora. 2000. "Between Ideology, Politics, and Common Sense: The Discourse of Reproductive Rights in Poland." In Susan Gal and Gail Kligman, eds., *Reproducing Gender: Politics, Publics, and Everyday Life after Socialism*. Princeton: Princeton University Press. Pp. 23–57.

Index